# College
# Girls

# COLLEGE GIRLS

## GIRLS

*A*

*Century*

*in*

*Fiction*

SHIRLEY
MARCHALONIS

*Rutgers University Press*
*New Brunswick, New Jersey*

Library of Congress Cataloging-in-Publication Data

Marchalonis, Shirley.
    College girls : a century in fiction / Shirley Marchalonis.
        p.   cm.
    Includes bibliographical references and index.
    ISBN 0-8135-2175-0 (cloth). — ISBN 0-8135-2176-9 (pbk.)
    1. College stories, American—History and criticism.   2. American fiction—20th
century—History and criticism.   3. American fiction—19th century—History and
criticism.   4. Universities and colleges in literature.   5. Women college students in
literature.   6. Education, Higher, in literature.   7. Women's colleges in literature.
I. Title.
PS374.U52M37   1995
813.009′352375—dc20
                                                                94-41573
                                                                CIP


British Cataloging-in-Publication information available

*To my mother,*

*Mae Parry Marchalonis,*

*with love and gratitude*

# Contents

# Acknowledgments

The ideas that led to my writing this book go back several years to the time when I read and enjoyed Bobbie Ann Mason's *The Girl Sleuth*, with its sensitive remembrance of the interaction of reader and text. While mine is not a similar exploration and I am not reacting to my own childhood reading, Mason's book gave me an awareness that eventually led to this study. Shortly after reading it, I stumbled on John O. Lyons's treatment of the American college novel, in which one fairly superficial chapter covers fiction about women in college. I was struck by the contrast in attitudes, and then, in the way such things happen inside the mind, other ideas fed what was still only a fragile thought. I began to look for fiction about women in college and even to write, although with no clear aim. Other demands intervened and I put my "college girls" away, not at all sure that I would go on with their story. But my interest did not fade, although my ideas have changed shape and direction many times.

I am grateful to the friends who encouraged me to keep on, and particularly to Linda Patterson Miller, a stern critic and good friend, who bravely read the unshaped manuscript and gave helpful suggestions. I also thank Leslie Mitchner, editor-in-chief at Rutgers University Press, for her patience and her willingness to give good advice, even when I have not followed it.

# College
# Girls

# Introduction

Between the 1870s and the 1930s, fiction about the experiences of women going to college constituted a small but significant subgenre. The earliest writings treat both a new opportunity for women and the controversy that surrounded it.

The opening of Vassar College in 1865 shocked many; the often ferocious objections ranged from fear that educating women would damage their "womanly" qualities to conviction that it would destroy society. Consequently, some of the fiction has an extra-literary element: to explain and make familiar a strange and disturbing venture for an audience that varied in age, gender, and class. At the same time much of the fiction, less consciously but more importantly, redefined women's space and offered role models for success within that space. Read chronologically, the fiction reflects differences in attitudes and behavior over the period on the part of the women themselves as well as those who observed them and those who wrote about them. The body of work examined here focuses on one area of women's lives and what that work reveals of their expectations for themselves and society's for them, and then the changes brought about by time and the outside world.

Vassar Female College (the "Female" was dropped a year later, thanks to the efforts of editor Sarah Josepha Hale) opened in 1865, to be followed ten years later by Smith and Wellesley, and Bryn Mawr in 1883; by the end of the century Mount Holyoke, a seminary since 1837, had become a college and the "annexes," Radcliffe, Barnard, and Pembroke, were established. Women were admitted into the large state universities in the 1870s. Smaller and less-noticed colleges, like Elmira and Wells, flourished.

In 1900, even though by then Vassar was thirty-five years old, Sophia Kirk, a contributor to important magazines like the *Atlantic Monthly* and *Harper's*, made her contribution to the attempts to explain "college girls" to a world that clearly still did not understand them.[1] In her first paragraph, after pointing out that higher education for women was here to stay, she wrote,

> The college girl, though golf and tennis have brought her nearer than of yore to her generation in society, and the sense of her being harder to talk to than other girls is wearing off, is still regarded curiously and a little askance. There is a certain myth afloat in regard to her nature and existence. She is subjected to three processes which in the eyes of the world at large are occult and mysterious, separating her from her kind, fraught with possibilities and dangers: she passes through a terrible ordeal known as the entrance examination; she plunges into the abyss of intellectual work; she is surrounded by the strange enchantments of college life.

Kirk went on to repeat the questions that so many had been asking from the day when Vassar's establishment and goals were announced: "Will her health, her spontaneity and joy, be forever ruined by the first? Will the second engulf forever her womanliness, her charm, her religious faith? Will she be unfitted by the third for home life, for social life, for the best of human life? These questions may sound portentous and absurd, but they are all floating in the air, sometimes without the interrogation-point, in the form of criticism." Higher education for women was once a socially disruptive phenomenon, one to which many and varied interests reacted, often emphatically, and authors tried, with varying degrees of subtlety and literary skill, to answer Kirk's questions.

In recent years much work has been done on reading, on the relationship of the reader to the text, and on popular fiction. Enough has been studied and written so that we can accept the importance of fiction as an influence, as a way of trying out other lives, directing behavior, setting and reinforcing standards, opening doors and providing role models.[2] All this was especially true in an age that valued books and reading as the way to knowledge. Because of that exploration of reader and text relationships, this study can rest on two assumptions: first, that popular fiction, perhaps even more than great literature, reflects the preoccupations and the attitudes of the immediate present, the time in which it is written; and second, that readers turned to the printed word for information as well as entertainment.

The fiction examined here, particularly the earliest, certainly wanted to tell a story, but it also wished to explain to an unknowing and often hostile society this new, frightening phenomenon: higher education for women. Although it is difficult today to understand the furious and emotional response to the opening of Vassar, that reaction was strong enough to frighten some, and those young women (and their parents) who considered a college education could not do so without questioning the act and the result. Fiction that was authentic, written as so much of it was by recent graduates, offered information about the life, the behavioral codes, and the ways to success. And as Alfred Habeggar points out, there is "an old and powerful truth about the act of reading fiction: lead characters are potential role models for the reader. . . . to read a novel was to try on a certain role—to think out with the help of a book-length narrative the potential life-consequences of being a given kind of woman."[3]

From any point of view, this college fiction is full of messages for and about women. Therefore, though it should not be read as historical record, it does legitimately convey some of the truths of an experience whose difference and newness cannot be overestimated and one that remained special for a long time. If we can assume that, although none of the accounts are factual, they contain or reflect truths, then it is impossible to miss the changes over this sixty-year period. The pioneer narratives of the early years gave way to the celebration of a special life, then to series books that exploited the women's college background, and finally to another, far less positive, set of serious examinations of the college experience. But the progression is not so neat as we might like it to be, for its movement is cluttered with and halted by contradictory attitudes, often existing at the same time, about what educated women were or should be.

Notably, most of the fiction, or at least that part which is serious in its intent, centers on the first four colleges of the group that would eventually be known as the Seven Sisters. While all women's higher education was controversial, the women's colleges fascinated outsiders as the coeducational colleges never did; because of that fact, and because more fiction is based on the women's colleges, my emphasis is there. I place further emphasis on the fiction written by authors who went to college between, roughly, 1890 and 1910; these tales celebrate the experience and present a kind of triumph unmatched by what went before and what came after. All these earliest writers find that the college experience itself is enough to carry their stories.

In the introduction to *The College Novel in America* (1962) John O. Lyons defines his "novel of academic life" as "one in which education is treated with seriousness and the main characters are students and professors." He rules out juveniles and mysteries, then comments, "There are a number of works for girls which strive to teach them how young ladies are expected to behave at college."[4] He is perfectly right in what he says, but he misses the significance of his own analysis, as his single chapter about women further indicates. It has been tempting throughout to set Lyons up as a straw man, but that would not be fair; given his thesis and the time in which he wrote, he simply shares a common viewpoint. The fiction written about the women's colleges did indeed partly aim at teaching young women how to behave there. The purpose was legitimate, perhaps necessary, for in the early days, as it is easy for us to forget now, the colleges were not just a novelty, but to many, a scandalous novelty. Stories served as maps of terra incognita, and they attempted to refute an image (or images) created by public opinion and a "press" that was frightened, hostile, or opportunistic. More, the fiction defined success in the new environment and ways to achieve it.

The short stories, novels, and juveniles examined here have one element in common: they all depict the life and experience of young women going to college. My choices have been made on criteria different from those of Lyons: major characters must be college students, whether or not they are presented with "seriousness," and the fiction must be immediate, as far as possible.[5] Since the only thing that connects all this fiction is the college experience, there are variations; literary quality, for example, ranges from excellent to cliché-ridden. But serious or superficial, well written or not, all the fiction makes statements about women's behavior, about rewards and punishment, and about social expectations.

My major points grow out of the sense that the early writers had an agenda beyond simply telling a story. Perhaps paradoxically, they wanted readers to understand this new and different experience for women at the same time that social attitudes forced them to insist that, in the language of these texts, college girls were just like other girls. Certain topics, therefore, are of major importance. Time, change, and varying degrees of commitment modify these topics, yet most remain in one form or another—and when they do not, their absence is in itself a statement. In their process of selection, what writers chose to tell about or emphasize from the material available to them, which was, of course, their own experience, indicates what seemed important and memorable to them (or perhaps sometimes what was tactful); that similar elements were emphasized by different writers underlines their importance. Significant, too, is the treatment of these themes and preoccupations in the hands of less-committed writers or the ways in which time and society changed or modified their aims.

The early writing presents a women's space that nourished community—a space, called the green world in this book, with its own rules; it offered women more room to define themselves than they could find anywhere else. This women's space is the core of all good in the early fiction, remains a vision even as it disintegrates or is distorted, and finally is inverted and lost. But the factors that create and destroy it reveal much about women's lives.

Another concern, sometimes conscious, is for image and definition: what should the "college-bred" woman, to borrow a commonly used though seldom defined term, be? How should she be portrayed? How was higher education to be reconciled with standards of womanliness?

Though most of the fiction does not address definition directly, it is implicit in all the works. The characters in the fiction are, with few exceptions, middle-class and white, with Anglo-Saxon surnames. Most come from financially comfortable families, with a few daughters of the rich and a few students with scholarships or working their way through school. This college population probably reflects historical fact, but wealth and class are seldom keys to success in the fictional college worlds, which do not promote exclusivity. It is certainly possible, in an America that foregrounded assimilation rather than ethnicity, that these young women, fictional or real, might serve as models for those aiming at upward mobility.

All the fiction, with the exception of the juvenile series examined in Chapter 5, was aimed at an adult audience. That the central characters were young women—girls—does not make this fiction for the young. Many of the collected stories published around the turn of the century appeared first in *Scribner's Monthly Magazine*; for a long time the "college story," male and female, was a kind of subgenre, reviewed in good places and treated as a legitimate literary classification. Too, as Richard Tebbel reminds us, "It was characteristic of the period that books which we consider children's classics today . . . were read at least as avidly by adults in the years of their greatest popularity."[6] The best-selling *Daddy Long-Legs* by Jean Webster, published in 1912, is a perfect example. It was reviewed as a novel, had a wide general audience, and was made into a Broadway play; it has never been out of print, and only in later years was it relegated to juvenile shelves. And earlier nineteenth-century letters and diaries make it very plain that fiction about young people (like *Huckleberry Finn*) was of interest to and read by adults; children, boys and girls growing up, were the next generation, to whom adults, in an age that believed in patriotism and perfectibility, felt a commitment. Serious women's college stories, the reviews indicate, were read as fiction, but also as a source of information.

Overall the total amount of fiction about women in college is small, especially in contrast with the enormous amount of commentary, serious or frivolous, on the subject. By 1890 issues of important magazines were seldom without some view of women and higher education, and later the popular magazines adopted the college woman as a feature. Serious studies of the aims of the women's colleges, or the advantages or disadvantages of coeducation were written by almost anyone with a connection or an opinion; those mentioned here, chiefly in Chapter 2, can provide only a sampling. More recently there have been several studies of the history of the women's colleges, notably Barbara Miller Solomon's *In the Company of Educated Women* and Helen Lefkowitz Horowitz's *Alma Mater*, as well as Lynn D. Gordon's *Gender and Higher Education in the Progressive Era* and an older one, Mabel Newcomer's *A Century of Higher*

*Education for Women.*[7] Although these and others have provided useful background for this study, I have tried not to make them reference points, preferring to use commentary that is contemporary with the works being discussed. My aim was not to make comparisons between history and fiction, but rather to try for a sense of the times, the experience, and the audience. I do occasionally refer to biography and autobiography, contemporary men's stories, and novels that include college life but were written much later, when such comparisons are useful.

The books and short stories examined here do not and probably cannot make up an exhaustive list. Discovering and locating all fiction about women in college is impossible; the problem is particularly great with juvenile series books for girls. Advertising in the backs of some volumes lists titles I have not been able to find; if these books still exist, they are buried in deposit libraries. Girls' series books have never been considered literary treasures.[8] Most of the juveniles examined here came from secondhand bookstores; while the search was delightful, I found only the occasional isolated volume and a few series popular enough or printed in large enough quantities to be found everywhere.

My approach is roughly chronological. Chapter 1 focuses on the earliest fiction about women and college and examines the special women's space, the green world, that the fiction presents. Chapter 2 looks at the interaction between the colleges and outside opinion, chiefly as it came through the press, and how it affected what was being written. Chapter 3 deals with the fiction written by authors who were in college during what seem to be the golden years, 1890–1910; it is characterized by a joyousness and pride and confidence in the consolidation of a women's community. Though I did not originally plan it this way, this rich body of fiction, the majority of which was published around 1900 as collections of short stories, is really the core of the study. As the high point, it sets standards for the rest.

Chapter 4 pauses to examine two particular themes of the turn-of-the-century fiction: prominence, which is really a name for power, allowing women to excel, to lead, and to control, though always within limits which are gender-determined; and the outsider, who for a variety of reasons remains detached from the magic world. Chronologically, a large gap separates the early, serious portrayals of college life and those that come later, and Chapter 5 examines the juvenile series books that fill that gap. The green world undergoes a disintegration, and many of its features are reshaped for a different audience. College, while still important, becomes more background than player. Chapter 6 examines the "others"—places where there is no green world or where it has been distorted, as in the stories with coeducational settings; or minimized, as in the developmental novel; or is, finally, under actual attack.

Men, romance, love, marriage, friendship, crushes, and lesbianism, real and perceived, are treated in various ways, and Chapter 7 discusses their presentation and significance in all the fiction. Chapter 8 examines the fictional treatment of a serious question: what to do with the college woman once she graduated into a world that seemed to have no place for her.

Readers will note that nearly all the quoted passages, fiction or commentary, call their subjects "girls"; it is the consistent terminology of all the texts and has a very precise meaning. Our awareness that the word is trivializing is fairly recent, although Henry Noble MacCracken, president of Vassar from 1915 to 1945, remembered the time when he was transferring power to the newly developing student government and there were questions about the students' ability to sustain responsibility. Professor Lucy Maynard Salmon urged, "'Call them women, not girls . . . and you'll see they will act like women.' So I did, and banished the term 'college girl' from my vocabulary." [9] But "girl" as used in these texts denotes a stage in female development, movement from child to girl to woman, and the term in context is not one of belittlement, but a definition of an age and status group: young and unmarried, characterized by innocence, unworldliness, virginity, and youthful freshness. The girls in this fiction are going to be women, but they are not there yet. They themselves know that womanhood awaits them after graduation. Times have changed and today the word applied to young college women would be nonsensical and offensive, since they no longer fit the description; the innocence, particularly sexual innocence, and the protected unworldliness no longer exist.

Although the fiction examined here and the speculation about the response of readers are of the past, the subject remains topical. The question of whether women can work together keeps recurring, each time as if it were a brand-new insight. Strong, well-educated women who assume leadership roles clearly continue to terrify some people. Women academics still have problems with tenure and promotion. In fact, it is sad to note that past commentaries on women's education still painfully resonate today.

The early and the turn-of-the-century fictional texts describe "a place that belongs to [women]. The surrounding society is not one where the sexes are equal," and "Women's colleges are first and foremost committed to the welfare and progress of women students." But the speaker of these words is not a voice from the past; she is Judith Shapiro in an interview with the *New York Times* on her inauguration as president of Barnard College in March 1994.[10] Current reexamination of women's education, such as the recent study done by the American Association of University Women, indicates that discrimination against women students still exists and reassesses the value of single-sex colleges.[11] Rising enroll-ments in the women's colleges, which one writer suggests are based on a "widespread feeling that parity with men is still an elusive goal" confirm changing attitudes.[12] So the debate over women's education that under-lies the works presented here continues, and the magical women's space of the early fiction seems once again desirable.

# · ONE ·

# *Beginnings*

Three titles can be designated the earliest fictional portrayals of women in college. These are *An American Girl and Her Four Years in a Boys' College,* by Olive San Louie Anderson (1878); Helen Dawes Brown's *Two College Girls* (1886); and Abbe Carter Goodloe's *College Girls* (1895).[1] Related to these are Elizabeth Stuart Phelps's magazine serial, "A Brave Girl" (1884), and a group of books by Elizabeth W. Champney whose titles begin with *Three Vassar Girls* (1882–1892).[2] The first three, in very different ways, explore the experience of young women in college, although only one, *Two College Girls,* presents the life as a different and wholly positive experience and offers models for success. This novel, an adaptation of a theme already popular in nineteenth-century fiction, is in a sense a prototype of the writing that will follow.

Although most of the fiction is about the women's colleges, the first offering is set in a coeducational institution. *An American Girl* is a roman à clef; its author graduated from Michigan in 1875 and her story is a fictionalized account of her life there. Dorothy Guies McGuigan, in her study of the first women students at the University of Michigan, comments:

> The authenticity of its picture of college life in Ann Arbor in the '70s was vouched for by various classmates of the author. Marginal notes in the copy in the University's Rare Books Room, originally inscribed by a friend of Louie Anderson, Cora Agnes Benneson, not only reveal the identity of all the personages involved—both faculty and students—but attest to the general veracity of the picture. Only occasionally has Cora Benneson noted "exaggerated" or "no longer true."[3]

Wilhelmina Elliott, called Will, the hero, is an unusual young woman, strong in mind and body; her name was probably deliberately chosen. She has splendid health, good looks, brains, and personality. She is able to assert herself, even though her strength pushes at the boundaries of womanly behavior. Her hair and her skirts are slightly shorter than those of other young women; she is an excellent rider and owns a gun, which she uses expertly. She thinks for herself and is an agnostic; the first chapter, in fact, portrays her finally successful efforts to persuade her mother, a Presbyterian fundamentalist, to allow her to go to godless college.

Will sets off for the university, where she has difficulty finding a place to live. Three boardinghouse keepers refuse her (they "could not think of taking a lady-student, it's so odd, you know; we can't tell what they might be like") before she finds one willing to "try lady-boarders" (36–37). A year later, she comments, these same landladies will advertise for women students, having learned that they were quieter than men, took better care of their rooms, "did not smoke and injure the wallpaper, nor spit tobacco-juice on the furniture . . . [or] reel upstairs half-seas over, and go to bed in their hats and boots." Women had become acceptable, "except in families where there were marriageable daughters" since the young women might be competitors for college men as husbands (87).

The trials of the first-year women students include dealing with professors, each of whom has his own attitude and therefore demands a different response. Will's student tutor in Xenophon becomes infatuated and tries to kiss her; she is regarded with dismay when she goes alone to hear Wendell Phillips lecture, and indeed is insulted by a male student on her way home after dark, but fortunately she has her gun with her. She describes parts of her life in letters to her sister: the first morning chapel, for example, was "a most uproarious din . . . the fresh and sophs in mortal combat." When the nine women students found seats, they were in the "direct line of the missiles between the hostile classes, which missiles consisted of hymn-books, sticks, anything moveable; a great apple-core struck me right in the eye . . . I was on the last step hurrying to get out of the crowd, when I was pushed violently against the bannisters, making my nose bleed in a most ghastly manner" (48–50). But in spite of the obstacles Will's first year is a success. She does well in her courses, finds the academic life stimulating, and makes several good friends.

Anderson faced some of the charges made against higher education for women. Will and her friends read Dr. Edward Clarke's *Sex in Education*, reacting with both disgust and amusement.[4] Will decides that he is right about the danger of corsets, however, and stops wearing hers. When one student kills herself, leaving behind a note explaining her inherited tendency to suicide, authorial comment is caustic; newspapers and general gossip insist that the act was caused by strain: "she had studied too hard to keep up with her class, and thus the evil effects of co-education were early becoming manifest. Others said that she had fallen in love with a classmate, and, because it was not reciprocated, she found life too great a burden to be borne; and another moral was drawn concerning co-education" (165).

Will is a good advertisement for higher education, however. While ice-skating, she rescues a young man who has fallen through the ice; his father, a state legislator who has actively opposed women's entrance to the state universities, becomes a strong supporter. After hearing "Mrs. Livermore, Mrs. Howe, and Mrs. Stanton" speak, Will favors women's suffrage, but in a debate speech and at commencement, where she is the only woman among the ten student speakers, her presentation on "Women in the Professions" is rational and appealing, not emotional and angry. There is an exchange of letters with a friend at Vassar in which Will criticizes the heavy supervision and isolation of the women's colleges and argues that the coeducational relationship with men students is more sensible and realistic. All these elements are presented as separate episodes.

The most sustained and cohesive part of Will's story is her romance. From the first she is attracted to Guilford Randolf, who scorns women students in general and Will in particular. While she offends his image of womanliness, he unwillingly admires both her achievements and her looks. "Don't get me started on her, for I can't bear her style," he tells friends who have called Will the "Queen of the Amazons" in wholly admiring tones (83–84). Although the two are constantly aware of each other, they do not meet formally until their junior year.

Though not explicit in the text, it is clear to the reader that Randolf is sexually attracted by Will's physical appearance and vitality. They meet formally at a croquet game; Will is suitably dressed in white cambric, and Randolf sees "the superior grace and symmetry of her figure, which was never embarrassed by any tight-fitting garment," the "pose of her head," and other physical attributes (184). He neither understands nor approves of what she is, and he resists the attraction as long as he can.

Will, too, has doubts, although she buries them. Earlier she had commented on a friend's engagement: "I tell you nothing takes the starch out of a girl like being engaged. She loses ambition right away. . . . That always seems to be the end of them, they settle right down and lose their individuality, and are as good as dead and buried" (111–112). She proves her own words as, after she and Randolf are engaged, she sadly and consciously gives up her dream of becoming a medical doctor: "I shall do the very natural and proper thing of forsaking a professional career for the one I love, and give up dreams of fame as a master of the healing art" (217). But when, as an indication of her love, she tells Randolf what she is giving up for him, his reaction shocks her; spontaneously and wholeheartedly he declares, "I'm glad to be your saviour from such a fate." Shocked, Will tries to explain her ambitions as much because she wants to make him understand her and her dreams as because she is upset by his complacency.

The scene is the most moving one in the novel, as Will honestly opens her mind and heart and Randolf pretends to understand, while under his agreeable surface he is sure "that he would save her from a life of hardship, and he wondered that she did not see this. . . . It might do for some women, but the one he cared for must never hold a scalpel or know anything about diseases." He was not, says the authorial voice, "more selfish, perhaps, than most men, in being unable to see that the woman he chose could wish to indulge any plans or wishes that might conflict with him" (219–221).

The reader realizes long before the characters do that this proposed marriage simply will not work, since the two have such conflicting values. The author, however, instead of leading Will to self-knowledge and action, contrives a scene in which she overhears a conversation that makes her break the engagement. Though there is no reconciliation, Randolf continues to seek her out, and the conflict between love and self-respect persists; in fact, the story ends equivocally, with Will going off to teach and earn money for medical school:

> "Bless my soul, does that girl think she is going to study medicine?" said Mr. Lewis, with an amused laugh. "If she don't marry that pair of handsome eyes that used to be forever coming to study off the same book with her, I'll miss my guess!"
> "Oh!" said Mrs. Lewis, "you men are so conceited! You think a woman never has an aim in life that she won't leave to go at your beck and call. I have more faith in our Will than that, and we'll see if I'm not right." (268–269)

The image of college women that Anderson's story presents is not the one that will be developed and sustained by later fiction. Will is too unusual. Her splendid health, queenly presence, intelligence and poise, thoughtful mind, courage in behaving according to her principles, and especially her willingness to stretch conventions separate her from her contemporaries, from the heroes who will follow, and possibly from the average reader—a young woman who carried a gun was not the norm in the 1870s—so that while the fictionalized firsthand account is certainly interesting, it does not catch the reader as good fiction might, nor does it provide a role model. Will's strength makes the other characters, even Randolf, shadowy: parts of the background against which the brilliant protagonist moves. Assuming that Anderson meant readers to see Randolf as an attractive young man, her characterization is a failure; he comes across as egocentric and snobbish, not worth either Will's affection or the sacrifice she is willing to make for him. The conflict is not equal and the reader feels that Will has had a narrow escape from an unfortunate sacrifice.

Anderson wants readers to understand an unusual experience, and she sets out the problems that she and others encountered as they entered male territory. She does not integrate her "issues" into a cohesive

plot; her lack of skill produced not an ongoing story but a series of episodes tied together with such awkward transitions as "At about this
time." Far too frequently she pauses to comment on what she has just
narrated. While this accumulation of incident makes interesting reading,
the novel is a flawed literary work, for the qualities that make a lively
record work against literary value, and at best the novel is pleasant but
amateur. It is the first attempt to tell the story of women in college, however, and the only one for fifty years to focus on coeducation.[5]

A few years later two writers far more skilled than Anderson turned
their attention to women in college. Elizabeth Stuart Phelps's "A Brave
Girl," was serialized in *Wide Awake*, a magazine for older adolescents
and their parents, in 1884; while the story is not really about college life,
it starts with its hero, Loto Rollinstall, a junior at Smith. Like so many
nineteenth-century novels written by and about women, the aim is to
show how bravely a young woman can deal with adversity. When her father's death forces her to leave school to support her mother and edu-
cate her younger brother, Loto tries crocheting and teaching, but these
acceptable womanly activities will not provide for the family. Finally she
learns to be a telegrapher, and although the work is not pleasant, it does
pay a decent salary. After her mother's illness and need for care ends that
job, she uses family recipes to start a small business making jellies and
cakes. Information learned in her college physics course enables her to
invent a better container, and the world beats a path to her door; by the
end of the story she is a well-to-do businesswoman, owning and managing
several small factories.

The opening scenes show the life Loto must give up. She loves college,
and Phelps presents the time at Smith convincingly. Loto balances her
life: "She worked as hard as she played, privately intending that her father should not be ashamed of her. She played as hard as she worked,
fully intending to have her education's worth, and having it" (30). The
reader meets her surrounded by friends, with whom she is clearly popular, at the exciting moment when she has discovered what she wants to
do with her life. She enthusiastically explains to them her plans to become a professor of biology.

Phelps ends the story by bringing Loto back to Smith to speak at her
class reunion as an example of a successful businesswoman. Her advice
to her classmates assumes that they, too, will go out into a man's world;
she tells them, "Be thorough. . . . There is no place in this world for
slipshod women's work anymore than there is for slipshod men's. . . . Do
it sensibly, not sentimentally, and *never* cry before a man." She ends by
reminding them of her dream of becoming a biology professor and says
that she could invent her container because of something she learned in
physics. "I thought you would be glad to see in what ways it pays to know
things, in this world. . . . I hated Physics. But I had to make the cans. And

I had to have a better cover than other cans—and so it came about" (161–162).

College represents the desirable and fulfilling life that the hero has to relinquish. That she gives it up bravely and without complaint is the point of the story. The brief college scenes picture an appealing life; the companionship of bright, spirited girls, the variety, the strength of friendship, the joy of learning, and the promise of an interesting future, all contrast with the misery and near-hopelessness of Loto's life after she is forced to leave. Her brave acceptance brings its reward and, since this is a popular magazine story, the ending has a hint of romance and marriage in her future.

The first real woman's college novel was published in 1886. Helen Dawes Brown's *Two College Girls*, though it skillfully deals with points of opposition to educating women, is a novel of character development, and it fits neatly into the general ambiance of the nineteenth-century "domestic" novel. But in an important way it is completely uncharacteristic of that genre, for the college is not background, but rather the working element in a story of growth and change. In fact, some of the best-written, most interesting, and amusing scenes in the novel are the "academic" passages, in which the reader is taken into the classroom to see the learning process at work.

Brown was a native of Concord, Massachusetts; her Vassar classmates nicknamed her "Emerson" Brown because the sage himself had written one of her letters of recommendation. She graduated in 1878, taught at Vassar, studied abroad and took her M.A. in 1890. She wrote novels, short stories, and essays as well as scholarly works on English literature. Her college novel seems to have been popular, since there was a fourteenth edition in 1893, and the review in the *Atlantic Monthly* was friendly, if tepid: "Vassar is responsible for this book, and one may by means of it get a glimpse into the interior of a girls' college. The book is written with feminine delicacy, and if not very strong is at any rate honest and wholesome." [6] *Two College Girls* neatly adapts a popular theme of nineteenth-century writing to the special conditions and quality of college life, and in spite of the review's faint praise, Brown's literary ability and her thoughtful presentation make this a pleasant book to read and one that makes significant statements about women and their abilities. The ending is unusual in its quiet insistence on the variety of choices available to educated women.

Edna Howe is the daughter of middle-class, upright, decent, though not well educated rural New Englanders, who support their bright child's desire to go to college. Relatives reflect more common views: Uncle Lemuel points out indignantly that he never went to college but seems to do well; Uncle Ira says, "We'll see if she cooks a piece of beefsteak any better for all her algebry" (15); Grandma begs her to go to Honeysuckle

Seminary, as two cousins did, "and now, I'm sure, they're well married and settled" (17).

Edna is, in her way, almost as narrow as her relatives; her desire for a formal education has blinded her to any virtues different from her own. Intelligent and well read as she is, she needs to learn about the world and its variety, and the learning begins almost at once when, after examinations admit her to the sophomore class at Vassar, she meets her roommate, the second title character. Rosamund Mills is a lively, frivolous, lighthearted westerner from Chicago whose purpose in college is to enjoy herself. Edna is self-righteously disgusted at her roommate's silliness, and her first real—and painful—learning experience comes when she discovers that Rosamund is equally dismayed at her: "That she would lie so lightly in another person's mind shocked her—she who had always taken herself so seriously" (51–52).

The story's path is clear: two dissimilar young women are going to grow and change, learning from each other as well as from their surroundings. Nineteenth-century fiction is full of stories about girls who mature into gracious womanhood through the influence of another character with whom they were first in conflict. And like many women writers, Brown creates and emphasizes community. But she goes beyond the commonplace, for it is an academic community that is the chief agent of change. Almost from the beginning the reader is drawn into that world; the third chapter presents students taking the entrance exams, and it humorously stresses the variety of young women and the confusion and vagueness of both their knowledge and their expectations. As Brown looks at them, her humor is mixed with affection and familiarity; she has been through the experience herself, and it is this familiarity that she shares with the reader, especially when she takes her audience into the classroom.

After the examinations, there is a chapter dealing with the relations between the two young women; then "Six Weeks Later," in a delightful, humorous, and crucial scene, the reader enters a history class.[7] Young women in varying degrees of preparedness are shocked when the professor uses the assigned reading as a Socratic point of departure to make them draw connections and conclusions—in short, to think about the facts they have learned. The picture of the class in action is rich and amusing, moving from the professor's mind to the shifting interaction between him and the students, as well as among the students themselves as they react to individual behaviors and the professor's direction. Stimulated and frightened by the mental exercise, the class moves on to Greek literature, where the lecturing professor, an "eloquent pleader for the old learning," clusters "about the name Greek such wealth and beauty of association as made it one of the charmed words in the language" (68).

Following the history class with indication of another kind of intellectual experience, Brown has clearly delineated the world in which the story will work itself out. She has also introduced the main characters, and the reader can easily believe in the personal growth and maturity of young women whose minds are being opened and made flexible in the ways shown. That this approach is never duplicated in other college stories may be partly a result of Brown's qualifications; as student and teacher, she knew both sides of the desk.

The history class reveals much about the different characters, but particularly demonstrates Edna's mixture of intelligence and inflexibility. As she leaves the class she feels humiliated, for the professor's method has made her see that while she is able to learn facts, she has not learned to think with them. But the humiliation is productive, as is the equal humiliation of the totally unprepared Rosamund, whose shame drives her to study. Their different embarrassments make the two feel some sympathy for each other. Rosamund is able to express her concern, and Edna begins to see beyond the frivolity to her companion's generosity of spirit. It is the beginning of self-knowledge and appreciation that will lead to strong friendship, just as it is the recognition and acceptance of differences. " 'It's a great pity,' [Rosamund] said meditatively, 'It's a great pity, I'm beginning to think, that you and I couldn't be added together and divided by two—or you toned up and I toned down. Do you see what I mean?' " (100).

Passage after passage illustrates the maturing process that Edna, Rosamund, and their friends go through as college life bombards them with experiences. Besides widening her mind, Edna develops social graces, learning to meet others without the old brusque intolerance of anyone with ideas differing from hers. She even has a romance; at the end of the novel she is engaged to Rosamund's brother, who has watched and appreciated her growth. Rosamund, who came to college to have a good time and who at first barely scraped through her classes, finds herself fascinated by zoology, and when the death of a friend forces her to serious self-examination, sees the lack of purpose in her life and decides to become a doctor. By graduation the girls are women, but they are also persons, understanding themselves and others, and, committed to the belief that their four college years were the beginning, not the end, of education, they are ready to do their work in the world.

In the process of telling her story, Brown, too, deals with several of the charges made against women's higher education. The whole thrust of her novel is that women can learn to think and can master the same subjects as men, but she also asserts that women can live and work together in a productive way and shows that the college experience can give them that ability. She quietly refutes the tendency of the outside world and critics to think and talk about "*the* college girl," as if there were only one kind, or the college cloned its students. This outsiders' point of view was inconsistent, since it existed simultaneously with such stereotypes as the bluestocking, studious frump, and beefy athlete, but logic was never a major component of the arguments against the women's colleges. "*The* college girl" persisted, and Brown and later writers did their best to show that it was wrong. By emphasizing different young women, different experiences, different interactions, Brown insists that the college can provide something for everyone; the mind opening that took place in the classroom can extend to all students but does not turn them into copies of some single vision. Instead, it provides what they need: the rough westerner, Rosamund, learns restraint and manners while the inhibited New Englander, Edna, learns to be gracious and respect others.

Almost at the end of the novel comes a scene that serves as a summing up of college life for all the main characters (289–296). With graduation near, the small group of friends want to spend their time together, meeting often to talk or read aloud and discuss their reading. In this case they are sewing as they listen to one of their number read aloud. All is pleasant until May, the reader, exclaims, "And *will* you listen to this! . . . 'Most women do with themselves nothing at all; they wait, in attitudes more or less gracefully passive, for a man to come their way and furnish them with a destiny.' " [8]

The listeners react with amused indignation to the idea that they will wait, "gracefully passive," until someone else establishes their fate, and the conversation turns to a discussion of their plans and hopes. None of them rule out marriage; most feel that it is the best life for a woman. They see, in fact, two "woman questions," different for married and unmarried women, and take for granted their ability to adjust to either. Clearly these young women value themselves as people who are able and prepared to make choices and to handle whatever comes, and each one has a plan for her life. They are neither defiant nor angry, simply confident that they have been given tools for a large measure of control over their own futures.

This wideness of choice and quiet self-confidence are far more radical than the resolutions of most nineteenth-century women's novels, and indeed more radical than anything that will follow. The attitudes probably reflect those of the first generations of college women, who knew that they were doing something unusual and exciting and were willing to assert their ability to handle this challenge. "It's a little odd," says Edna at one point in the long conversation about the future, "that we don't talk more here about the education of women. We hardly ever mention the subject." A friend answers, "Because the argument is ended. We are here; that is the conclusion." But Edna muses, "I'm not sure this is the conclusion. All the rest of our lives will have to be the conclusion" (291).

Like her characters, Brown does not editorialize about education, but she transmits her own sense of adventure and the importance of the experience through her story.

As a novel, *Two College Girls* fits into the category called domestic fiction, domestic realism, or literary domesticity—that is, the kind of novel that nineteenth-century women writers produced out of their social reality. The narratives follow the pattern that Nina Baym has shown to be characteristic of the nineteenth-century woman's novel, which reflects the structure of the initiation process in which the initiate is separated from home, undergoes tests and ordeals, learns the lore and codes of the culture, and finally returns to his or her society as a responsible adult.[9] Brown's characters, however, are initiated within and for a special world that does not replace but is added to the normal one. They are both women and college women; more is offered to and expected of them, but they must still conform to a basic, if widely expanded, vision even as they have a wider range of choices.

Even Phelp's Loto in "A Brave Girl" illustrates this point. When she is thrown upon the world, she first tries all the suitably womanly means to earn money, only to find that none of them work. It is not until she combines family recipes with college physics that she succeeds—and succeeds in the "man's world" of business. Anderson's Will Elliott is headed for teaching, then medical school, but she can marry if she wants to. In Brown's novel Edna and Rosamund and their friends, rich in a variety of opportunities, make their choices with confidence that whatever happens, they are ready.

A major difference between Brown and Anderson, other than the content itself, is their ability to center their stories on a believable and accessible protagonist, one with whom the reader can identify and therefore hold as a role model. Brown succeeds, but Anderson's portrayal raises some questions. Perhaps for the 1870s her Will is interesting but too exceptional—too vivid and strong to be a "normal" young woman; the character suggests that to survive in the coeducational world, one must be almost a superwoman. The author's focus on her, leaving the other less spectacular young women as shadowy background figures, strengthens that message. Brown, on the other hand, has two central characters, the reserved, inhibited Edna and the boisterous, outgoing Rosamund, who has never bothered to use her mind. Both are flawed and human. Other characters are given enough emphasis and delineation so that the reader can see growth in different young women and in different directions. These are not superwomen, but ordinary bright young women who still need to learn, like Edna and Rosamund, to use their minds, modify their behavior to make it socially acceptable, and respect and value differences. Again, Brown quietly stresses the fact that the women's college provides for difference, and later writers will reinforce her point.

Between 1882 and 1892, a series of books by Elizabeth W. Champney told the experiences of *Three Vassar Girls . . . Abroad, in England, at Home* and other similar titles. In spite of the titles, however, these are not "series books," which usually recount the experiences of a continuing single hero with her subordinate friends; the Vassar students are different in each book, although there are always three of them. Nor are these stories about women in college. In reality they belong to what was for a while a popular subgenre, lightly disguised travelogues. A great many established authors sent characters abroad, producing fairly thin plots embellished with much description and anecdote. There is no exploration of college life; Vassar simply connects the three travelers who journey and have adventures. Advertising material for *Three Vassar Girls in Russia and Turkey*, for example, sets the story "during the exciting scenes and events of the late Turko-Russian War, with many adventures, both serious and comic." The illustrations underline the point: they are all of highly romantic scenes—mountains, glens, chasms, beaches—or of picturesque towns. Occasionally the face of a character appears sketched in the text.

The significance of these books lies in their assumption that the boundaries for women—college women—are open. When the protagonists of *Three Vassar Girls in the Tyrol* plan their trip, they can find no chaperone for one part of it. One character says, "what a self-reliant girl, clad in all the womanly dignity of Vassar, needs of a chaperone is more than I can make out" (21). Like Edward Everett Hale's protagonist in his short story "Susan's Escort," they feel annoyed that anyone with their background should be thought to need chaperonage.[10] The lack of a chaperone does, in fact, cause some embarrassment by exposing them to overfamiliarity, but the situation is one they can easily handle.

Champney graduated from Vassar in 1869, a member of the first class; though she chose not to explore or re-create college life, it is clear that for her, Vassar graduates are not to be judged by the standards that apply to others. It was not socially acceptable for young women to travel alone in the 1880s and 1890s, at least not young women of good family who hoped to make good marriages, yet for Champney the Vassar label—its "womanly dignity"—proclaims a privileged and separate status. Since she was writing for a popular audience, it seems that by the 1890s the women's colleges, though still misunderstood, scolded, and ridiculed, had gained their own kind of prestige.

The last of the early attempts to interpret the world of the women's colleges to the public is Abbe Carter Goodloe's *College Girls* (1895), a collection of short stories, several of which had been previously published in *Scribner's Monthly Magazine.* Goodloe graduated from Wellesley about 1888 and wrote at least one novel and essays for several magazines; her book is a handsome volume illustrated by Charles Dana Gibson, whose drawings of girls frequently decorated the walls of college rooms.[11]

At first reading these stories seem an honest attempt to explain and share the experience of college, but this first impression is both true and deceptive. Goodloe has an unstated thesis that college women are no different from other young women in that they are waiting to get married—"gracefully passive" perhaps, as the characters in *Two College Girls* refused to be. In the meantime, going to college is a good way to keep busy. In fact, all but a few stories present college as a kind of pleasant storage vault for girls while they wait for marriage and adulthood. Of the fourteen tales, the majority are simply love stories that could take place anywhere; they tell of romances, of self-sacrifice, of misunderstandings, of feminine rivalries, with the college functioning as an unusual background that brought the characters together. Even "The College Beauty," a powerful story about an extraordinary young woman who seems to have everything, including a wonderful future, but lives with the knowledge that she is trapped in a youthful secret marriage to a well-meaning clod she has long outgrown, is enriched by the college setting, but does not need it. Her tragedy is that she now loves and is loved by a man who is clearly her ideal mate.

Another story, "As Told by Her," needs the college setting but rejects what it stands for. A graduate, back for a reunion, seeks out a professor she had revered. The younger woman has "lived"—married, borne a child who died, battled poverty, illness, and danger at her husband's side—and as she praises the professor's intellectual attainments, the older woman sees herself as dried up and useless because her life has missed emotional experience.

Love, romance, and marriage are of first importance, and the author asserts that education does not make women unfit for all that belongs to their sphere. Some of the stories are serious examinations of women's lives and relationships with men; these young women are, in the male-defined sense of subordinating everything to love, womanly. They have not become mannish, desexed, or desiccated. But certainly education, college life, the finding of identity, and the stretching of the mind are not their chief concerns, nor do the stories emphasize community, shared lives and goals as Brown did and as later fiction would do. Goodloe writes well, but with a slight touch of satire that effects a distancing from her characters and has a faintly patronizing tone, as if they should not be taken too seriously.

Three of Goodloe's stories, however, are different; they turn their humor against those who maintain stereotypes of educated women. In "An Acquarelle" young Allardyce of Harvard, returning from a tour of Europe, stops off to visit his sister, who for reasons he cannot understand has chosen to go to college. As he waits for her, he sees an attractive young woman unlocking a boat and offers his help, explaining who he is and why he is there. She invites him to join her. During the boat ride, while his companion gathers water lilies, Allardyce entertains her with his man-of-the-world conversation. Her smiles and appreciative murmurs encourage him, and if he sometimes suspects that she is trying not to laugh, he credits his own wit. He describes a cousin's Parisian boarding school where the girls really know how to flirt; advises his listener that college women get too concerned about things that really don't matter, like doing well in their studies; talks about a scrape that his sister got into and mocks her concern lest it be discovered; discourses on the horrors of mathematics in general and for young women in particular. When they return and he meets his furious and despairing sister, he learns that the attractive companion before whom he had shown off all his college-man sophistication is not only faculty, but a brilliant young mathematics professor.

The same theme is treated differently in "La Belle Hélène," told in letters. A Baltimore society matron anticipates a visit from a niece she has not seen in years. Since Helen is a college graduate and has spent a year at Oxford studying mathematical astronomy, her aunt knows just what she will be like: "One of your hard students, engrossed in books, without one thought for dress or social manners! I am afraid she will prove a sore trial" (41). She plans to introduce her niece to society at a small dinner, with eligible young men for her daughters and some "old fogies" for Helen. But the "ugly duckling, strong-minded, college-bred and all that" (47) is none of these; she is beautiful, she wears Paris gowns, and she is so poised and charming that all the men, young and old, are enchanted by her. As one of them raves to a friend, "She's stunning! . . . She's different from any girl I ever knew" (63–64). But even as Goodloe attacks a stereotype she does not quite subvert her own thesis, for the point is that these young women are, in spite of their intelligence and learning, appealing to men and therefore womanly and marriageable.

While these two stories humorously undermine the bluestocking image, "Revenge" tackles another misconception. With exercise and sports well established by the last years of the century, Miss Atterbury, captain of the senior crew and a formidable tennis player, is indignant over a newspaper feature mocking women's attempts at athletics. "To read this article one would imagine that we were imbecile babies. One would think that a girl was weak as a kitten, and didn't know a boat from an elevator. . . . He—whoever wrote this ridiculous article—seems to think that all our training and physical development is a huge joke . . . he isn't even aware of his unutterable, his colossal ignorance!" (167).

One of her friends has met the young man, and they invite him to the campus saying that they hope to benefit from his expert views on athletics. His flattered response does not last long, for assuming his interest and ability in sports in a way that he cannot contradict without losing face and treating him with exaggerated respect, they outdo him in every category. He is made to walk the several miles from the train station to the campus, in his formal dress and town shoes, because so athletic a man would naturally want to walk; hot and tired, already regretting an article written only to fill up space, he is taken to the tennis court and given a racket so that he can demonstrate the best form. Though his tennis and later his golf are clearly inferior, the politely respectful attitude of his audience does not change. As he displays running form on the track and rows the heavy observation boat to see the crew at work, "he decided within himself that the physical development of women had been carried to an absurd and alarming extent . . . and that he had made the mistake of his life when he wrote that article on athletics in girls' colleges" (185). Outclassed in every activity, he escapes at last to the city, loudly declaring his regret that an appointment prevents him from demonstrating the techniques of gymnastics, basketball, and pole vaulting.

Goodloe wanted to make it clear that college women remain womanly, and therefore acceptable and unthreatening. That she succeeded is indicated by a favorable review: in these "graceful sketches, the American college girl is a most attractive creature," the reviewer writes, but what she insists the book proves is that "life is more important than books" and that, somehow, college life is not life at all. She concludes with reassurance: "The whole atmosphere of the book is pleasant and stimulating. It so completely takes away the formidable terrors of college life, that any doubting mother, who is afraid of launching a pedant into the world, should read it. She will learn that possession of a degree has not power to deprive a girl of human emotions and aspirations."[12] None of the opposition in these stories—the Harvard brother, the society matron, or the young newspaperman—is malicious or angry; they have simply accepted the stereotypes that were prevalent and that Goodloe seems to support in most of her tales.

Curiously, she contradicts herself in another piece of writing about college life. She is a contributor to an 1898 series published in *Scribner's* which aims at providing a general and truthful look at life in the women's colleges; her piece on Wellesley, after moving from description of the town and the physical plant, begins its focus on the student herself by declaring that " '[g]oing to college' is yet so new and important a thing with her, and is so frequently for the purpose of studying, that she conscientiously decides upon the institution where she can get the hardest and most thorough course in her most difficult elective."[13] This emphasis on the desire to learn certainly does not appear in Goodloe's stories, and the omission suggests that in tailoring her message for a wider audience, she chose to downplay what her article presents so positively.

The first two deliberate attempts to show life in a woman's college have, in fact, different, almost oppositional goals. Not merely does Helen Dawes Brown celebrate intellectual experience and Goodloe suppress it;

rather, Brown sees it as so integral to the whole that classroom, social, and personal learning cannot be separated, while Goodloe's presentation sets formal learning apart, perhaps to avoid frightening those doubtful mothers. Both treatments acknowledge the importance of womanliness, though they might define it differently, but Goodloe's young women bring with them and retain the quality, while Brown's grow into it.

Nothing in Goodloe's tales offers an image or role model that differs from the the accepted perceived image and role of women. Brown, on the other hand, offers several over and above the variety of young women themselves, ranging from the popular teacher, Miss Ireland, whom the students respect for her knowledge and good teaching and value as an understanding friend, to Mrs. Powers, the wife of a professor, who finds her satisfaction and uses her intelligence in running a home well. These are balanced alternatives, for both are happy, fulfilled women.

There is, of course, more room in a novel than in a short story, even a collection of stories around one theme, to develop characters and to explore growth, change, and the influence the young women have on each other. Goodloe does not attempt any such coherence, although a few of her characters appear in several stories. Rather, her episodes are discrete, nor do her young women influence each other in the text, whatever they may do outside the pages; caught in a moment in time, they seldom seem to have pasts or futures.

In fact, although the separate stories are moving or amusing or "pathetic," to use the reviewer's term, the collection as a whole suffers from a lack of consistency. The episodes do not always work together; "Revenge" and "An Acquarelle" undercut the overall effect of the collection by suddenly presenting both a separate women's space and men as intruders into it, almost as if Goodloe is not sure what impression she wishes to make. What she clearly does not want to do is to show college life as a special experience that cannot be duplicated and that is bound to leave its mark. In this she differs from Brown and Anderson, and from the writing about the women's colleges that would follow in just a few years.

The greatest difference among the college worlds portrayed by Anderson, Brown, and Goodloe lies in their treatment of women's space. Will Elliott's college world is a town that has a university in it, but it also contains men and women students, professors, landladies, doctors, storekeepers, and farmers. There are streets and roads, shops, houses, and farms, with woods and fields surrounding; Will lives in a boardinghouse in town and interacts freely with people who could exist in any setting. Though she can carve out a personal space for herself, there is no women's space for her to enter; she is an intruder into a man's world.

Goodloe's college world, though physically a separate place, is one with which most of the inhabitants seem uninvolved as they wait to get back to real life—a kind of pleasant, vaguely defined preparatory space for entrance into women's sphere of marriage, home, family. There is little significance to this women's space except in the two almost subversive stories that do present a women's community with men as intruders. Brown's world is very different.

Although the beginnings of coeducation nearly parallel the opening of the women's colleges, coeducation never drew the attention that the women's colleges did; it was never a major subject for the popular media and did not inspire fiction. It was the women's colleges, the communities of young, marriageable women, isolated and concentrated, successful versions of Tennyson's *Princess*, that were unusual and provocative and caught the public's attention and curiosity.[14] Certainly the fascination with the topic and the mixed subtext of scorn and envy in journalistic writing suggests so, and suggests as well a point made by Nina Auerbach in her *Communities of Women*: "Women in literature who evade the aegis of men also evade traditional categories of definition. Since a community of women is a furtive, unofficial, often underground entity, it can be defined by the complex, shifting, often contradictory attitudes that it evokes. Each community defines itself as a 'distinct existence,' flourishing outside familiar categories and calling for a plurality of perspectives and judgments."[15] Auerbach's comment enlightens the reality as well as much of the early fiction about the women's colleges. While the colleges were not underground in Auerbach's sense, perhaps because they asserted their right to exist, they were fascinating and threatening, so that outside forces, including administrators (usually male), tried to control them, even as they suspected that part of this life was hidden from outsiders. A review of one collection of college stories that came out around 1900 begins with the statement that the "college girl is rapidly accumulating a library of her own. Of course, she is a girl like all others, but for all that, she has had several years of existence in a purely feminine environment, which has its hieratic meaning not understanded by the lay woman."[16] The inflated language and the equation of the college environment with sacred mysteries reveals awareness of (and perhaps discomfort with) separate experience and separate woman's space, coded, self-contained, and different—a woman's world in which her chief duty and obligation, at least for a while, was to focus on herself.

In his study of college novels Lyons uses the metaphor of the vernal wood, applying it to some of the masculine fiction he is examining.[17] The romantic term is useful for his purposes but does not suit the fiction portraying the women's colleges. It is not Wordsworth's vernal wood that serves as the most appropriate metaphor for them, but an older and lovelier one: the Forest of Arden, a wood outside Athens, the country of Illyria.

In the best—the most readable, most attractively presented—college fiction, the women's community bears a striking resemblance to what

Shakespeareans know as the green world.[18] This in itself is an adaptation of the magic forest found in medieval romance, into which the untried knight enters to begin his quest, and that this parallel existed in some minds is indicated by the passage quoted at the beginning of Lida Mc-Cabe's 1893 study of the women's colleges: "All the adventures of knights will not prove one lady's valor. She must fight her own battles." [19] This challenging and romantic view informs the early fiction, especially the turn-of-the-century short story cycles that followed Brown and Goodloe. Crossing the boundaries into an enchanted world, journeying from the known into the unknown, brings the traveler into a space that has its own rules: it is away from the "real" world and has its own reality; there can be movement in and out of it, but always with the sense of crossing borders; it is beautiful, mysterious, and magical; it has its own laws, which are not those of the world outside and must be learned; most important, it is the place of transformation, where its temporary inhabitants grow, change, seek identities, and find solutions. Entrance to the green world involves a journey; exit from it is accompanied by festivities. For some the green world is a stage that sends them back to society strong and ready for life; others postpone departure and a few never leave. Some cannot belong to it, but that does not mean they are not affected by it. It is not a perfect world: there are lions in the Forest of Arden, and there are problems in the college world—those created by the world itself and those brought into it. Imperfect though it may be, however, this green world that becomes woman's space has more to offer than anything these young women have encountered before, and it offers something they will never find again.

Annis Pratt's study of women's archetypes defines the green world as a response or return to nature, a primal source of strength.[20] The green world of the college stories is closer to Andrew Marvel's "Gardener upon Gardens," in that its natural beauty and energy is mowed and manicured—controlled, intellectualized, perhaps, and certainly asexual, without becoming less beautiful or beneficial; the presiding deity is Athena rather than Pan or Eros. For while the green world of the college stories is certainly an enclosed physical space, a garden of trees and flowers and handsome buildings, it works its transformational magic through spiritual and mental, not natural, means, and its core is the mysterious entity that is finally reduced in words to the trite phrase, "the college spirit." But although the context is different, Pratt's declaration that the "green world is thus the primary agent of the hero's quest for authenticity" is certainly true (127).

Fiction and reality are close here. Helen Lefkowitz Horowitz, whose work on women's colleges is based on her interest in "the places and spaces designed for women's exclusive use in the late nineteenth century," points out that both Vassar and Wellesley were designed like

Mount Holyoke Seminary, with one enormous building that held rooms, classrooms, offices, faculty housing (for women faculty), dining hall, and even long, wide corridors so students could exercise indoors in bad weather.[21] The grounds had walls and limits, and the entry of outsiders was controlled. Whether the purpose was to guard or restrain, the result is a self-contained and exclusive unit, physically separated from the world. In one story, a Wellesley student and her professor, returning from an evening walk, see "the giant bulk of College Hall loom[ing] before them into the night; the whole great shadow, high on the black hill, dotted with even rows of lighted windows, 'like a ship at sea,' Miss Haviland said."[22] Even at Smith, where the model was an academic village rather than a fortress, and even after increasing enrollments begot other buildings and the creation of a campus, the sense of self-containment, of a separate world, remained. And, with another kind of reality, President MacCracken of Vassar noted that trustees and gift givers, primarily male, had a Ruskinian vision of the college as "a fountain sealed, a walled garden," and did not want to hear anything that might damage that image.[23]

Control of space is noticeably different in fiction about men's colleges. In the collections of men's college narratives published around 1900, young men roam.[24] Harvard men do meet in each other's luxurious rooms, but as well they go to Springfield, to New Haven for the boat race, to dinner parties in Boston, or to an evening of burlesque at the Old Howard in now-vanished Scollay Square. They gather over beer and cigars in a favorite bar. The freedom reflects reality; the Yard might be a small green world, but Harvard is not isolated and men were not confined. Even Bowdoin students, who certainly were geographically isolated, have adventures away from their campus. Several of the men's collections even range in time, telling stories of alumni who fought in the Civil War. Simply, the patriarchy placed no real restrictions on men, who did not have to be guarded and protected, and as a result their stories show a base but no boundaries or sense of enclosure. While there may indeed be social and class distances between college men and others, there is no self-contained and separate world.

Not all the women's college stories share the green world, but where it is present it gives both a center and a vitality to the depiction of experience; it marks the best of the women's college stories, those that convincingly present this female world as a place of delight, stimulation, and a stretching of the self without romanticizing the truth. Discovery of this separate world is a feature of the early stories; for Molly, a Vassar first-year student learning the new territory,

> College may be a small world and a narrow one, but while a girl lives in it she neither knows nor desires any other. The fall of the Chinese

Empire moves not a whit her who is striving with all her might to bring about the fall of a too ambitious office-seeker in her own class; and Cecil Rhodes' speech on imperialism leaves cold a heart hot with rage over Prexy's last chapel talk on the powers of the Faculty. Should it not be so? A girl has all her life to live in the world without, but only four short years in college. And, too, it is all her own. The "Olympians," to whose number she will herself be added appallingly soon, are responsible for the outside world, but she alone can make or mar college.[25]

As the passage indicates, to this women's space is added women's time, for in the best of the stories there is a tension between the magical, separate women's world and the world outside, a tension that is expressed in the melancholy of graduation, the exit ceremony marking final rites of passage. There is always consciousness that this short stay in Illyria has fixed limits, and that while the place can be revisited, the experience can never be recaptured since its boundaries lie in time as well as space.

Brown and Anderson, of course, reflect their separate realities. Edna Howe and her friends live in a clearly marked, separate world—the green world that Brown presents with such skill, from Edna's transitional train journey into it to the graduation festivities that mark her exit. In between she learns new codes and is transformed, returning to the outside world ready to deal successfully with whatever it brings her. Even Phelps, who did not have the college experience, is able imaginatively to re-create the separate green world from whose enchantment Loto is suddenly barred, so that her attempts at adjustment are even more poignant; significantly, it is what she learned in college that brings her success.

Anderson, Brown, and Goodloe, in different ways and with varying degrees of caution, do argue the same broad thesis: that higher education does not harm young women. Anderson, the most defiant, does it by presenting a hero who combines physical womanliness with intelligence and force. It would be years before there were stories about women students in coeducational institutions, and never again a hero as strong, strong-minded, and outstanding as Will Elliott. She can learn, she can take care of herself—but she can also attract men. Brown, by fitting her intelligent and capable young women into a traditional women's novel pattern and then going beyond its restrictions, is even more positive in her covert insistence that higher education does no damage. By tying together intellectual and social learning she asserts that a good education produces a more complete, finer end product—womanly in the best sense of the word, a marriage partner rather than a toy. Goodloe is curiously divided. Overall her stories seem to prove that college has no effect at all on her young women, since her characters are chiefly involved in romantic relationships with men. Yet three among them and much of her other writing suggest that the narratives were carefully chosen to present an image that would reassure rather than alarm readers.

The college fiction that followed these earliest stories used Goodloe's format, the collection of stories around a single theme, but their spirit comes from Brown's *Two College Girls*. Her modification of the domestic novel and her evocation of the green world of the women's colleges, a space separate and rewarding, set the pattern for much of the fiction to follow, and provides a standard for evaluation of the portrayal of women's college life.

# · TWO ·

# *The World Outside*

P art of the aim of those who wrote about women in college was to answer the charges of critics. Before going on to discuss the next chronological group of college stories, I shall examine the variety and force of public opinion against the colleges themselves, since that opinion probably inhibited writing about them in the first place and then influenced what writing did occur. The enemies of change tried to prevent the foundation of the women's colleges and then, when unsuccessful, worked to control and shape college procedures to fit common perceptions of the acceptable product of women's higher education. Whatever had been thought before about educating women, the announcement of the establishment of Vassar and its goals triggered a rush of response, creating in press and pulpit what we would today describe as "hype." When direct attacks failed to stop the young colleges, many commentators, especially in the popular women's magazines, moved to trivialization aimed at reducing the special to the commonplace.

Even before it opened its doors, Vassar was controversial. The alarmed reaction was created by the declared intent of its founders to coopt the male curriculum and provide young women with the same education that their brothers were receiving at Harvard or Yale. That women should study mathematics or science was bad enough; that they should trespass on the sacred ground of Latin and Greek, those hallmarks of a gentleman's education, was outrageous.[1]

There had been women students at Oberlin and Antioch, most of them neatly segregated in a woman's curriculum; Mount Holyoke Seminary had since 1837 prepared "informed Christian women" to teach; Elmira College quietly and unobtrusively educated young women. There were any number of seminaries, ranging from such rigorous ones as Hartford, Ipswich, or Troy to the more common ones that specialized in the "ornamental branches"—the skills that made women appealing wives. In a study called *Perish the Thought; Intellectual Women in Romantic*

*America, 1830–1860,* Susan Phinney Conrad has shown that while "intellectual" women did most certainly exist before the opening of the colleges, their education was private, usually offered by their fathers. She also makes clear the isolation of these women and examines the stereotypes:

> The idea of an "intellectual woman," that favorite phrase of her enemies, haunted nineteenth-century women who happened to be thinkers. As of today, both the scholarly and the popular mind still rely on the common stereotypes to characterize women intellectuals. "Salon women," old-maid schoolteachers, "lady" writers, "headhunters," hysterics, headmistresses—all form a vast sisterhood whose members are identified as "intellectual women." Drab, aggressive, unloved, and usually pitiful . . .[2]

For the women whose lives Conrad examines, there was none of the community that the new women's colleges would offer.

Vassar opened in 1865, then Smith and Wellesley in 1875, and Bryn Mawr in 1883. It must be emphasized that the hostility toward these and other colleges was not primarily against schooling for women, but against a curriculum that asserted women's intellectual ability and equality. Judging from the furor the women's colleges inspired, tightly held masculine insecurities or conservative convictions were severely threatened.

Today, when financially able young women in the United States take for granted their right to be educated, it is hard to understand the furor created by the opening of Vassar—the media "hype" and the thunderings from press and pulpit that portrayed higher education as a factor destined to bring about the collapse of civilization. Bright young women and the parents who cherished them needed both understanding and reassurance. Undoubtedly the underlying cause of all the attacks was a conservatism that feared change, a phenomenon not confined to the nineteenth century; the attacks themselves fell into several categories.

The first and for a while the strongest ground was medical. Articles and sermons insisted that woman simply could not manage; her smaller brain, frail body, and unstable nerves would not support her through such an unnatural experience. More specifically, the smallness of the female brain meant that a woman was physiologically incapable of learning in the way that a man learned, and the strain of effort followed by inevitable failure would destroy her already fragile nervous system. Even more chilling was the medical opinion of which Dr. Edward H. Clarke was chief spokesman: woman might be able to learn, but she was not physically constructed to stand such mental activity, for the energy used by her brain would be diverted from her dominant organ, the uterus, and she would be incapable of fulfilling her true function. Clarke said some useful things about women's health, urging, for example, that women stop wearing corsets, but clearly he wanted them healthy for what he regarded as their only real purpose, childbearing.[3]

Interestingly, the issue of health, originally the major and most ferocious point of attack for hostile critics, did not retain its force very long and hardly surfaces as a topic in the fiction, probably because that battle was fought outside the colleges as well. While the image of women exercising offended some, the argument that healthy female bodies produced healthy children was a soothing answer.[4] There had been strong midcentury voices for the physical development of women; Dio Lewis, a well-known medical doctor, emphasized in the *Atlantic Monthly* and other important magazines good food, exercise, and outdoor life for everyone, including women and girls.[5] Whether from the urging of Lewis and others like him, the growing opportunities, or the model of the women's colleges themselves, which from the beginning had stressed exercise, young women eventually stepped out of their corsets and went hiking or camping, pleasures that eventually, to jump ahead in time, were institutionalized by the founding of the Campfire Girls (1910) and the Girl Scouts (1912). High schools offered gymnastics of a sort and, to the real horror of many, girls began to play competitive team sports like basketball.[6] Each of these innovations was severely criticized and was often the subject of journalistic opportunism, but in spite of the furor each became an accepted activity. This change affected the college fiction by substituting for concern over health a focus on athletics, sports, and rather carefully controlled competition, and it generated innumerable camping and hiking stories for girls, many of which share with the early and turn-of-the-century college stories the sense of the magical transformational green world; often lonely girls find friends or spoiled unpleasant ones find, like Mary of *The Secret Garden*, that living with nature brings self-realization, the desire for change, and finally happiness.[7] Many of these books assert an increasing physical freedom for young women who learn to be comfortable with their bodies.

In modern terms, the college women, faculty, and writers of the early years were dealing with problems of image and public relations, and they show their awareness of it, especially in the fiction written around the turn of the century. One college story begins, "Because Timothy was so correct, he particularly detested and disapproved of college girls. They represented to his mind a mixture of bespectacled phenomena of learning, and of cheering, basketball-playing New Women. In either capacity he found them peculiarly objectionable. He often said of them, with a fervent horror he might have expressed toward Wild Indians, 'I sincerely trust it will never be my misfortune to meet one.'"[8]

Before the story ends Timothy's picture of college women will change; several tales have this conversion process as their direct goal. In another story in the same volume, Catherine Neville, the clever daughter of a prominent Philadelphia family, decides to go to college and the family is horrified: "A daughter of the Nevilles in college! Preposterous! It is all very well for a girl who has her own living to make. But a Neville!" After the entrance examinations which only a "Monstrosity" could pass, she enters "into that atmosphere of social depravity and advanced ideas that old-fashioned conventionality has associated with a woman's college."[9] Quite a few stories make deliberate attempts to examine and disprove the stereotypes or the reasons for antagonism, although in the better ones awareness of image is more skillfully incorporated into story, or provides background or amusing anecdote. Young women discussing their homes point out problems: "I live in a town where not one man in a hundred goes to college, and I, even I, am the only girl that's ever been. . . . [the neighbors] send over to ask me how to pronounce new words."[10]

Some stories, especially those in a collection set at Bryn Mawr, address the question of image directly—so directly, in fact, that the thesis obscures the narrative and the stories read as propaganda. "Her Masterpiece" tells of Ellen, a graduate busy and active in various causes, who agrees to give a talk on college life at a social science conference. After interviewing various classmates, she prepares a paper full of facts and statistics but feels that although her information is correct, she is not really giving a picture of the life. Before leaving for the conference, she and some classmates spend a few days at Bryn Mawr and, going on to the conference full of her happy memories, she gives not her prepared speech but one on "The Poetry of the College Spirit." Unfortunately, she does not know what she is saying, nor can she remember it afterward; it is, the author suggests, as if the "college spirit" has spoken through her. Lacking the speech itself, however, the story seems contrived and unconvincing.[11] In "A Diplomatic Crusade" in the same volume the undergraduate hero, Marjorie, after a weekend at home, enlists her roommate in an effort to teach the outside world what college women are really like. She describes an anticollege gentleman at a dinner party and her determination to impress him, showing herself to be a perfect lady, socially adept, knowledgeable on every subject discussed: "The point was to convince him, as thoroughly as possible in one short evening, that I, in the character of college woman, was neither a bit of thistle-down nor a fearful prig."[12] In other words, no pedant; the ideal college woman, with every conceivable virtue, wears her achievements lightly. The other half of Marjorie's crusade is to encourage bright, studious young women to become involved in other activities as well, so that they will not fit the pedant stereotype.

Though never so directly voiced as the concern for health, which may indeed have been a disguise for it, the underlying fear was for loss of conventionally defined femininity or womanliness: marriageability. Popular wisdom knew that a well-educated woman would hardly be a woman at all. As a creature of emotion and intuition, she would be ruined by learning to reason and to discipline her mind. She would become mannish, desexed. Furthermore, she would destroy the family. As Conrad points out, the image of the female scholar was the "bluestocking," authoritatively spreading her knowledge, or the scholarly frump, dowdy, unattractive, all graces gone, intent on the pursuit of knowledge rather than of a husband. Who would want to marry her? Popular contemporary novelist Amelia Barr has a male character say, after his brother has admired the modern woman, "I greatly disapprove of women who lecture and write books. I could not love a woman who met me at intellectual sword-point. I like a girl to have the bloom of womanhood upon her." And later, "Ellen is unselfish, clever, dutiful, and reads Emerson and Ruskin. Men have a high opinion of such women, but they do not love them." [13] Given the fact that at the time there was no future other than marriage for most women, there is a logic to the fears, and this attitude pervades much of the criticism. But a curious subtext underlies the expressed concern: provide women with alternatives and they may choose not to marry. It is almost an unspoken admission that the institution of marriage has not served women well, and that given choices they might not care to be unpaid housekeepers in their separate spheres.

The belief that men would choose not to marry educated women, or that those women themselves would avoid marriage, fed fears that the end of the "race" was in sight, as indicated by two *Ladies' Home Journal* features entitled "Does the Girls' College Destroy the Wife?" and "College Women and Race Suicide." [14] The race meant, as it usually does in this kind of rhetoric, the white, male, Protestant middle class, which, by not reproducing itself, would clear the way for some unspecified "them" to take over.

All these ideas fueled the attacks and, though each might be individually rejected, they had their cumulative effect. The need to remain "womanly" was present in the minds of many students, parents, and probably all administrators, with the possible exception of Bryn Mawr's scholarly, forceful, feminist president, M. Carey Thomas. It needed to be demonstrated that women could take advantage of these new opportunities and still remain womanly, a necessity that continued to influence the process and product of women's education as well as the literature it produced. As late as 1912, a character in a novel set at Vassar comments in a letter on the day's sermon:

> Just back from church—preacher from Georgia. We must take care, he says, not to develop our intellects at the expense of our emotional natures—but methought it was a poor, dry sermon . . . . It doesn't matter what part of the United States or Canada they come

from, we always get the same sermon. Why on earth don't they go to the men's colleges and urge the students not to allow their manly natures to be crushed out by too much mental application? [15]

This kind of comment so often appears in the fiction that it is clearly a reflection of reality. Even when there is tempered and qualified approval of higher education on the (male) speaker's terms, the approach is sometimes more insidious than outright attack.

Some commentary connects womanliness with economic status. A piece in the *Independent* signed by "Miss C. S. Parrish, Professor of Philosophy at Randolph Macon Woman's College" and entitled "The Womanly Woman" (1901) is a spirited and logical attack on male definitions of womanliness, aimed at pointing out their inconsistencies. As an example she quotes one voice: "An 'old Virginia gentleman' once said in the presence of the writer that the higher education of women is unwomanly. Begged for reasons, he said that when a woman is well educated she is capable of supporting herself. As soon as she is able, she wishes to do it, and that is destructive of all true womanliness, for the essence of womanliness consists of being supported by a man." Parrish ends with her own wide definition of womanliness and sums up: "She may be a man's friend and companion, his helper and co-worker. She is never, voluntarily, his dependent or his plaything." [16]

The words of the "old Virginia gentleman" are echoed by William DeWitt Hyde, president of Bowdoin and therefore not directly menaced by college women, who wrote a book called *The College Man and the College Woman* (1906). The title is misleading, since only two of the chapters are addressed to women, but Hyde's stated aim in his preface is to provide "sympathetic interpretation and intelligent appreciation" for both. His arguments, which accept woman's higher education, are positive on the surface, but he not only repeats the need for women to remain womanly, he, too, grounds his definition in economics: "Happy is the woman who as daughter, sister, wife, mother, finds herself excused from the task of direct economic production by the generous devotion of father, brother, husband or son, and can find the economic justification of her life in this ministry and superintendence of the common household consumption."

Hyde goes on to make his definition even more precise:

> The feminine ideal, to make toil tolerable, and leisure enjoyable, and home habitable, and, in Stevenson's phrase, life liveable, by the benificent ordering of consumption, and the gentle ministry to individual persons, whether in the home or in some not too exacting and impersonal vocation,—this is so supremely precious that the woman who risks it for an attempt to imitate or rival the activities of men in conjunctive production wrongs her own soul, and in doing so robs the world of her most distinctive and valuable contribution. [17]

This appeal, which really translates into the need to keep women out of the workplace and at home taking care of men, has at least a kind of honesty, but is less easy to combat than outright attacks.

The early fiction does share a concern for "womanly" standards, though the implied definitions are broad and they vary with author and time. Attempts to refute the stereotypes of educated women were complicated by the complexity of the stereotypes themselves, which were multiple and inconsistent. Bespectacled frump, dessicated student, pompous bluestocking, beefy athlete, or the general feeling that "real" women did not go to college—all existed at the same time.

For the end of the nineteenth century and the beginning of the twentieth, a single definition of "womanliness" is difficult to find, and certainly this fiction presents no unified image. An insistence on modesty and self-abegnation in some of the fiction invokes the memory of the Cult of True Womanhood; the energy and sense of mission in other portrayals suggests the energy and fervor, if not the goal, of what Ronald Hogeland has called evangelical women.[18] Times were changing; women ran households and brought up children, but they also were active in the clubwoman's movement and in a few states could vote for and serve on school boards. Some held jobs, through necessity or choice, and even those not directly involved in the women's rights agitation must have been affected by it.

In her study *All-American Girl*, Frances Cogan argues for a midcentury ideal that she calls Real Womanhood:

> This popular ideal advocated intelligence, physical fitness and health, self-sufficiency, economic self-reliance, and careful marriage; it was, in other words, a survival ethic. . . . The ideal of Real Womanhood was a popular, middle-of-the-road image that recognized the disparities and the dangers protested by early feminists but tried to deal with those ugly realities in what it saw as a "female" way. It placed itself, therefore, firmly in the "separate sphere" controversy by claiming a unique sphere of action and duty for women, but one vastly extended and magically swollen past the dimensions of anything meant by that term to devotees of competing True Womanhood.[19]

Though Cogan locates this ideal in midcentury and feels that it weakened later, her definition comes closest in a general way to the young women portrayed in the college stories. And though today we might, correctly, see as New Women those who went to college when it was a daring thing to do, who learned, thought, traveled, played competitive sports, and prepared for an active future, the writers carefully and consistently avoid using the term.

Understandably, then, the image of womanliness is inconsistent in the books and stories because it was confused everywhere: "The predominant form of Victorian writing about women is not pronouncement but debate. Moreover, the arguments in this debate were both more complex and more fluid than the model of a single cultural myth would indicate," according to Elizabeth Helsinger.[20] And Lynn D. Gordon, addressing the question in her fine study of women's education, notes that, like women today, the turn-of-the-century women "attend[ed] college during an era of changing gender roles and confusion about the meaning of those changes," thus making it harder for women to define themselves.[21]

The review of *College Girls* quoted in the preceding chapter makes the point that Goodloe's stories will reassure anxious mothers that their daughters will not become pedants. After Brown and, to a lesser degree, Anderson, almost no writer even attempted to integrate intellectual experience into story; they chose rather to present the kinds of learning and growth usually described as character development, more compatible with attitudes about "womanly" behavior. And as they tried to answer critics, they wanted to present the experience truthfully yet invitingly to readers of all kinds. Perhaps what is surprising is that they tried at all.

In one sense the writers of college stories could legitimately avoid facing the question of definition directly; they were dealing with what they and their culture thought of as girls, not women, and girls—as children—could be allowed more freedom. The fictional students themselves accept this definition; an occasional passage shows them looking ahead to graduation and the transition to a woman's status and responsibilities:

> [There was] a sudden chill realization that it was all over now, the work and the fun, the happy-go-lucky, free, careless, warm life of College . . . they would be dignified, sensible women of the outside world, in a little house in a little corner of that world somewhere; and gone forever would be the dear old tribal life, with all its things in common, from ideas to umbrellas, its intense happiness and its woes so overwhelmingly great that they were almost a kind of pleasure, its hail-fellow-well-met acquaintances and its close enduring friendships.[22]

The outside world, therefore, could reassure itself by looking at the four college years as a kind of harmless aberration, an irrelevant or even a preparatory period before a girl returned to life and womanhood. Popular writer Amanda O. Douglas's Helen Grant series heavily projected that thesis; at one point a professor comments that one of the great values of going to college was that it prevented girls from making youthful and "imprudent" marriages, with the implication that prudent marriages represented success for women.[23]

Yet while a definition of womanly behavior is never formulated and the expectations vary from story to story, one element in the standard definitions of ideal woman is fairly constant: her role as nurturer. The majority of protagonists display real concern for others and feel an obligation to offer help when needed. Even in the stories written around 1900, which most strongly advocate finding and celebrating one's self and one's talents, the subtext is always that women care about and help others. In the best stories, the need or duty to nurture sits comfortably with the idea of self-realization, as if both elements are necessary for the final product, a redefined woman.

That the goals were various is borne out by male analysis. In his autobiography, Henry Noble MacCracken, president of Vassar from 1915 to 1945, looked back on the history of the college and described the type of student encouraged by his predecessor, who presided from 1886 to 1914: "It was, indeed, against M. Carey Thomas's ideal of intellectualism as the keynote of Bryn Mawr, that Dr. [James M.] Taylor set up his ideal of the 'well-rounded' woman. Vassar graduates were to be cultured but human, not leaders but good wives and mothers, truly liberal in things intellectual but conservative in matters social. And this most of them dutifully became."[24] Later MacCracken summed up a progression for Vassar students, and by extension for those of other colleges, as first the "'strong-minded' women who claimed equality of mental powers with men, and who insisted that good minds were meant to be used. . . . Then there were the 'dangerous women,'" like Harriet Stanton (Blatch) and Inez Milholland, the women's rights activists. After them came the Taylor-nurtured "well-rounded" women ("some of them took one elementary course in each of the twenty departments") and finally what he calls the "liberal" women of his own administration, concerning themselves with social and political movements, "hospitable to new ideas and experi-ments . . . enlightened in social problems, and free to take up the struggle for justice which is the human task of our age" (164–165).

MacCracken may not be entirely objective or exact, and he works from an ideal of woman, however her horizons have expanded, as a nurturer whose concerns and devotions are chiefly for others. The idea that educating women might make them even better nurturers, however, was seldom voiced in the early days, and those who wished to go to college— and their parents—had to ask questions. How did a young woman who wanted to use her abilities but not disqualify herself from courtship and marriage find support for breaking, however moderately, with traditional views of her role? Were going to college, learning, and, as time passed, hiking, playing basketball, and still later driving a car or flying an airplane compatible with being a good—womanly—woman?

Doubts were certainly reinforced by newspapers, magazines, books, lecture platforms and pulpits, making the choice hard and conscious. Nevertheless, the colleges opened, and defenders were able to argue, as time went on and more and more women entered and graduated, that four years of college had not ruined them. From the first none of the colleges had trouble attracting students; in fact, there was hardly space for those who appeared on the first day. And they stayed, got their educations, and graduated. Some indeed could not stand the mental rigor, some could not get along with other women, and some did suffer bad health, but never in numbers sufficient to back up the charges of the attackers.[25]

But even as the colleges proved themselves, they and the college woman were never quite out of the public eye. From the early years, when the question was whether she should be allowed to exist, the female college student remained a topic of serious concern. Some worried about what she was learning, whether she was capable of such learning, and, the constant, whether her learning made her unfit for marriage. Later critics argued the merits of single-sex schools over coeducation, the morality of "secret societies" (honor societies, sororities, and fraternities), and the growth of snobbery in the schools. Later still there was concern over what to do with the college graduate in a world that had no place for her. Approaches might be scornful, satirical, trivializing, or serious, but these were the major issues and points of attack that women's higher education generated.

By 1900 colleges for women were a fact. A young woman who wanted an education could get it, subject to normal restrictions: her ability, preparation, parental support, and financial means. For some lack of money was not a hindrance, for several colleges provided work for those who needed it, as some seminaries had done. In the early days, in fact, having all students take part in domestic management was a way to cut costs and keep tuition low. One student, entering Wellesley in 1880, had as her "domestic work" the clearing of four tables after lunch; the next year she and her roommate were responsible for "lighting the gas all over the house. She takes two floors and I two. We found it tonight very pleasant, much better than real *domestic* work." [26]

The women's colleges remained the subjects of serious debate, but with their secure establishment they also became topics for journalistic opportunism. The young newspaperman in Goodloe's "Revenge" had no hostility toward women's colleges and knew absolutely nothing about women's athletic ability; he needed a feature to fill some space, and college women were fair game. Both administration, concerned with image, trustees, and gifts, and the students themselves understood their vulnerability to misrepresentation by the press, and to be the subject of newspaper articles was particularly painful to well-brought-up young ladies reared in the tradition that said a lady's name was in the paper three times: when she was born, when she married, and when she died. While features about "college girls"—or, more often, "*the* college girl"—did not mention names, they did call attention to activities that might seem to flout womanly standards. What college women did was news and remained so for years—the kind of news that could provoke laughter or criticism, ridicule or alarm. After physical and mental health stopped being a real arguing point (although as late as 1900 S. Weir Mitchell was still pondering "When the College Is Harmful to a Girl"[27]), observers had other topics. In the "serious" magazines articles about the men's colleges discussed curriculum, values, ethics, and the influence of the colleges on the future of the country; those about the women's colleges dwelt on studies of marriage patterns, children, employment, and the use of education, although there were occasional attempts to understand the life.

With the existence of the colleges secure the tone of the press changed. It is a human protective strategy to reduce the terrifying to manageable size, and one method is to make it laughable—to trivialize the unusual and bring it to a level at which it can be controlled. A no doubt unconscious campaign against women's academic communities was carried out chiefly in the feature pages of newspapers and the new popular women's magazines like *Ladies' Home Journal, Women's Home Companion,* and *Good-Housekeeping,* which sprang up late in the nineteenth century. College women made legitimate material, but journalistic pieces stressed girlish fun, not learning.

Representative of the less serious press was the *Ladies' Home Journal.* The magazine had a clear policy: girls remain girls whether they go to college or not, and the value of girls is that they become women and, perhaps, consumers. Its targeted audience was woman as homemaker and light of the home, and the editor, Edward W. Bok, firmly and consistently held that higher education could be tolerated unless it were to interfere with woman's destined role as wife and mother.[28] Besides its fiction, which tended to be about love, romance, marriage, children, the *Journal* presented famous people—actors, singers, artists, writers, politicians—at home: "Kate Douglas Wiggin As She Really Is As a Woman."[29] Wives and daughters of famous men were written up, but never the details of a woman's career or her achievements outside the home. Topics of advice columns ranged from cooking, sewing, and fashion to social etiquette and behavior; all features and fiction saw as a general goal the womanly woman, noble and nurturing. Separate spheres were alive and well at the *Journal.*

Around the turn of the century the magazine featured versions of Charles Dana Gibson's famous Girl; these pictures frequently hung on walls of college rooms. Yet an article in 1904 called "Daisy Miller and the

Gibson Girl" lamented that the modern (Gibson) girl had given up her superiority to men and made herself their equal. While the contrast seems an odd one and suggests that people were not reading Henry James very carefully, the article echoes an earlier one by Caroline Ticknor in the *Atlantic Monthly* called "The Steel-Engraving Lady and the Gibson Girl," a dialogue in which the two types (the steel-engraving lady is the womanly woman) scornfully examine each other's lifestyles, closing with the sentence, in capitals, "WOMAN, ONCE MAN'S SUPERIOR, IS NOW HIS EQUAL." [30] The conclusion reflects a position taken by many: women's nobility and natural superiority would be lowered by such masculine activities as, for example, learning or voting.

In fairness to Bok, he did know what was going on in the world: that young women went to college and that more and more of them were joining the work force. This regrettable reality was acceptable as long as young women remained girls and girlish even in their unnatural surroundings. "A womanly woman," Bok wrote in answer to a request that he define the creature, "is she who is gentle, tender and considerate; a woman with sufficient strength of character to allow neither her head, her heart or her home to be disturbed by any claims other than those belonging to her womanhood and wifehood." [31] He then, predictably, went on to quote the appropriate verses from Proverbs. Later in his column he answered a query about woman stenographers from a young man concerned that jobs would go to women instead of men. Bok was fair: the job ought to go to the person best qualified. He added some comfort, however; he was sure that the unfortunate situation of women working would soon be resolved and that in ten years they would all be back in the home.

Bok's ideal of womanhood was consistent; he is even harder on clubwomen than on young college women, declaring that women's clubs "have produced a type of woman who in her self-culture is an absolute danger to herself, and especially her children." [32] Clubwomen were what college graduates might easily become. He advises moderation and dislikes their issues; there is a hint that the latter feeling is the stronger because those issues do not agree with his. How much is principle and how much is concern for advertisers is, of course, impossible to tell, but whatever the motives, Bok's voice had a wide audience.

One of the *Journal*'s regular columnists, the Reverend T. DeWitt Talmadge, also in answer to a query, said that he never bothered to discuss women's rights in his column because he "did not feel the importance of the subject. . . . God, who can make no mistake, made man and woman for a specific work, and to move in particular spheres—man to be regnant in his realm, woman to be dominant in hers." [33] And in 1900 "An American Mother" answered the question about the value of a college education for Our Girls resoundingly: bad if it failed to prepare a girl for "her womanly work." [34]

Clearly once woman as college student was accepted as permanent, she had to be made manageable and nonthreatening. The effort was consistent: change her from something formidable into something cute. She became a feature of the magazine, often presented in spreads with pictures. "Fetes of College Girls" included "Float Day at Wellesley," "Daisy Chain at Vassar," and "Ivy Day at Smith"; "Inside the Rooms of College Girls" showed their surroundings; a series running over seven issues, entitled "What a Girl Does at College," emphasized special events, although there is one picture inside a classroom with the students sitting rigidly in their seats, wearing fixed smiles.[35] Titles show the degree to which the approach was belittling and trivializing: "College Girls' Larks and Pranks, as Retold by a Graduate," "The College Scrapes We Got Into," "When College Girls Have Their Fun," "Christmas Pranks of College Girls," "The Dainties at College Girls' Spreads," "Madcap Frolics of College Girls," and "What College Girls Eat."[36] Neither titles nor content constituted any threat to the established social order; there was no need to worry about these girls, and if Bok could not have them at home becoming women, he made the best of the status quo by emphasizing girlishness and ignoring academic and career achievements or growth into maturity.[37] The winners of Bryn Mawr's European fellowship for study abroad or fellowships in various disciplines were never mentioned.

Bases for attack were not consistent. In one of the college series, the students are incensed at a newspaper article by a journalist named Beatrice Slammer. "The article occupied a full page under flaring headlines: THE PRESENT DAY COLLEGE GIRL NO LONGER A PLEASING FEMININE TYPE. SHE IS VULGAR, AGGRESSIVE, SLANGY. COLLEGES FOR GIRLS THE RUIN OF AMERICAN HOMES." Accompanying the text are

> drawings of wildly dishevelled beings in gymnasium suits playing basketball and hockey. One picture, also, represented a blousy looking young person in a sweater, carrying a bundle of linen under one arm and a bottle of milk under another. In still another this same blousy model was yelling "Hello" to her twin sister across the page. They saw her again in the drug store dissipating chocolate sundaes; and once more, chewing gum; hobnobbing with the grocery boy, too, or perhaps it was the postman.[38]

None of these activities seem particularly startling today, but clearly from the text these are examples of unladylike behavior and therefore disgraceful. Although the story does not develop the point, the young women who read about themselves in this way were angry and offended, but, in a sense, not surprised to be so targeted.

Later, as conditions changed, the magazines found new topics to treat semiseriously. When wealthy and socially prominent young women found college an acceptable way to spend four years and entered in numbers, "democracy" and snobbery became issues, just as they did, for that matter, in some of the fiction. After Havelock Ellis made sexual behavior a topic, young women and girls were warned against "extreme" friendships, although the dangers were seldom clearly stated.[39] By the 1920s, with wealthier students attracted to the colleges, fashion magazines and the interests they represented were viewing college women as a profitable consumer group.

Not all the voices that spoke about women's higher education were hostile; from the beginning there was powerful support for Matthew Vassar's experiment. In 1859 the young but already prestigious *Atlantic Monthly* published Thomas Wentworth Higginson's "Ought Women to Learn the Alphabet?" with his radical thesis, supported by innumerable historical examples, that there was no difference between male and female intellectual capacities if women were given the same chances to learn.[40] He concluded with the judgment that woman had only two choices: she had to be man's equal or his slave. Since Higginson commanded enormous respect, the forthright voice of his essay and the prestige of the magazine in which it appeared must have encouraged interested women. Other support was equally impressive. Women such as the formidable Julia Ward Howe, whose name and "Battle Hymn" were household words, and the intellectual Elizabeth Cary Agassiz, along with other Boston social leaders and thinkers, not only supported women's higher education but led the efforts to allow women to enter Boston University and to establish the Harvard "annex," which later became Radcliffe.

Sophia Kirk's 1900 article in *Lippincott's Magazine* had rationally examined the reasons why "the college girl is still regarded curiously and a little askance."[41] The excellent series of articles in *Scribner's* (1898) allowed the authors, who were recent graduates, to show all the facets of life in their own colleges at considerable length. That these authors were aware of press and public attitudes is indicated by Margaret Sherwood's piece on Vassar:

> The problem, What is to be done with the college woman? has of late been troubling critics and reviewers. Much discussion of the problem has perhaps given the public the mistaken idea that she does not know what to do with herself. As a matter of fact, during her undergraduate life and after, she is too busy to be seriously troubled about the uses of her existence, and nobody is less perplexed in regard to her future than she is. In college, the serious undercurrent of work and the bright life out of doors and in, absorb her. It is only when she is forced into it by pressure from outside that she becomes self-conscious, and stops to wonder if she is "a little queer."

That she is slowly being awakened to a sense of the supposed antagonism between domestic and intellectual pursuits is evinced by a few faint signs, such, for instance, as the debate held not long ago at Vassar on the problem, "Does a college education unfit men for domestic life?" . . . The newspaper joke, that leader of thought in American life, has established two widespread convictions: first, that colleges for young men are entirely given over to muscular exercise; second, that life in a woman's college is a shadowed existence, into which girls are plunged in their youth and freshness, from which they emerge pale, sharp-nosed, spectacled. The fact that both these beliefs are untrue, perhaps lends charm to them. . . . Of the warmth and light and color of the life in women's colleges only the initiated know.[42]

This is the view of the college world that would shape the fiction published around 1900, confident, full of "warmth and light and color," but still influenced by the attitudes reflected in the newspaper features and popular magazines. The authors carefully selected the content of the college stories, choosing topics that recur, regardless of institution, and that assert women's abilities to live and work together, to learn, and to remain eligible for romance and marriage, as "initiated" authors tried to show the joy of the experience.

Since there was no consistency in the stereotypes or the attacks it should not be surprising that still another demand was made of educated women: they, unlike men, were expected to show results almost at once. By 1890, with Vassar twenty-five years old and Smith and Wellesley fifteen, critical voices were asking why the college graduates were not producing any great literature. Helen Gray Cone, in a long survey of American women writers for *Century Magazine*, ended her essay by answering the question:

The deed, and not the word, engages the energy of the college women of today; but as these institutions grow into the life of the land that life will be everywhere enriched, and the word must follow in happy time. . . . It would be idle to expect that the cases in which nature, power, and an adequate preparation go hand in hand will be frequent, since they are not frequent among men. The desireable thing was, that this rare development should be made a possibility among women.[43]

The fact that college women did not at first produce any fiction explains in part why they were not writing about the college experience. Still another reason may be indicated by Arthur Bartlett Maurice's review of Josephine Daskam Bacon's *Smith College Stories* (1900), which reveals some attitudes and responses to college fiction when it did appear.

Bacon's lively, well-crafted, and tightly woven collection of stories opens with the basketball game between the first- and second-year classes, a tradition that welds the new first-year students into a unit by joining them against traditional rivals. Maurice begins his review "weighted down by a great solemnity and sadness, and with a realization of the fact that the college woman is not a subject to be lightly touched upon. . . . There is enough in the very first story of the volume, 'The Emotions of a Sub-Guard,' to fill our soul with an awful wonder." From there he quotes at length passages describing the game, the "riotous carnival of blood and brutality" for which, he says, the "sensitive reader of the male persuasion" is not prepared, emphasizing players running, shrieking, falling, bumping into each other, grimly determined to win. Fearing that basketball "as played by the young women of Smith College is rather too harrowing and exhilarating a spectacle," he turns to "the gentler athletic pastimes of the male undergraduate," describing football for comparison. Since his language becomes completely technical, with all emotions and human reactions shut out, the account of the football game is indeed bland and unexciting.

Maurice's final paragraph reveals more about him and the attitudes he represents than it does about Bacon's book:

> The gravest feature of the whole matter is, that after careful consideration it is impossible to accept the story in question as a bit of highly imaginative writing. . . . No. It is very much to be feared that all this did take place, and that Miss Daskam has not evolved this out of her inner consciousness, but has described it just as she saw it from the gallery above, like one of the Roman women who gathered in the Colosseum to watch and to applaud the battles of the gladiators. In this conviction the present writer is strengthened by a little personal experience of his own. Some time ago he was introduced to and fell into conversation with a very charming and amiable young undergraduate of Smith. Did she discourse to him in the words of Plato or Socrates? Did she chant to him the songs of the troubadours? Did she whisper darkly to him of the esoteric wonders of the Orient? Did she attempt to solve for him the great questions of all time—the riddle of the Sphinx, who wrote the letters of Junius, who was the Man in the Iron Mask—who hit Billy Patterson? She did not. *She promptly challenged him to run her a hundred-yard dash.*[44]

The emphasis is Maurice's; so, it would seem, is the failure to make unbiased literary judgment. In the same essay he reviews *Stanford Stories*, and while he is occasionally caustic ("what we demand in American undergraduate stories is a hero of brawn, a bayard of the gridiron, the diamond, or the track—in short, we want the man in the 'varsity sweater"), he treats this and other mentioned books seriously; when he comes to *Smith College Stories* his tone changes to mockery. He either misses or ignores as not suiting his purposes the story's focus on the thoughts and emotions of the first-year Theodora, the substitute who is finally sent into the game and whose playing rallies the team that cannot win but can at least show courage and spirit. So the review is distorted and out of context as well, for the first story and its characters are tightly woven into the book as a whole (which, one would guess, the reviewer never finished).

The collection is not judged as fiction at all, but rather as it fits Maurice's vision of young women. If they do not behave as he wishes, in this case as attractive entertainers, discussing subjects that interest him, then they are targets for his satire and their stories (and lives) do not need to be taken seriously. Athletic young women offended an image of womanliness and deserved amused superiority and mild contempt for their deviation from male-defined standards of womanliness.

During the ten years that Vassar was, if not the only woman's college, the most noticed one, there were reasons to avoid fiction. The pioneers of the women's colleges were, as the very act of entering college proclaimed, fighters aware that they were being watched as they ventured into forbidden territory. They had good times—the "warmth and light and color" of Sherwood's essay—but they needed to present themselves to the world as serious, healthy students, and they had to combat the view that women could not think, concentrate, or stay committed to anything, much less anything intellectual.[45] The good health of Vassar and the establishment ten years later of Smith and Wellesley in 1875 may have signaled permanence; in spite of the attacks, colleges for women were going to stay. But the critical voices influenced what was finally produced, as the earliest fiction shows, by creating a felt need to answer, one way or another, the points of attack.

Finally, there was an internal as well as an external inhibition felt by those who wanted to fictionalize the college experience. However hard combating public opinion might be, an equally great difficulty was summed up in conversation among editors of the Vassar college magazine:

> "Why don't the girls write brisk, up-and-coming college tales instead of cowboy stories when they haven't been west of Utica in their whole lives, or extraordinary love effects?" asked Mary.
> "Because, my friend, the college story is the hardest in the world to write. If you explain customs and general surroundings enough to enlighten the world without, the grads. are bored. If you don't explain, the public are bored," said Rose, who knew.
> "Yes, and if you write about the work people say 'how women grind in their narrow conception of an education.' And if you write

about the fun they say 'only silly boarding school girls after all, with no earnestness or cultivation.' Thank you, I'd rather write two purpose novels and a tract on higher mathematics than one college story," said Anna, who also knew.[46]

It was not merely identifying and suiting audiences that troubled writers, but the fiction, again especially that written around the turn of the century, makes clear a sense that nothing they could write would properly convey to those audiences the real nature of the experience, just as the students themselves could never quite explain what the life was like and what it meant to them. This difficulty is woven into several stories, as if letting the characters voice it would make it clearer to readers. Josephine Daskam Bacon, for example, creates humor out of the inability of outsiders to understand the life in her story "Point of View." Mary, a popular and prominent Smith junior, is opening her mail; letters from home are full of advice on using all her spare time. Various aunts suggest rest, dancing classes in Boston, or scriptural readings; a former teacher hopes she is keeping up her scholarly rank; her sister urges more golf practice; an old friend chides her for not writing to friends at home more often: "It isn't as if you lived in the city and had church work and dancing classes and all that. Way off there I should think you would *want* to write! There are just six of us all together, you see, and why couldn't you write to *one* of us every day? . . . Why not do it in the evenings—there's nothing else to do, is there?" The same batch of mail includes reminders: work to be done for her campus society, the date of an exam in history, the demand for revision of a Shakespeare paper, the announcement of extra choir practice, her promise to meet a friend's visiting family, and finally her own birthday party. The stated message is that Mary has no spare time, but the subtext is, again, that outsiders just do not understand.[47]

The best of the college series books, Margaret Warde's account of Betty Wales and her friends, offers the same perception; the author makes the point with a scene in which friends, toward the end of their first year, try to write letters home. They want the letters to reflect the range of activity and the mixture of seriousness and fun that is their world, but they find that none of their accounts satisfy them. One student sums it up at the end of the letter-writing session with humorous despair; speaking of the variety of their experiences, she mourns, "That's what they don't understand . . . and they don't know either how fast we can go from one thing to another up here. Why, energy is in the air!"[48]

The writers who did tackle the subject understood these problems; in spite of difficulties, they obviously felt the communication was worth the effort. The newness of the experience created a need for these stories, these maps of uncharted territory, and, even without precedents for this unique life, the authors used their fictions to make the unknown familiar. That they succeeded is sometimes suggested by the fiction itself; series hero Jane Allen, for example, during the long train trip from her Montana ranch home to her eastern college, reads *Beatrice Horton's First Year at Exeley*, a "series . . . about Eastern college life," to prepare herself for what she will find when she arrives.[49]

Against the hostility and attacks, graduates who wanted to interpret the college experience could not simply tell their story; starting with a handicap, they had to combat certain attitudes without destroying the integrity of their fictions. For the most part they succeeded, and in the process they offered a new and attractive version of women's space.

The years between 1900 and 1905 produced a spate of college books, male and female, written for a general audience. Those who depicted the women's colleges wrote with a different kind of consciousness than Brown and Anderson had had. Although they attempt to present a many-faceted experience in their stories, above all they stress the ability of women to live and work together and to profit from the venture—to exploit that community, symbolized here by the metaphor of the green world, that provided a new and different women's space. As a theme, this ability to live and work together within their special space is the most complex and protean; it goes beyond simply getting along together to include such specifics as learning the codes of the new world; emphasizing differences, probably in response to reportorial insistence on "*the* college girl"; female bonding; and the transformational power of the college itself.

# · THREE ·

# *Living Together:*
# *The Celebration of Community*

I n *Two College Girls* Helen Dawes Brown presented to the reader a
women's community, purposeful and, in its larger aims, harmonious;
individual problems and flaws do not conflict with the college world,
but are solved or alleviated by it. Young women make their adjustment
to each other and to the college as part of their learning. These were the
eager and courageous pioneers, for whom going to college was an adventure in itself, one that included the establishment of community as part
of the experience. They presented themselves to the world seriously, as
Brown did her characters.

Nowhere in the fiction is the sense of women's community as magical,
transformational green world so strong and celebrated as in four collections of short stories published around 1900: *Smith College Stories, Vassar
Stories, Wellesley Stories,* and *A Book of Bryn Mawr Stories.* With them belongs
one juvenile series, the Betty Wales books.[1] These interpretations belong
together because of publication dates, but even more because all the
authors were students during the 1890s, and their joy in the experience
is so great that the reader feels this must have been the best time to be
in college. Sharing the sense of celebration are a novel, *Daddy Long-Legs,*
a collection of stories about Patty, and to some extent another series, the
*Molly Brown* books.[2]

The turn-of-the-century short story collections are the high point of
writing about the women's colleges; they combine delighted discovery,
celebration, and the assumption that college life is important enough to
be the main reason for telling the story. While the writers try to be honest
and show dark as well as bright, they assert that college is a unique and
positive experience and opportunity, and they display love of and gratitude to the institution itself.

Perhaps this celebratory approach is a result of the times, for women's opportunities expanded during the last years of the century. By 1895 Vassar was thirty years old and educating the daughters of its first graduates; Smith and Wellesley were twenty and Bryn Mawr, twelve. They were healthy and secure as institutions, and while the outside world still did not understand them, their students no longer had to prove the right of the colleges to exist or their own right to attend. At the same time, total enrollment remained comparatively small, so that all the students in a class could know one another. The changes that would come with a larger student body and an influx of those who found college fashionable were beginning, but their effects were still minimal.

The writers of these stories all display confidence in what they are doing, and along with that confidence is a willingness to say that the experience of college is not just important and rewarding, but fun. If the message of Helen Dawes Brown and Olive Anderson is *women can*, then the message of this fiction is *of course they can, and they can enjoy themselves in the process.* But a shift in emphasis from the academic to the social shows in the selection of the events that make up the narrative. The focus is on interaction within the community: from a comic story about borrowing to a serious account of choosing new members for an honor society, young women are portrayed analyzing and reacting to others, functioning within a highly ethical world, making choices, and deciding their own behaviors. Light as some of the topics may seem, the stories explore human relationships and the development of character.

Of the four collections, the most interesting and the best from a literary point of view is Josephine Daskam Bacon's *Smith College Stories* (1900). Josephine Daskam graduated in 1897 and had a respectable, if minor, literary career, publishing stories and critical essays in the *Atlantic, Scribner's* and other serious magazines and writing several novels and juveniles. She writes well, and part of her strength in the stories lies in avoiding direct confrontation with issues; she prefers to substitute narrative for argument, focusing on character and attempting to show the integrated facets of college life. Her technique is to "drop in" on a group of young women at various points in their four years, using the same people, but varying her emphasis and focal character. Her first story, for example, is about Theodora Root and the basketball game that creates an identity for the freshman class; Theodora appears in passing in other stories, then is the point-of-view character again in the last one, set at her graduation four years later. Bacon turns an episodic approach into coherence; the separate tales hold together so well that the result is more like a novel than a collection of stories, with each facet contributing to the vision of a whole. And although her preface states that "the college girl is very much like any other girl," the fiction contradicts her by insisting that the college experience is unique and individual. *Smith College Stories* is a successful and appealing book; it was reprinted several times and followed by a second collection, *Her Fiancé, and Other Stories.*[3]

*Vassar Stories* (1900), a collection by Grace M. Gallaher, who graduated in 1897, most closely resembles in literary format and style the Smith collection. It has a similar approach; there is the same brisk, affectionate humor; and the author keeps continuity by having characters appear throughout, although she lacks Bacon's ability to connect the episodes into a whole. Her unity is created by the image of Vassar rather than by literary focus. All the collections celebrate the alma mater and typically display love for their school, but Gallaher deliberately makes Vassar the primary actor.

Grace L. Cook in *Wellesley Stories* (1901) does not attempt anything beyond a group of stories that, though interesting and well written, lack any connection beyond the sharing of an unusual and delightful experience. *A Book of Bryn Mawr Stories* (1901), with two editors, Margaretta Morris and Louise Buffum Congdon, who put together stories by different authors, is disappointing in comparison to the others. As might be expected, tone and quality are uneven; several stories are very well written, but in too many the thesis and the desire to combat the stereotypes are distressingly obvious. These four collections do not stand alone; they are contemporary with *Harvard Stories, Stanford Sketches, Yale Yarns, Princeton Stories, Tales of Bowdoin,* and *Cornell Stories,* as if every publisher hurried to cash in on an interested audience.[4]

The Betty Wales books (1904–1911) may be the first college series for girls.[5] Under the pseudonym Margaret Warde, the author wrote books for older girls and short stories for *St. Nicholas, Youth's Companion,* and *The American Girl*; under her own name, Edith Kellog Dunton, she was a regular contributor of essays to the more prestigious magazines. She graduated from Smith in 1897, a classmate of Josephine Daskam's, and her fiction has the same kind of energy, affection, and literary skill. Like the collections, her series celebrates student life, and with more space to develop individual characters and relationships, she defines success and gives the formula for it. If the standard for judging these narratives is their ability to create the world of magic and transformation that foregrounds women's abilities, this is by far the best of the series books and, though aimed at a younger audience, ranks in quality with *Smith College Stories.*

The four collections and the Betty Wales series display what Margaret Sherwood called the "warmth and light and color" of the women's colleges. With far less emphasis on serious purpose and academic achievement than the fiction of Helen Dawes Brown or Olive Anderson, with romance consigned to the future, the focus is on character and interaction, displayed against a bittersweet awareness that this lovely world offers only a short time for women to find something unique that will forever change them. The emphasis is on female bonding: on young women not just making friends, but learning to value each other as persons and learning in the process to value themselves. The glorification of the green world here reaches its height as they are given the opportunity to discover and stretch themselves, to broaden their lives, and to value other women as more than competitors for men.

With a few exceptions the fiction is so well written that direct response to outside attacks, stereotypes, and false images, while certainly present, merges into the whole. The thrust is to counter a generally negative view of women, not just those in college, but everywhere: the belief that women could not live and work together. Women, as everyone knew, were unable to be cooperative and loyal; their friendships could not be real or lasting. In groups, so ran popular wisdom, women cackled and ran off in all directions ("hen" parties); their friendships were not strong enough to weather disruptions and today's intimate would be the subject of tomorrow's malice. They displayed what Marjorie Pryse has described in another context as the "traits misogynistic convention has considered characteristic of women—vindictiveness, vanity, and verbal cruelty."[6] Women could not work together for a common objective because they were unable to rise above the level of personalities—and these qualities were, of course, innate rather than the effect of their conditioning. "Girls" by their nature had all these faults, and youthful silliness and irresponsibility besides. To send them to college was absurd, since they were incapable, not just mentally and physically, but socially as well, of getting anything out of a college education. One might argue elements of truth in this view since social and economic conditions forced women into competition, using whatever weapons were available to them, for marriage partners and security. Perhaps the exclusion of men from the green world removed one source of hostility and allowed these young women to expand in their own directions, placing self-realization and friendship as high and important values.

The ability of women to live together constructively, ethically, and enjoyably is certainly the most thoroughly explored topic in the stories that attempt an honest presentation of college life. And the topic includes not just the details of daily interaction; it involves as well learning the behavioral codes of the new society, recognition and acceptance of difference, and the transformational power of the college itself. As a topic, living together has so many ramifications that the distinctions made in this study overlap and should not be seen as discrete, although it is more convenient to examine them that way.

Being part of a community of women, living intimately with other than family, was new and therefore probably both anticipated and feared; girls and young women were still strongly supervised in and by their families,

and most of the people they met were of their own social status and background. Few had wide travel experience; a young woman from a small
town might never have seen a city and might be accustomed to a class
structure that assigned levels from which friends would come. In some
of the juvenile fiction that shows girls going to high school, it is very clear
that only the well-to-do are educated even at that level.[7] (When there is
an exception, she is an object of concern and perhaps charity for the
"good" girls and a target of scorn for the bad.) And there were geo-
graphic limitations: the daughter of a wealthy New England family might
have been to England or Italy but might never have seen Ohio. Part of
the challenge, then, was to meet and get along with—to establish community with—all kinds of women, in a group that had, in the beginning,
little in common but gender and the desire to learn.

Meeting and adjusting to a roommate is the simplest version of the
process of learning to live together. In *An American Girl* Anderson does
not stress this point for obvious reasons: Will is too individualistic to
share the stage with anyone and in her case, the roommate comes with
the place to live. The two young women seem strange to each other at
first and must adjust, but the roommate remains a kind of adjunct; like
most of the other characters in that novel, her story is never developed
and she remains shadowy. The opposite is true in Brown's *Two College
Girls*, where the difference and incompatibility between the coheroes
makes the story; Edna and Rosamund introduce each other to different
lives, and they must break through misunderstanding and hostility before they are rewarded with real friendship and the widening horizons
that each new experience promises them. Part of their learning process
begins when they realize their differences and develop a desire to overcome them and is voiced in Rosamund's wish that they could be "added
together and divided by two—or you toned up and I toned down." They
make a paradigm for the process of growth that Brown sees as one important reason for being in college.

Adjusting to roommates or finding a solution if there is a real problem
is one element of success in college life, and the situation has built-in
dramatic value as well. Gallaher's Vassar collection begins with "In the
Matter of Room-mates," the story of Molly Olmstead, arriving from California into eastern autumnal rain, confused, shy, homesick, and longing
for the roommate who will be an instant and special friend. When she
finally appears, she is "moist, and dank and crumpled, and crumbly in
all sorts of unexplainable ways. Molly's perceptions were not keen, but
even she knew at once that the room-mate was an impossible person. A
big, rosy, vigorous girl herself, she shuddered at the unwholesome little
creature before her" (*Vassar*, 8). While outgoing, friendly, athletic Molly
absorbs with delight all the new experiences, the roommate whimpers
and clings. When they finally separate, a new roommate arrives and un-

packs her trunk: "'My set of frogs' as if they were shirt-studs, 'six young toads, my rattlesnake—what's the matter?' " (15). Besides her zoological specimens she brings a talent for arguing anything at all. After her departure the "new girl was lovely in Molly's eyes because she could not argue if she tried. When she left because of illness, Molly grieved sincerely. The fourth roommate was as entertaining as a play, but she considered College a land where it is always afternoon, and, the Faculty having other views on the subject, she departed before Finals" (23). The succession of unsuitable roommates goes on, but it is balanced by delightful discoveries; Molly has made friends, has thrown herself into college life, and loves what she is finding. There is no didactic message here, no how-to-get-along formula; rather, the story says that all kinds of things can happen, that they can be dealt with, and above all, that the life more than compensates for the occasional difficulty.

In "Biscuits Ex Machina," one of the most amusing stories in the Smith collection, two sets of mismated roommates cause chaos in their house and psychological damage to each other (and their housemother) until B. S. Kitts, a clever observer of life, persuades the housemother and then the young women themselves to switch roommates. The story is humorous, but it is also another exploration of difference.

Series hero Betty Wales, like Molly, has a roommate problem: "She had imagined a pretty girl like Eleanor Watson, or a jolly one like Katherine or Rachel; and here was this homely little thing with an awkward walk, a piping voice, and short skirts." But Helen Chase Adams, her assigned roommate, is just as disconcerted; in her "limited experience, all pretty girls were stupid. The idea of seeing crowds of them in the college chapel, much less rooming with one, had never entered her head. A college was a place for students" (F 28–29). Warde will, in fact, use Helen as a means of showing the growth of friendship and self-discovery, proving that the most unlikely people can find success as the college world defines it.

Although roommates are featured in some and part of the background of many stories, sharing a room does not need to involve close friendships. Since roommates and rooms are random, their effect on individual lives is not predictable, nor is the effect of location. In a Vassar story called "The Clan," Lydia Waitely's college life is shaped by the location of her single room: "If Lydia had roomed at Strong, where there was a handful of serious, studious girls like herself, she might have been happy at once. If she had roomed in first South, the noisy, lively set that ruled that corridor would have extended to her its friendship, simply because she was a freshman and within its precinct" (*Vassar*, 185–186). Instead she is among girls who share wealth, background, and class, and although they are friendly and even adopt her into their group, she knows she cannot afford to live as they do. Her own intelligence saves her from more than a bittersweet longing as she dissociates herself from them and finds her own kind of success.

Success in the fiction circa 1900 meant being happy and at home in the green world. That, in turn, depended on each young woman's getting the most out of everything offered, fulfilling her own needs and dreams, earning the respect of peers, in ways that enriched both herself and the college. The latter point is stressed in these stories; the honor societies, for example, take in outstanding young women, but part of what makes the chosen students outstanding, rather than merely popular, is their enhancing of the college itself.

One of the means to success in a new world with its own rules is, obviously, learning those rules and following them. These are not laws made by the administration, like the hated ten o'clock rule or compulsory chapel attendance (the first things to go with the establishment of student government); they are codes: understandings and acceptances, seldom spelled out, that govern behavior. Even when restrictive they are acceptable because they were, if not student-generated, sanctified by usage that made them into the traditions defining college life. In *An American Girl* and *Two College Girls* there is little emphasis on codes, logically, because the latter is about the people who created the codes and traditions that came to govern interaction, and in the former the codes in place are masculine and exclude women. The author of *College Girls* deliberately keeps to the codes of the outside world that emphasize women on the way to marriage.

Among the fairly elaborate system of codes firmly in place was designation by class—not socioeconomic class, but college status, a hierarchical arrangement of importance for first years, sophomores, juniors, seniors. A student's class established her primary loyalty, encouraging the students to think of themselves as belonging to a group: Smith's "ninety-yellow" or Vassar's "ninety-blank," as they are called in the stories. And the class divisions create codes within codes: seniors, and to a lesser degree juniors, are treated with respect amounting to reverence. They are the standard setters and arbiters, and the lowly first-year student who is noticed by an upperclasswoman is flattered indeed.

The two first-year Smith students who expect a visit from the distinguished "Miss Biddle of Bryn Mawr," known in the college world for grace and ability, are greatly daring when they plan a tea for her, for they invite several graduates, some faculty members, and, after much discussion, a few seniors. When at the last moment Miss Biddle cannot come, the two are horrified, not at the reactions of graduates and faculty, but because their presumption in inviting seniors could be justified only by the strongest reasons: "'And they say freshmen are getting so uppish anyway . . . they'll laugh at us and be bored.' They felt that they were doomed to endless joking at the hands of the whole college" (*Smith*, 68).

In the Molly Brown books, a first-year student named Minerva, who wears her high school medals, imperils her reputation by addressing upper-classwomen by their first names, joining groups without invitation, and even leading conversations: " 'She is taking great chances,' [said] Nance, who had a thorough respect for college etiquette and class caste. 'Every pert freshman must be prepared for a call-down; and if she doesn't take it like a lamb, she'll just have to expect a freeze-out' " (J 54). Seniority and survival demand respect.

Far more serious are the codes that govern ethical behavior, for these green worlds have the highest ethical standards. Abbe Carter Goodloe, in her article on Wellesley, compares the insouciant and open cheating of male undergraduates with the absolute standards of her own school: "I have known girls who did clerical work for professors to have in their desks copies of the papers for the examinations which their room-mates were to take the next day, and they were as safe as if locked in the President's private office . . . one cannot help contrasting favorably the standard of morality in a woman's college which would ostrasize a girl for taking into class a literal translation of the original" with various examples of male cheating.[8]

Transgressions of class codes can be amusing, but none of the writers find any humor in abuse of the ethical codes; it is a tragic mistake. The story of Arna Kellar, a Vassar student who seems to have everything but who destroys herself by cheating, typifies the attitude. Arna is described as the "embodied spirit of youth itself" to her admirers, who "followed her as one follows a cool wind on a languid summer day" ( *Vassar,* 73) Besides beauty and charm, she "has a nimble wit that flew faster in dangerous situations and a luck which was fairly often ominous" (74–75)— ominous because she cannot bear the image of herself as someone who needs to study. When her cheating is discovered, her shocked and disappointed peers take on the responsibility of punishment themselves; she is sent to Coventry, and for the rest of her college years, no one speaks to her. At the end she tells Barbara, her former roommate who, after agonizing between her affection for her friend and her own commitment to the ethical codes, had finally reported her, why she cheated:

> I wanted to be considered a great scholar and a genius. I couldn't bear to have the girls think me just like everyone else who had to grind over Hygiene and freshman English, or flunk. I planned to cheat all that semester. . . . I never dreamed the girls would cut me. I was such a fool in those days. I didn't believe love of truth and a high standard of honor would win against me. I thought I held the girls so fast they couldn't get away. . . . What did I care about honor, or Vassar's standards, or anything, so long as my reputation for brightness was safe, my power over the girls unshaken? I was one of those "feeble souls" Emerson describes, who want to be loved,

but don't care about being lovely. I wanted praise, and influence, and friendship that I hadn't earned, that just came to me because I had certain ways of speaking and looking, not because I was really fine.   (96–100)

Both her action and motivation are wrong; they transgress the codes that the students have chosen to uphold, and Arna's terrible punishment is not official, but is administered by her peers. And, characteristic of this fiction, her act is unforgivable because it is not against another young woman but against the college itself.

The codes that apply to all do not create conformity, however. The recognition of differences and the ability to understand different kinds of people and to learn how to deal with them are major connected themes, perhaps in reaction to that objectionable journalistic habit of talking about "*the* college girl." Clearly it was important to show readers that different kinds of young women could fit into the college world, that it had something to offer everyone who approached it correctly, and that one could learn to understand, accept, and get along with all these differences. This point is implicit in all the early fictions and is spelled out in the *Scribner's* article on Smith, written, like the others in that series, by a recent graduate:

> To avoid turning out girls cut by any one pattern has been the great desire of the president and of the members of the faculty most influential in college affairs. A brand of girl, put through the mill and turned loose upon the world, stamped and labelled "Smith" would be their greatest disappointment. For a symmetrical, well rounded woman, in every way *developed as the need of her own personality dictated*, has been their hope for the alumna.

The emphasis is added, but the author might be setting out a thesis for her contemporary writers. Later she adds that "college activities are so complex and various, that girls of every description and character may find an outlet for their energies." [9]

Those who fictionalized the college experience made "difference" a major theme, and the writers are so consistent in presenting it as a strongly positive fact of college life that its importance to them is unmistakable. "A Few Diversions," in the Smith volume, makes the point directly. Young Marjory does not want to go to college; she has seen her cousin Georgiana, who "had short hair and was such a frump and she wore such hideous spectacles and talked about Socialism—or was it Sociology?—all the time. I remember she was always trying to get us to join clubs and protest against something or other—it was very wearisome" (206). But she accepts the invitation to visit the campus from a Smith junior, a friend of her family; Nan quietly arranges for her to be entertained by a variety of young women, from elegant Ursula with her Parisian coiffure, to athletic Nan herself. At a favorite haunt,

> In one corner four girls with rumpled shirtwaists and dusty golf stockings squabbled over scores, and illustrated with spoons preferred methods of driving and putting. Their voices rose above the level prescribed for drawing-room conversation and they called each other strange names. In another corner a tall, dark girl with a grave expression talked steadily in a low voice to her companion, a clever-looking creature, whose bursts of laughter grew hysterical as the dignified one continued, with a perfectly impersonal manner, to reduce her to positive tears of mirth. . . . Near them a porcelain blonde, gowned in a wonderful pale blue stuff with a great hat covered with curly plumes, ate strawberry ices with a tailor-made person clothed in white pique, mystic, wonderful. She was all stiffness and specklessness, and she looked with undisguised scorn at the clamoring athletes, a white leather card-case in her hand. Near one window a gypsy-faced child in a big pink sunbonnet imparted mighty confidence to her friend, who shook two magnificent auburn braids over her shoulders with every chuckle. (213–214)

By the end of Marjory's visit her image of the college girl as obnoxious bluestocking, or any other single image, has crumbled. "She was used to them now, used to pigtails and puffs, shirtwaists and evening dresses, Western rolled r's and Eastern broad a's, handsome matronly young women, and slim, saucy little chits, solitary walkers, devoted pairs, and rollicking bands" (223). She has met a highly civilized world in which young women are free to develop their own talents and styles with acceptance and understanding from their peers. One need not like everyone equally to appreciate the richness of variety.

Just as the stories stress the differences in the young women who come to college, so they stress the many ways that this world offers to exploit, in the best sense of the word, those differences so that everyone benefits. There are, at Smith, the Sutton twins, "the recognized jesters of the class," the terror of the housemother but able to maintain high standing in their classes while they star on the basketball court (95). There is B. S. Kitts, "called Biscuits as soon as she had found her own particular little set of girls," the intelligent observer, "one of five or six clever girls. . . . The house president spoke of them bitterly as blasé and critical . . . the collector for missions found them sceptical and inclined to ribaldry if pushed too far; but the Phi Kappa banked heavily on their united efforts, and more than usually idiotic class meetings meekly bowed to what they themselves scornfully referred to as 'their ordinary horse sense' " (87). Martha Augusta Williams deplores her commonplace name and specializes in ennui: her shelves hold French novels and on her desk is a skull with a Japanese paper snake winding through it, while Beardsley drawings instead of Gibson Girls adorn her walls. Her poses are a source of fun for everyone but the faculty, who note that they keep her grades low (87–88). There is the immensely talented Suzanne, artistic and eccentric: "people who disliked Suzanne called her unprincipled and shallow and lazy; people who admired her called her brilliant and irresponsible and lazy; people who loved her called her fascinating and spoiled and lazy. . . . She was never without two or three admirers, but her class disliked her, and it took all their self-control to bear with her to the extent that was necessary to profit by her special abilities" (257–258).

There is Jean Webster's Patty, presented first in *Scribner's* pages, then in a book, who has almost made a career of "psyching out" the faculty: "By her senior year she had reduced the matter of recitation to a system, and could foretell with unvarying precision the day she would be called on and the question she would be asked. Her tactics varied with the subject and the instructor, and were the result of a penetration and knowledge of human nature that might have accomplished something in a worthier cause." [10] Her method fails, finally, with her philosophy professor, who has no system for her to analyze, and she is forced to turn to studying. In literary terms Patty is a trickster; in other terms she is a con artist, determined to get by without effort. She gets away with her pranks because she has charm, because she is not malicious, and because, with all her tricks, she does not cheat. College is the theater in which this early antihero plays out her own dramas; that she is not typical is made clear by the portrayals of her roommate and friends, whose attitude toward her is affectionate, amused, and totally without illusion, for Patty is one of the interesting phenomena that can be encountered in college. Her nice normal friends consider her a delightful source of amusement, to be neither condemned nor imitated. The important point is that no effort is made to change these and other different students; they are to be understood and enjoyed.

Betty Wales, very much a "well-rounded girl," comes to college "without any particular enthusiasm for it, though she was naturally an enthusiastic person." She is armed with advice from a friend of her older sister's: "You'll like college, Betty. . . . Not just as Nan and I did, of course. Every girl has her own reasons for liking college—but every nice girl likes it" (F 11–12). For Betty the liking begins as she meets the other inhabitants of Chapin House, who indeed represent variety. There is humorous and outgoing Katherine; merry, capable Rachel; pale, quiet Roberta, who may be "snippy" or only shy; impish, clever Mary, the only sophomore, who leads and teases the first-year students. Betty is fascinated by the beautiful and difficult Eleanor Watson, brilliant, spoiled, and bent on being a power in the college world. Later the author adds Madeline, the talented daughter of cosmopolitan artists, who has traveled widely, knows all sorts of people, and acts as a useful author's persona, commenting in a detached way on people and events. These are the characters around whom the story will work, and for Betty at first college means getting to know these new friends.

Molly Brown, herself a sweet Southern lady, also makes friends chiefly through location; later the friendships are refined by time and compatibility. Her roommate, Nancc, is a pretty, staid New Englander, while Judy, who as the daughter of a civil engineer has never had a permanent home, is tempestuous, brilliant, and overdramatic; she is unstable, she claims, because she was born on a ship crossing the Pacific. She will get into "scrapes" from which her friends must rescue her. Unlike though they are, the three become close friends. Other girls in the group include Margaret, daughter of a senator and herself a politician and women's rights activist (a promising idea that is only slightly developed); Jessie, who is so pretty that everyone expects her to marry rather than finish college; two bright and witty sisters; and finally the Japanese Otoyo Sen.

Different though they are, nearly all the young women in these fictions have Anglo-Saxon names and "normal" American backgrounds, differentiated only by economic levels or as urban or rural. There were, however, by this time, noticeable numbers of foreign students attending the four women's colleges, and Otoyo represents them. She is welcomed, but at first she is almost a toy: "the most charming little doll-like creature the girls had ever seen, so unreal and different from themselves, that they could hardly credit her with the feelings and sensibilities of a human being. So correctly polite was she with such formal, stiff little manners that she seemed almost an automaton wound up to bow and nod at the proper moment" (F 26–27).

Otoyo is delightfully presented. She has learned English but has trouble with grammar when she speaks; when her trunks arrive, "'Oh,' exclaimed Miss Otoyo, clasping her hands with timid pleasure, 'my estates have to this place arriving come.'" Nance and Molly must control their laughter so as not to hurt her feelings, and as they know her better they take pains to correct her "early participial-adverbial faults." She is adopted into their group, yet even after the friendship is long established, and charmingly presented as she is, her nationality defines her; there is always the suggestion that she is cherished as a doll or a token— not quite real. But she is cherished—by the friends she has made and by the college, which has a place for her.

Not all the differences are so positive, nor all the people who are revealed so delightful. In "A Lyrical Interlude" Rebecca has succeeded in conning Wellesley students into believing that she is a model of literary talent and taste. Her pretentiousness causes some amusing moments; after she dramatically reads a submitted poem to the Rhymesters Club she has founded, she searches for its depth and significance until its author points out that it is supposed to be funny. But to those who know, she stops being amusing when a real poet's verses are attributed to her and, though she does not claim authorship, she does not deny it, either. When the real author confronts her, Rebecca slides wide-eyed out of the "misunderstanding." She continues in her way, and others continue to worship her. "Clorinda" is another Wellesley charmer, a young woman who wants popularity and can find it only in the admiration of lower classwomen; she eventually cheats another student out of a large sum of money. And in "The Evolution of Evangeline" the title character, after having been transformed from dowdy obscurity to statuesque beauty for a Smith "girl-dance," achieves enormous popularity even though, as one of the agents of the transformation notes, she remains "an essentially uninteresting person" (268). But part of the learning experience is to recognize the meretricious, or even be fooled by it, as well as the meritorious.

The author of the Betty Wales books consciously and deliberately voices the attitudes that serve to incorporate codes and differences and, in fact, spells out the steps to success. As she discovers her way around, making friends, learning the codes, becoming a part of this increasingly delightful world, the unintrospective Betty stumbles on the ancient truth that using one's abilities to the fullest creates happiness. Everyone has a talent of some kind, and happiness and success depend on finding that talent and using it to express self and at the same time make a contribution to the college as a whole. Stretching of self, acceptance of the codes, and appreciation of differences make up the behavioral manifestation of the "college spirit" just as the campus itself is its physical manifestation. And like all the magical green worlds, it has the power to transform.

The idea of the college as a place of transformation dominates this fiction and is accompanied by its corollary, love for the college and obligation to it. The idea is an underlying constant in the Smith collection and the Betty Wales books, the unifying theme in the Vassar stories, and is present although not so heavily emphasized in the other works. Smith's basketball game against the sophomores welds the new students into a class entity; Theodora Root has the joy of hearing her world sing its tribute to her and though it is only "flattering doggerel . . . anyone who has had that experience knows the little contraction of the heart, the sudden hot tightening of the eyelids, the confused, excited desire to be worthy of all that trust and admiration" (21). By the final chapter, at their dinner when the graduates are singing to each other, Theodora, as individual and representative, looks back on experiences that were both individual and shared. For her and her classmates there is "a little of the first faint conviction that the college owns all her classes, the feeling that grows with the years" (343) and so their final cheer and song is no longer for themselves but for their college.

In the Vassar collection this love of and gratitude to the college and its power to transform is so strong that it becomes the unifying theme. It is spelled out in "A Sense of Obligation," for example, in which Lucretia, brought up in one of those rural towns that come off badly in these stories, has been so isolated because of her intelligence, sensitivity, and love of books that she believes there is something wrong with her mind. She is discovered by a teacher and comes to college:

> What can express that which Vassar was to her? Land to the ship-wrecked sailor? Water to the desert traveller? These know the bitterness of her deprivation, but not its years of endurance. Vassar gave her books, instruction, inspiration. Its great gift was respect for herself, the assurance that she had a right to her individuality, though it differed from that of every other human being. . . . She absorbed all that Vassar could offer, in work and in fun. She did everything that one mortal, hampered by time and space, could. Her little body was exhausted often, but her spirit never flagged. . . . She even spent her vacations at Vassar, that she might not miss one experience of College, not even that of bare, lonesome corridors and deserted campus. (107–108)

The transformation of character by the mysterious entity of the college spirit informs many of the stories and is made explicit in several others. In "Within Four Years" Lillian, as the daughter of a fundamentalist preacher, brought up within a rigid group and being educated to be a missionary for the sect, comes to Bryn Mawr full of disapproval of everything that does not fit within her narrow guidelines. Her father's creed is "wholly negative, in its exclusion of all that makes for the brightness of life" (103). Lillian does not realize that she is changing, that as she learns and observes this world, her mind is becoming too wide and generous to accept the dogma in which she has been reared. In a meeting she attacks the frivolity of her classmates and the falseness of their aims. She leaves the meeting knowing she has gone too far: "for the moment there could be nothing but alienation from one who had found tongue against the college·spirit—for [the students] felt that the attack was really against this vague, shadowy, stern, beloved thing of many hues and forms—the spirit of the college" (116). But the outburst is a catharsis; it forces Lillian to look at what she has denounced and to examine herself. Gradually she lets her mind open; she accepts and even seeks out new experiences. By the end of her senior year she has made friends, accepted the legitimacy of beauty, joy, and pleasure, become part of college life, and proved herself a fine scholar. Awarded a fellowship in history, she graduates joyfully, knowing that she will come back to the college that has given her so much and that she need never return to the angry, limited world of her childhood.

If the transformational power of the college is a given in all the fiction, nowhere is it so clear as in Jean Webster's best seller, the popular and long-lived *Daddy Long-Legs* (1912), which is still in print, though now relegated to juvenile shelves since it lacks sex, violence, or a fragmented universe. The novel was made into a successful Broadway play and later suffered the indignity of becoming a 1950s musical film, about which the best that can be said is that Fred Astaire always danced well.[11] The hero is a Cinderella figure and the novel equally balances its suspenseful love story with college life; the play, which restricts its "college" element to having the girls clean their room by shoving everything under the bed, is simply another love story, but the novel exalts the power of the college to transform.

Judy Abbott has spent the first seventeen years of her life in an orphanage. When the story opens, one of the trustees, convinced by her writing ability that she is talented, decides to send her to college. He will remain anonymous, but she is to write him once a month describing her experiences. All she knows of him is his tall shadow, which gives her the name she uses for him. After the introductory chapter the story is told through her letters, and the plot offers the reader the happy experience of knowing more than the character does. One of Judy's suite mates is rich, stuffy Julia Pendleton, and when her young Uncle Jervis visits and is particularly interested in Judy, it does not take the reader long to realize that he is the mysterious benefactor, although Judy, locked into her assumption that all trustees are old, white-haired, and pompous, never suspects.

The popularity of the novel rested on more than a well-handled Cinderella plot and believable characters. It remains fresh because the reader shares Judy's sense of discovery, her amazed delight at what is happening to her. Her letters are charming and humorous as she tells of each new intellectual and social experience; at times they are very moving in their revelation of the longing for someone to love, which impels her to transform her unknown trustee into a family of her own and so erase, for moments, her loneliness.

Her new experiences move her from nameless orphan to secure, confident, well-educated woman. She can even write finally that her trustee may give her love to the hated orphanage: "When I first came to college I felt quite resentful that I had been robbed of the normal kind of childhood the other girls had had," but now she sees that she has a "vantage point from which to stand aside and look at life," in contrast to "those who never know they are happy. They are so accustomed to the feeling that their senses are deadened to it, but as for me—I am perfectly sure every moment of my life that I am happy" (270–271).

Even today the appeal of the novel, innocent though it is in late twentieth-century terms, is evident. Because of its enormous popularity, the message it carried about women in college was widespread. Judy Abbott's situation was unique, but the story presents the college as a magical place, the green world in which she and others might mature and find identity. It is not simply that from a frightened, eager, separate being who knows nothing she becomes popular, successful, a member of an honor society, and an editor of the magazine who in the future can write a successful novel and marry a wealthy and cultured man without any sense of inferiority; the college has changed her potentially limited, wasted life to something rich, secure, and positive.

The already-mentioned Betty Wales books are contemporary with the college collections. Series books, like the popular novel, reached a wide audience and of course, a specific one, juvenile readers. Those who study children's literature seldom give series books much consideration, and it is easy to understand the reasons: many are superficial, episodic, unskillfully written, and presented in the cheapest possible formats. But they were popular and widely read, so that whatever messages they carried went to a large and receptive audience.[12] Whatever their quality, their circulation alone argues their importance as a means of bringing other lives to readers and widening their worlds.

None of the negative qualities listed above apply to the Betty Wales books; they are very well written indeed, and Warde creates characters and situations that later series writers would attempt (or copy) with varying degrees of success. She is particularly good at balancing kimono-clad girls at "spreads" and fun of the "larks and pranks" variety with serious issues of ethics, self-examination, and maturity.

In her main character Warde establishes a central figure who both does and does not fit the insistence that the college woman is just like everyone else of her age and gender. Betty Wales's outstanding talent is general unselfconscious niceness. She is intelligent but not intellectual; she will eagerly participate in sports, dramatics, writing, politics, or any other areas in which her friends excel, though she will never star in them. But she will draw around her by her goodness, charm, only those who do excel. One friend says to her, "It's no use at all, you, Betty Wales. . . . You always twist the things we don't want around until they seem simple and easy and no more than decent" (201). Betty is, in short, a figure with whom it is easy to identify, a kind of Everygirl, not out of reach of any reader, nor, as good characters so often are, priggish or pompous. She has faults: at the beginning she is so naïve as to seem callow. Rather frivolous and imperceptive, her lack of awareness often means that she does not anticipate the effects of her actions, and though she is always kind, she can get caught up in her own affairs and pleasures and miss some very obvious feelings and needs of others. What could be unpleasant, however, is redeemed by her good instincts and real caring when she does see a need. In short, she is flawed, human, and likable. And as she acts and learns, the author can use her naïveté and her sense of discovery to speak to the reader.

Warde stresses what others, Brown and Bacon especially, have suggested: female bonding. She offers a most joyous and concentrated por-

trayal of a community of women. Living together is defined chiefly as the
making of strong friendships, initiated by proximity but developed by
shared activity and insight into each other's characters. And awareness
of differences is handled with great skill. All Betty's friends are clear and
definite personalities, with their own directions, and Warde flanks her
agreeable hero with two other young women, Helen and Eleanor, who
in their separate ways have to deal with their relationships to the college.

Perhaps most interesting about the series, the quality that gives it both
its strength and appeal, is that message articulated by Betty and carried
out in all the intertwined stories: the way to succeed in this world (and
by extension, all worlds), is to find one's own talents, strengths, abilities
and interests, then foster and use them. Betty is certainly a nurturer,
though an easily distracted one, but like the short story writers, Warde
emphasizes self and self-discovery. She sets out a strong, positive message
for women, and perhaps even a subversive one, for all the conventionality of its context.

With four volumes rather than one to work within, Warde can explo
fully the transformational power of the college, the importance of
codes, the ethical universe, and the value of difference. She does so
her presentation of the college lives of Helen Chase Adams, Bett
"freak" roommate, and the brilliant, beautiful Eleanor Watson. Betty
the nice normal young woman who has nevertheless worked out and
voiced the formula for college success and who grows steadily and without drama, is the pivot between these two extremes. Helen and Eleanor,
"unlike in everything else, were at one in being self-centered" (S 111)
Betty feels at one point that she has as much trouble from one
the other. Because these two lives are so carefully and pr
worked out and are so clearly designed to carry a message, i
examine them in some depth; they exemplify what other
trying to say within their smaller spaces.

Helen Chase Adams with her three-part New England nam
ward, rigid, shy, unappealing on the surface, but sensitive enou
be aware of her own inability to make an impact. Even Betty, with al
her kindness, often forgets that her roommate exists. Helen is both a
"freak," an obvious misfit, and a "dig" who studies too much. She cannot at first balance studying with pleasure, and she is slow to pick up
undercurrents and subtleties. Because she is plain and plodding, in contrast with the pretty, secure young women around her, she assumes that
she cannot be part of the green world. But Helen has intelligence and
her own kind of integrity. When a snub that only her naïveté permitted
to happen makes her wonder if her housemates are kind to her only out
of pity, she does not complain, she simply withdraws, and the others assume that she would rather study than join in their entertainments. Betty
finds her roommate's behavior exasperating, but like the others, accepts
her surface.

Confidence begins to grow when a woman faculty member invites her to supper and Helen interprets the act as an indication that there must be something interesting about her, rather than as the impulse of pity it really is. Miss Mills, asked by a colleague why she bothered with someone so drab, says her questioner wouldn't understand: "You were president of your class when you were a freshman. I was nobody in particular, and I know what it's like" and then, "When girls are happy they are cruel . . . or perhaps they're only careless" (F 245–246). Helen's friendship with Theresa Reed, another apparent freak, moves her closer to understanding her own role. Theresa was "homely and awkward, she wore dowdy clothes and wore them badly, and she was slow and plodding" (F 247), but she is also T. Reed, the dazzler on the basketball court, whose brilliant playing turned the inevitable defeat of her class team into a splendid moral victory, and who is the pride of her class and the admiration of the college.

Helen realizes that her friend has followed the Betty Wales formula of finding one's talent and using it; further, she realizes that she can do something similar. Her new confidence leads to an honest talk with Betty, so that the two understand each other and Helen again joins her housemates in their fun. There is no fairy-tale transformation, but Betty helps her find a nicer way to fix her hair and Madeline lures her into gym class to improve her posture, so that while she never becomes "exactly 'a marvel of grace' . . . she was erect and supple, with considerable poise and dignity of bearing, when she left Harding" (S 47). She remains a "dig" but because of her new insights she works to discover and use her talent, which turns out to be exactly that ability to work faithfully and dependably.

Eventually the roommates separate. Betty gets a single room and Helen rooms with T. Reed; it is a friendly parting and both are pleased that their rooms are near. In fact they come to rely on each other and their friendship strengthens. Helen makes friends outside the original group, and as appreciation for her abilities grows,

> Helen blossomed out. She saw that at last the girls really liked her for herself, and enjoyed her quaint little fancies and original ideas about persons and places. And so, as Mary Brooks put it, she let herself go; she forgot to be frightened and sensitive and ill at ease, and before she knew it all her dreams were coming true. She was somebody "at last"; the class of 19— and the clan both wanted her and were proud of her.

The end of the process is that the "shy, awkward, unfriended little freshman had become that envied and enviable person, a 'prominent girl' " (J 326).

At the end of her junior year Helen achieves one of the college's highest honors by becoming an *Argus* editor. Reputation presents her as quiet, clever, resourceful, a young woman in whom the college community takes pride. She has learned who she is and that the person she is has value. Her particular mission, she decides, is "being queer. Sometimes she hated it, sometimes she laughed at it, always it seemed to her a very humble one, but she honestly tried to live up to its responsibilities and to make the most of the opportunities it offered" (Sr 106). She never forgets "the loneliness of her freshman year," and with more insight than most, she can take quiet pleasure in her own status, her solid contentment built on success, and the affection of her friends. The text tacitly insists that Helen has not been changed into another kind of person; the transformational process has found and developed qualities dormant within her.

A passage comparing Helen and Eleanor begins, "It is odd how positions shift. Eleanor Watson had spoiled all the chances that had seemed so brilliant at the beginning of her college course" (Sr 26). Unlike Helen, Eleanor entered with everything in her favor. Strikingly beautiful, brilliant and charming, but undisciplined, spoiled by her prep school experience that gave her rewards for very little effort, Eleanor expected admiration, status, and power without effort.

She is the inversion of Helen, for whom she has nothing but contempt, in more than looks and personality. A brilliant student, she, like Arna Kellar and Jean Webster's Patty, relies on her wits; in her eyes it is somehow disgraceful to be seen to study. And her desire to be first makes her snobbish; after a thoughtless and catty remark about Katherine, she

> bitterly regretted having antagonized the girls in the house, when she had meant only to keep them—all but Betty—at a respectful distance. She liked most of them personally, but she wished her friends to be of another type—girls from large schools like her own, who would have influence and a following from the first . . . who could control votes in class meetings and push their little set to first place in all the organized activities of the college. . . . She saw now that she had indulged her fondness for sarcasm too far, and was ready to do a good deal to win back the admiration which she was sure the Chapin House girls had felt for her at first.   (F 41–42)

Unaware that her housemates see her goals all too clearly but do not care enough to be other than polite and friendly, it never occurs to her that, far from admiring her, they are simply not interested.

Eleanor understands politics, but not the college codes. Betty, for whom the codes are givens, may be fascinated by Eleanor, but when the latter wonders if she should try to hire Helen Chase Adams to write her themes for her, Betty does not even try to hide her shock; when Eleanor breaks rules, Betty's horror indicates that she is going wrong. Words she overhears from a prep school friend describing her as a "general failure here" (F 330) finally break Eleanor's complacency and make her want to change herself. It is a suitable ending for her first year, but the reform only deepens her conflict, for her desire to follow Betty's open enjoyment of everything wars with the old need: "She had not lost her worldly ambitions in one summer; and she had not gained, at a bound, the concentration that enabled the other girls to get through an amazing amount of work and fun with perfect ease. She knew infinitely less of the value of time than Betty Wales; she had less sense of proportion than Helen Adams; and she was intensely eager to win all sorts of honors" (S 56).

Pressured as she tries to make up her work and tempted still by her need for admiration, she plagiarizes, taking a story from an obscure literary magazine, making slight changes, and submitting it to her theme course, where it is praised and published in the *Argus*. She leaps into the prominence she wanted, even becoming an early choice of an honor society. For a tense, bitter year she lives with the knowledge that her fame rests on a lie; when her plagiarism is discovered, she must face open contempt. Betty stays loyal and the acquaintances from Chapin House, now scattered around in different dormitories but still a "crowd," remain politely friendly. But when the original group—all of whom by now are on the way to the prominence that Eleanor so much wanted—and a few new friends who have informally joined it along the way form themselves into a kind of club, they do not include Eleanor. It is the detached observer Madeline Ayres who fully understands what Eleanor has done to herself:

> "I suppose," remarked Madeline, irrelevantly, "that if it wasn't a lot more trouble to find things than to lose them people would be even more careless than they are now. But it seems a little hard sometimes to have to hunt so many times for a thing you lost in a minute."
>
> Betty stared at her uncomprehendingly. "What kind of things do you mean, Madeline?"
>
> "Oh, all sorts," said Madeline. "Handkerchiefs and fountain pens and gold beads and reputations." (J 279)

Eleanor does change, but it is too late; her reputation hangs like an albatross around her neck. When Helen Chase Adams is elected an *Argus* editor, along with others who had worked and proved their abilities, it is a terrible blow to Eleanor: "Ever since she had entered college, fully informed by her upperclass friends about all the ways of putting herself forward and all the offices and honors that a clever girl might aspire to, Eleanor had looked forward to the day of the 'Argus' elections as her hour of greatest triumph" (J 302). But she forces herself to overcome her resentment, to acknowledge that she has caused her own downfall, and, indeed, to give the traditional celebration dinner for Helen. Not until graduation does her class as a whole forgive her, and even then there is as much pity as respect in their act.

The parallel stories of Helen and Eleanor, like the collected stories, reinforce the message that the green world has so much to offer those who play by its rules; it is a testing place that honors and forms those who belong in it. These pleasant and positive fictionalized accounts present a separate world of women within which each, regardless of differences, can find a place and know that she belongs; all that is asked is that she accept the world's standards. Yet these writers are honest, and they admit flaws: some women will always remain outside. The kinds of outsiders and their reasons for being so vary; decisions about who are "out" and who "in" are unspoken judgments made by peers and usually mean that they do not seek out the outsiders as friends, though they feel no hostility toward them.

Honor, recognition, self-realization, and reward come to those who follow Betty Wales's discovered truth: each young woman needs to find out what she can do and then do it to the best of her ability. The emphasis on the development of individual talents and strengths and the fulfillment of self, all in a socially acceptable manner, reverses the direction of so much nineteenth-century fiction by and about women, in which the self is totally denied. In its quiet way, it is another radical message, for the precepts of individualism and self-reliance are here arranged for women: a sense of self and a high value for that self.

What the authors of these fictions selected for inclusion in their narratives clearly was significant to them. Of course there are other points made and other topics included in these stories, but all the writers are alike in their emphasis on what seem to be main, significant topics: women's friendships and female bonding, not turned inward toward exclusivity, but opening out to a wider world; pride in an ethical system and their own ability to maintain it; the pleasure of difference—different people, backgrounds, attitudes, behaviors—that make the college years so rich an experience.

The green world presented by these recent graduates of the women's colleges is its own domain, with its own emphases, codes, languages, and values; it is not wholly isolated, for it has ties to the outside, but self-contained and full of opportunity. Here is the safe place for women to find their own identities. Perhaps there is a parallel between the green world and women's sphere, and once again women are isolated within their separate territory, but this small world with its rules and codes for living, its values, standards, and expectations, its encouragement to these young women to stretch themselves to their limits, is something new and different. Awareness of that truth accounts for the reluctance to leave and the sense of limited time that pervade these stories.

In a fictionalized autobiography published in 1945, but looking back on her Bryn Mawr years, Margaret Emerson Bailey, a 1907 graduate, tells a story that supports many of the points made by the fiction writers. But since those years are simply part of Meg's whole life, the text has a distance that makes it a kind of commentary on the college fiction.[13] There are elements of the roman à clef in the novel, notably the presence of M. Carey Thomas, the strong, intellectual, feminist president of Bryn Mawr, as a character. Meg discovers the kindness and concern hidden under the president's formidable and somewhat eccentric exterior.

Before graduation President Thomas tells the assembled students, "The test of a good college . . . is that a Senior Class should have outgrown it and be bored by it" (271). At first Meg does not understand, but finally realizes that "President Thomas was quite right. A girl should outgrow Bryn Mawr. If she was honest, Meg was glad that she was through with it. All the same, there were people whom she wanted to remember. Mostly people. Besides them, a way of tackling work. And perhaps a few ideas" (280). The college has marked Meg and she has grown to love it, but she can accept the idea of moving on unsentimentally.

Her realization is in strong contrast to the Smith, Vassar, and Wellesley collections and the Betty Wales books, all of which end with a graduation scene—the exit festivities from the green world. The Bryn Mawr collection does not, but one story has alumnae looking back with love and nostalgia, and even Goodloe's *College Girls*, with its mixed emphasis, shows seniors at their commencement banquet, with

> a curious disagreeable sensation and a queer tightening in the throat, accompanied by a horrible inclination to shed tears over the closed chapter of their lives . . . they wished that the President would get on her feet and say something funny to make them forget that this was the end, . . . that they were being gracefully evicted, as it were, and could never be taken back upon the same terms or under the same conditions. (69–70)

Even Webster's effervescent trickster, Patty, "suddenly grew sober as the thought swept over her that in a few weeks [the college] would be hers no longer. This happy, irresponsible community life, which had come to be the only natural way of living, was suddenly at an end. . . . She wanted to clutch the present and hold it fast" (264–265). Graduation stories are alike in mixing the spring beauty of the campus, the rush of last activities, pride in achievement, and reminiscences of the four years with the heartbreaking realization that this fulfilling, wonderful time is about to end and can be recaptured only as memory.

Even with the occasional flaw this turn-of-the-century fiction presents the special separate world of women at its best. Expectations are different from those of the outside world: women are to find and respect themselves, to value and use their abilities. It is significant that all these authors are preoccupied with the inability of the young women in college to communicate the experience to anyone outside; the difficulty declares that nothing out there can compare with this unforgettable and unique experience. So the authors present a glorified moment, a kind of Camelot, and at the end of their stories the young women in the collections are reluctant to exit from the green world. They have proved, and the authors have in a sense documented, that they can not only learn but live and work productively, can appreciate a widened world, and can maintain an ethical standard. And their authors in fact leave them without any sense of the future at all, except the painful feeling that nothing will ever be like this again. They can revisit the place, but they can never recapture the time.

When Bacon, thirty-four years after her college tales, wrote her juvenile novel, *Kathy*, she began it with a gently ironic scene in which the contemporary Smith students comment on the returned alumnae, making it clear that ownership of the green world has passed into younger hands.[14]

# · FOUR ·

# *Living Together: Rewards and Limits*

The college collections, the Betty Wales series, and Jean Webster's fiction are celebrations of an expanded women's world, and nothing illustrates that expansion of opportunity better than what these authors call "prominence." As they use it, the term suggests not just fame, but power as well, although it is power with restrictions, for even in the most positive accounts there is a subtext of limitations within the women's spaces. The colleges welcome everyone, but just as there are those who, in different ways and for different reasons, stand out through their achievements, so there are those who remain outside the experience even though they are inside the space. Reward, limitation, and status are significant in the stories about young women that these authors tell.

The "prominent girl" appears regularly throughout the turn-of-the-century fiction and the books that follow. While no author defines the term, it is clear from the contexts what prominence means: it is the reward for "right" behavior, and it generates recognition, influence, respect, authority—in short, power. The prominent girl moves from the margins to the center. Prominence is not the same as popularity and it can be earned in a variety of ways. Each young woman is free to develop some quality within herself that makes her distinctive, and if she stands out from the crowd for the right reasons she wins approval from all elements of the college world. Achieving prominence, she becomes a role model to others and what she says is listened to with respect. She has positive identity as an individual and she can control others.

The term is not used in the earliest college fiction. Will, the hero of *An American Girl,* undoubtedly achieves a kind of prominence. She is successful in meeting the demands placed on her, as are her friends, but

Will stands out because of qualities she brought with her. However, all the "coeds" stand out because they are a small and different group within the masculine norm. They do not enhance their institution, as prominent students at the women's colleges do later, but only because the institution does not want them to. In later books set in coeducational schools women can win a kind of prominence by belonging to a sorority and attracting men.

*College Girls*, with its particular agenda, pays more attention to popularity than to prominence. The author describes a character who is popular: "She was a stylish girl, with New York manners and clothes, and a pretty, rather expressionless face, strongly addicted to fads, and after almost four years still something of a fool. She had become popular through her own efforts and the fact that she had a brother at Harvard. If a girl really wishes to be a favorite in college she must arrange to have some male relative at a neighboring university" (4). Another young woman is known for "her good looks and her wealth and her evident superiority" (250). But these young women, though their names and faces are recognized, are popular rather than prominent.

For very different reasons, neither does *Two College Girls* show the same kind of prominence that appears in the stories just a few years later, although the novel anticipates it. Perhaps in 1886 simply being in college was in itself such an achievement that nothing more needed to be added to it. More likely, the first classes at the women's colleges were so small that all students could know each other and so in a sense were all "prominent girls." As enrollments steadily increased and the size of the classes grew, simply being there became less of an achievement and when the intimacy of the earlier classes vanished, young women with talent surfaced as more opportunities for achievement developed, particularly through the establishment of student government, the acceptability of dramatics and athletics, and the founding of college magazines.

In the collections and the Betty Wales books, those fictions that celebrate the experience of women in college, the concept of prominence is spelled out in the events of the narrative. It is a reward for work or talent, but always with the provision that these young women have added something to the life of the college. They contribute their talents and their abilities to their community, and they become important and powerful within its boundaries because they enrich its life. Opportunities are many and varied; as well as through athletics, dramatics, government, and writing, students are valued for artistic talent, gracious demeanor, and a balance between academics and activities. They are, of course, role models for others.

The contemporary collections of men's college fiction rather overwhelmingly suggest that there prominence is achieved through violence. The first of the Princeton stories, "The Winning of the Cane," involves traditional class rivalry, but it is not a matter of outwitting another class as it is for the women's colleges:

> Then, while the referee was shouting, "Get back! Get back!" the freshman was suddenly seen to rise on his knees yelling shrilly, like a wild beast in pain. "You would bite me, would you, you——." He sprang to his feet. The blood from his nose was smeared all over his face. A furious wrench jerked Parker from the ground. With what was extraordinary power Hill whirled him; part of the way the feet dragged, although some like to tell that Parker was clean in the air all the way round; he whirled him about, as you would whirl a pillow with both arms; then, suddenly reversing all his big weight and simultaneously twisting the hickory, he snapped the sophomore off in the air and lifted the cane high and dry above his head. "The freshman has it," shrieked a shrill voice.[1]

The freshman indeed has it and has established himself as a prominent and respected figure for the rest of his college life and probably beyond, since his achievement provides entry into many different male networks.

Physical strength and athletics provided a clear path to prominence for men; the Maurice review, quoted earlier, emphasized the public liking for the "man in the 'varsity sweater," and Margaret Sherwood's piece on Vassar mentions the stereotype of the male student as athlete. The importance of the athlete is overwhelmingly clear in the popular and contemporary Frank Merriwell books, with the athlete-hero dominant and all energies directed toward victory on the playing fields.[2] Merriwell-type heroes live complicated lives; it is all in the day's work for Frank to be kidnapped (by big-time gamblers or jealous classmates) on the eve of the Big Game, to be held prisoner, to make a bold escape, and finally to appear at the last moment (when all seems lost) and play spectacularly, in spite of having been tied up and starved for the preceding twenty-four hours. If he goes to class at all, it is so that he can be accused of cheating—an accusation that threatens to keep him out of the game until the real culprit is discovered, again at the last moment. Frank Merriwell is perhaps the ultimate in prominence achieved through athletic competition; any number of heroes, however, follow his path.

For women students the path is, fortunately, not so single. There are many more opportunities, and the honor societies in the women's colleges recognize their own definition of prominence—outstanding ability that brings luster to class or college—as they choose new members. As a sophomore, Betty Wales watches the traditional choosing by the honor societies of the "first four": sophomores who distinguished themselves in their first year. The choices are Eleanor, for her brilliant (though plagiarized) short story; Emily, a scholarship student who performed superbly in a humorous debate; Babe, described as a "prod" (prodigy), fun, and "she can do such beautiful pantomimes"; and Marion, already respected as a writer (S 132). Though not chosen herself, Betty is perfectly happy; she sees the justice of the choices and knows that there are future opportunities for her.

Again to make a comparison with men's stories: Owen Johnson's *Stover at Yale,* roughly contemporary with the women's collections and the early series books, is a well-written, well-constructed version of a Frank Merriwell saga.[3] Classed as a novel and reviewed seriously, it is considerably better crafted than the Merriwell stories, but the kinship is there. It is a novel of physical contact, and the reader can never be sure whether the hero has a field of study other than sports. Possibly the most self-centered protagonist anywhere, Stover's athletic talents lead him to nearly total focus on them; his only other preoccupation is his questioning of the importance and fairness of the exclusive senior societies. His cause is a good one, perhaps, since it ostensibly involves finding and pursuing individual directions rather than conforming for three years to other people's standards, but having nobly decided not to conform, our hero, who retains his prep school nickname of Dink, finds himself at the end of his junior year, having gained a reputation as a great athlete, anxiously waiting to know if he will be "tapped" for a senior society. The tapping scene is psychologically brutal—all the students gather and watch while a few of their number are chosen. Presumably maturity is shown by the restraint of the chosen and the stiff upper lips of the rejected majority. But after Dink has questioned the value and morality of the societies for three years, the author undercuts his own thesis by ending the story immediately after the hero is tapped. The reader never finds out about senior year, or whether Dink's soul-searching was as futile as it now seems. What the author tried to present as a moral-intellectual concern turns out to be not a questioning of the societies, but worry over whether he will be chosen.

In the course of his college years Dink gradually and in a highly unimpassioned way falls in love with an intelligent, thoughtful young woman (not a college student) and near the end of the book they become engaged: "Then he knew that he held in his arms one who had never given so much as her hand lightly, who came to him in unflinching loyalty, whose only interest would be his interest, who would know no other life but his life, whose joy would be the struggle that was his struggle" (378). But winning this male-defined paragon is only the penultimate episode of Dink's fictional life; getting into the society is its culmination.

The means of selection define the difference between men and women; there is one opportunity for men, and their world becomes a place of intense competition. There are many chances for women, so they can wait and work. Betty Wales hears her class sing to honor a friend's achievement; she longs for the time when she will be worthy of hearing her class sing to her with confidence that she has chances to deserve the admiration of her peers. Just as the stories stress the differences in the young women who come to college, so they stress the many ways to achieve prominence that their world offers. No single pattern of behavior brings success, and none depends on exclusivity. In this diversity of women, each has the opportunity to find her talent and use it.

The Sutton twins, who appear in several of the Smith College stories, are "the recognized jesters of the class, and their merry, homely faces were sure of answering grins wherever they appeared"; their pranks delight the other students: "it was they who left the gas brightly burning and the door temptingly ajar at 10:15, so that the long-suffering woman [their housemother] pounced upon them with just recrimination, only to find her stored-up wrath directed at two night-gowned figures bowed over their little white beds, as it were two Infant Samuels. It is doubtful if a devotional exercise ever before or since has roused such mingled feelings in the bosom of the chance spectator" (*Smith*, 95). But the Sutton twins are more than pranksters delighting their friends and terrorizing their housemother; they maintain high standing in classes, and they prove themselves almost at once by their skill as basketball players, contributing a victory to their class in the psychologically important freshman-sophomore game. So the playfulness that entertains others rests on solid achievement.

The young women themselves are aware that not everyone wants, needs, or is capable of the achievements that bring notice. The honor societies that recognize ability and contribution also recognize difference; in a serious discussion before a vote on candidates, one Smith member analyzes other students:

> There are girls who are queer and erratic and somewhat solitary and perhaps discontented, but they get into a prominence of their own and you call it a "divine discontent," and make them geniuses, and they get a good deal out of it, after all. There are girls who are queer and quick-tempered, but good students and devoted to a few warm friends, and their unpopularity doesn't trouble them particularly. There are the social leaders who don't particularly suffer if they don't get into a society, who are popular everywhere, and get the good time they came for. (44)

Others who find nonconventional paths to their own kind of respect and fame appear throughout the stories. At Smith, B. S. Kitts, who solves someone else's roommate problem, and her friends establish themselves as observers, quiet, clever, in control of their time and lives, clear thinkers and problem solvers, while the eccentric Suzanne, who is not much liked, is honored for her artistic ability. Although all these young women differ in ability and attitude, common to their portrayal are the celebration of individuality, recognition of differences, and the assumption of freedom to be oneself and to win respect for precisely that. As these authors establish the validity of difference and variety, they make it clear that there is no one way to prominence.

There are, of course, some obvious activities that, if participated in correctly, will bring recognition and respect. Student government was a comparatively late development, a radical change that came into being about 1900, but its beginnings show particularly in the tales of Smith and Wellesley.[4] In the earliest days students were protected, supervised, and regulated; their time was totally structured and they moved to the ringing of bells. Vassar's Lady Principal, Hannah Lyman, for example, controlled every phase of life outside the classroom during her reign.[5] Women teachers lived in the dormitories (male professors lived outside with their families) and patrolled the halls, enforcing such regulations as quiet and the lights-out rule.[6] When Will Elliot wrote from Michigan to her friend at Vassar it was precisely this kind of supervised life that she scorned as a chief drawback of the women's colleges. Regulations are a normal part of the life portrayed in *Two College Girls*, although they are unobtrusive there, perhaps because they match the attitudes about women still prevalent outside the green world.

Possibly as long as there were rigid standards for womanly behavior off the campuses, there was little rebellion inside, but as the place and activities of women outside changed through the entrance of women into the work force, the growth of the clubwoman movement, and the extreme of suffrage activism, the rules became harder to bear. When student government moved both rule making and enforcement into the hands of students, "lights-out" and compulsory chapel disappeared; other elements, however, such as the standards that forbade cheating, were just as strongly upheld as they had ever been. Responsibility, in fact, created a stronger sense of belonging and obligation to the college. The authority to run their own world, even within limits, the establishment of governance and judgment systems, and the bestowal of actual authority and power on students created leadership positions for those with managerial talents and political interests.

In a Vassar story Lydia, forced to separate herself from the friends she would prefer, falls back in her loneliness on her studies; then she

> began . . . to feel the life of the college as it is for all its members, without distinction of class or clique, to understand, albeit dimly, the relation of the students to the place. Self-government committees, editorships, presidencies of student associations, did not come into being primarily, she reasoned out, to give popular girls a

chance to have an outward and visible sign of their hold on the af-
fections of two hundred or so others, nor ambitious little Napoleons
a field in which to show how they could handle their fellow-beings,
but that the business for which Matthew Vassar built his College
might get on happily and successfully.   (214)

It was a short step from that realization to participation, done with her
usual intelligence and dedication, so that finally she "grew to be a power,
though she never suspected it" and in her last year was elected president
of students, as the "strongest, coolest, broadest girl in the class" (216).

In many of the stories young women achieve prominence through dramatics, and this area of achievement, too, is based on fact. In the early
days plays were performed for a strictly female audience, with women
who took men's parts wearing long black skirts instead of trousers. When
they did finally wear men's clothing, men, even faculty men, were excluded from the audience, since appearance in such garb before them
would have been indecent. But the world changed; house and society
plays flourished and eventually a senior play became a feature of graduation ceremonies and appears in much of the fiction. Often professionals
were called upon for help and the plays might even be reviewed in
newspapers.

Athletics, too, offered opportunities for those so gifted. From the
opening day of Vassar, the necessity for exercise was stressed. At first it
was individual; students were honor-bound to walk a mile a day, for example.[7] Later they worked out for a certain period in the new gymnasi-
ums that appeared as alumnae gifts, and finally they took up golf and
tennis, learned to row, and played such team sports as basketball. Goodloe's "Revenge" displays their range of ability and opportunity, just as
the opening story in the Smith collection establishes the psychological
importance of the class team and class rivalry.

In all these activities, while outstanding performance brings about
a kind of stardom, honest participation is equally valued. The young
woman who paints scenery or holds the promptbook, like her counter-
part on the basketball subteam, is making her contribution to the whole
effort; not only stars but contributors matter. This is, of course, the
strength of Betty Wales, who, outstanding in nothing, is enthusiastically
engaged in all the college has to offer and wins her prominence that way;
younger readers without or unaware of any particular talent could identify with a character who is nice and ordinary, and is rewarded and made
happy through her eager participation.

The young women who do not stand out in any area are seldom characters in any of the fiction, but they come to see the plays, cheer the
team, and read the magazines. Often, and consistently throughout the
collections and the series books, they are the students who live off

campus and therefore find the campus-centered activities more difficult and less accessible. But they are never deliberately excluded, and they are not scorned unless they do something that detracts from the college or violates the codes. The defining mark seems to be sincerity, and the punishment of even popular young women like Arna Kellar and Eleanor Watson, who want to win others through charm and who cheat to preserve a false image, prove the importance the codes had assumed.

Like so many elements of college life, the opportunities to lead, to shine, to be admired rest on the bittersweet knowledge that these chances belong to the world of college and that graduation will leave them the memory of fame, not fame itself:

> Senior year had come, and with it the presidentships of clubs, the chairmanships of committees, and, most onerous burden of all, the responsibility for that mystery known as "the tone" of college. Some Seniors are so impressed by this that they never get back to a normal state. Their whole after life is spent in alternately moralizing over and trying to alter "the tone" of the place they happen to inhabit. Other Seniors, the more lightminded, refuse to be as gods while in college. These same, however, gasp with consternation when they find how little the big world cares about them, or their college, or their beautiful degree. They begin to wish they had lorded it more regally while yet their little day endured.[8]

The future may give satisfactions of other kinds, but there is a pervasive awareness that never again will their environment give them the chance to stretch themselves to their limits.

The activities that lead to true prominence have in common the fact that they add to the luster of the college itself, but more personally important and more unusual, they empower these achievers to act as decision makers. The power is indirect: the important student should influence rather than order. She can exert control over other lives through approval, friendships, or more obviously through committee placements and society memberships, always, of course, in a ladylike manner and for the good of the group. She can inspire others. Even more satisfying than the actual wielding of power within her world must have been the respect and approval that she gained by doing so; this green world of college not merely permitted but encouraged her to fulfill herself, and she had as well the power that comes from confidence in her own abilities and approval of peers.

As fine as all this sounds, with its positive picture of the opportunities for women to use their talents, there are two major caveats. Almost nowhere in the stories are there activists. Lynn D. Gordon describes the Progressive Era as "a time of profound social and cultural change. Throughout those thirty years, American attitudes, values, and styles slowly and gradually transformed; as they did so, younger women, the inheritors of progressivism, changed with them. Women students' separate organizations and spirit of social meliorism looked much the same in 1895 and in 1920, but their personal concerns and conceptions of gender politics evolved over time into a new cultural consciousness."[9] But this kind of change is not reflected in the fiction. There are women who see problems within the college world and who work to solve them, but there is no commitment to causes, and no real awareness of any political concerns in the outside world. Radical as the colleges may have seemed in some eyes, within themselves they remained extremely conservative, and the fiction avoids issues that are disruptive or even unconventional.

The closest thing to political awareness occurs in Brown's *Two College Girls* when the students become passionately involved with a presidential election campaign, but this is a stunt rather than political involvement.[10] One Bryn Mawr story, "Epoch Making," finds comedy in students who try to refute the charge that women are incapable of acting politically by turning the election for class president into a political campaign; the result is chaos.[11]

Brown's fictional stunt, however, had some basis in reality. One of her classmates was Harriot Stanton (Blatch), a "dangerous" student as perhaps a daughter of Elizabeth Cady Stanton was bound to be; her autobiography makes no attempt to hide her disappointment in Vassar. Underlying her affectionate memories of the faculty, notably Maria Mitchell (also considered dangerous) is a kind of despair: "Comparatively they [her college years] were a slough of despond." Fresh from a home where the "dining table was a platform for debate, our mother acting as arbitrator on moral and sociological issues, and our father as referee in political and historical debates . . . we were trained to feel no loyalty to family when individual conviction was at stake," she entered "an institution composed entirely of a disfranchised class which was definitely discouraged by the authorities from taking any interest whatever in its own political freedom."[12] Years later on a suffrage campaign (1908), she was not allowed to speak on the campus; Inez Milholland, then an undergraduate, arranged to hold the meeting in a nearby cemetery (108).

Stanton did make a mark, however. She quotes her classmate, Helen Dawes Brown, who "exclaimed, to my astonishment, 'I owe to you the implanting and growth of a habit which has proved of great value to me. You taught me to read a daily paper.' It seems I manoeuvered a meeting of the class, of which I was Freshman President, into passing a resolution that each member must read the newspapers twenty minutes a day or pay a fine. Miss Brown, when referring to her predicament . . . explained with a laugh, 'I was too poor to pay the fine, so I had to do the reading. I've profited and feel grateful'" (40).

Only one other fictional example suggests political awareness. In the Molly Brown series Margaret, besides being a "politician"—in the best sense, of course; she is class president for four years because her classmates know her to be the best person for the job—is an active crusader for the cause of women's suffrage. When she learns that Nance, Molly's roommate, is the daughter of the "most famous suffragist and clubwoman in the country," she thinks she has found an ally. But Nance, hesitantly, states her case:

> "I've been fed on clubs until I feel like a Strasberg goose. I've had them crammed down my throat since I was five years old. When I was twelve I was my mother's secretary, and I've sent thousands of just such pamplets as you are distributing now. I learned to write on the typewriter so I could copy my mother's speeches. . . . So you see," she added, simply, frowning to keep back the tears, "I think I'll take a rest from clubs while I'm at college and begin to enjoy life awhile with Molly and Judy."    (F 104–105)

Tactful Margaret does not press, and the friends remember that Nance has grown up in boardinghouses, since her mother is too busy to make a home for the family.

But the cause is not condemned. When Mrs. Oldham comes to speak at the campus, the students, ready to feel hostile for Nance's sake, find an exhausted woman whose energies are totally channeled to her purpose. Her exhaustion and vagueness disappear when she speaks: "She approached the front of the platform with a composure marvelous to see, and in a cultivated, trained voice—not her everyday voice, by any means—she delivered an address of fervid and passionate eloquence; a plea for women's rights and universal suffrage so convincing that the most obstinate 'anti' would have been won over" (F 207–208). But the author carries the theme no further; she simply presents the situation which beyond the chapter has no effect on the lives and actions of her characters.

No doubt Harriot Stanton, with her unusual background of political consciousness and activism, was an extreme, but she suggests, as do other firsthand accounts and the absence of these topics in the fiction, that the activist could expect disapproval, even punishment. Institutions are essentially conservative, and the women's colleges remained conscious of the world outside where womanly standards, however fluctuating, were determined and defined by the patriarchy. The majority of college presidents and faculty were men. More important, as Vassar's President MacCracken had pointed out, the majority of trustees and gift-givers were men, and men who had a different way of looking at the green world; to the trustees the college was that "walled garden" and they wanted to hear only pleasant and suitable accounts. It was, in other words, fine to urge young women to stretch themselves, to develop their talents, as long as they did so within acceptable boundaries.

Even more telling, given attitudes about women and womanly standards, was the strongest limitation of power: while young women might and should become prominent, they must never strive to do so. When Eleanor Watson in the Betty Wales books deliberately sets out to become prominent, she has almost guaranteed that she will not succeed, for both her intention and her methods offend the codes; she has made a goal out of what should be an unsought reward. Here indeed is a paradox: prominence is desirable, but it must not be sought. Honors and recognition must come naturally and unnoticed. One student becomes a "power" but "she was never aware of it" and another "was more prominent than she ever realized"—statements that argue an incredible lack of awareness or an excess of womanly modesty.[13] So in the Betty Wales series "Eleanor had said that she came to college for 'fun,' but 'fun' to her meant power and prominence" (F 41); she aims for power and gets disgrace while Helen Chase Adams seeks and uses her own abilities and becomes a prominent senior. Arna Kellar cheats to maintain the image that she feels brings her admiration, and is punished by her peers. Clorinda, in one of the Wellesley stories, actively seeks prominence and power, leading her peers to know and despise her. When she arrived, "She meant to be the most popular girl in Wellesley" but she went at it so openly that "after repeated trials she was branded 'sham' by the instinctively fair-minded girls who form public opinion in a great college." By the end of her sophomore year Clorinda, "always a noticeable figure in the corridors, was as unimportant in college affairs as the timidest of Freshmen. She had received no society invitation—an omission to which this ambitious, self-dependent young woman could not easily become reconciled" (10–11). It is not until she is a junior and new students arrive who do not know her history that she can summon a crowd of younger admirers. Women who try for power are "little Napoleons," and there is no mistaking the scorn in the epithet. The emphasis is on the process of achievement, not on the goal.

What this means in reality is that women must never compete; even on the basketball court they must play for the team and the class, not for themselves or against their rivals. When Molly Brown and her class are ready to elect their sophomore class officers, Margaret, the talented politician, is "too well-bred to declare herself openly as a candidate for the place of class president" even though she is the best choice and everyone knows that she wants to be elected. Anyone who deliberately strives for honor is condemned by her peers, for she has gone beyond the acceptable bounds of womanly behavior.

In her study of the women's colleges, Liva Baker charges that they have failed to train women for leadership positions. The Seven Sisters, she

claims, have prepared women to marry leaders, but not to lead themselves. They provided no expectation of success or outstanding achievement outside the campus; instead they bred into women a passivity and
avoidance of success:

> The women's colleges offered an elaborate selection of extra-
> curricular activities and exploited the fact that in the absence of
> men—who traditionally dominated the coeducational campuses—
> all these activities were accessible to women as tools with which to
> learn organizational skills and to test leadership capacities. Lacking,
> however, the input of the traditionally dominant faction of society,
> it seemed more like playing house. Further, in the name of psycho-
> logical support, there was a vital element missing—competition, on
> which middle-class boys have traditionally been nurtured as prepa-
> ration for competitive careers. As a substitute for competition
> women were offered the cooperative enterprises on which little
> middle-class girls traditionally have been nurtured from the time
> they began to play nurse in preparation for a lifetime of adaptability
> to the lives and careers of others, a perpetuation of a double stan-
> dard which is easily and often carried to psychological absurdity.[14]

Whether Baker's charge is true, and there are those who would disagree
with her, is not the subject here.[15] The fiction of the early years does seem
to support her charge by its emphasis on performance as contribution
but never for reward, and modest, noncompetitive behavior.

Nor, it should be added, must achievement change behavior; honors
must be handled modestly. In *Peggy Parsons, A Hampton Freshman,* a single
volume probably set at Smith, Gloria is elected president of the freshman
class, chiefly because the other students are impressed with her good
looks, tasteful clothes and pleasant personality.[16] The leap into prominence makes her lose her common sense; she begins to feel she must act
a part and, in order to dress well, runs herself deeply into debt.

"President Jefferson," in the Wellesley collection, is almost a paradigm
of acceptable behavior as defined by Baker's thesis that women were restricted to "cooperative enterprises," those that fit the image of womanliness, where sharing, nurturing, and contributing to the common good
were the chief values. Mary Jefferson hesitates to run for freshman class
president because "although she was conscious of a certain power over
the impulses of those about her, she felt that her own lack of charm, of
what she called brains" (68) seemed to make her unfit. She is elected
anyway, and her mixture of joy that she should have been chosen and
doubt that she is worthy dominate her thoughts until mathematics class
brings an unannounced test. She fails the test and her mind is made up.
Calling a class meeting, where her control of procedure and "the force
of her personality, the undeviating directness of her judgment, and a

strange, new poise and purpose in her manner, dominated the minds of her admiring subjects" (86), she announces that she will resign the office because she is conditioned in math and therefore is not the best choice. There are protests, but she is adamant. Born leader though she is, Mary Jefferson does not seek office, judges herself in terms of the good of the whole, and assumes her obligations to work and to the college. Yet, the story says, her qualities and her sacrifice are rewarded and she is an example to others.

Only one of these writers saw this issue as worth communicating directly to her readers and perhaps questioning. In *Betty Wales, Sophomore*, Betty and her friends discuss obliquely their chances of being selected as one of the "first four" sophomores to be chosen by the honor societies. The eligible students are uncomfortable with the discussion, and finally Madeline Ayres, the "Bohemian," who "had never lived more than three months in any one place, and . . . had grown up absolutely without reference to the rules and regulations and conventions that meant so much to the majority of her fellow students" (40), asks them to explain:

> "But in general, I mean, why will you never admit you want a certain thing, or hope to get a certain thing?"
> "It is funny, isn't it?" said Rachel. "Wild horses couldn't drag it out of any junior that she hopes for a place on the 'Argus' board or the Senior Play Committee."
> "Nor out of any sophomore that she hopes to make a society," added Christy Mason.
> "I suppose," said Babbie, "that it's because nothing is competitive here. You just take what people think you ought to have. You stand or fall by public opinion, and of course you are never sure how it will gauge you."
> "College men aren't that way," said Katherine. "They talk about such things, and discuss their chances and agree to help one another along where they can. And if they lose they never seem to care; they joke about it."
> "But we never admit we've lost, because we never admit we were trying for anything," put in Nita.
> "I like the men's way best then," said Madeline decidedly. (S 127–128)

All are analytical enough to see their own behavior, but only unconventional Madeline is able to approach the taboo subject without discomfort, and it is never clear in any of the fiction whether the feelings and ambitions are suppressed because competing is unwomanly or because of the fear of failure: if they don't try, they can't fail.[17]

Comparison with stories about men highlights the difference; Dink Stover's life is an accumulation of competitive activity approved by his world, while Betty Wales, Judy Abbott, and the numerous heroes of the story collections live in a place of quiet achievement and delight, turned inward to their own self-growth. Their world is ideally nonviolent, noncontroversial, and noncompetitive. Dink's triumphs are external, physical, and based on rivalry. They bring clear and obvious rewards while for a young woman success is internal, personal, and individual; though she wins admiration, her real reward should be her own sense of worth.

There is another significant lack in the achievement of prominence. While the talented, particularly those with literary ability, are treated almost with reverence, the intellectual woman is hardly considered at all. Perhaps not surprisingly, the young women who win the most respect, even if they are eccentric, remote, or selfish, are those who write. Story after story reflects the honor and prestige given to "literary" women, whether they be editors of Smith's *Monthly* and Vassar's *Miscellany*, contributors to these magazines, or creative writers, especially if they give promise of a literary career. Kate, who doesn't much care for college and who is not particularly liked, is respected for her excellent writing ability and so is included in the college world; the much simpler Molly picks her as a student who will bring honor to the college.[18] And the story of Rebecca, the dilettante who has created a literary image for herself, makes very clear the importance of the quiet and unobtrusive Janet, who is the real poet.[19]

But the intellectual young woman, the kind who may become a scholar, is absent everywhere but in the Bryn Mawr collection, where several stories do clearly value intellectual achievement, as one would expect from the college presided over by M. Carey Thomas. In "Within Four Years" Lillian, reared within a rigid fundamentalist sect, finds her mind opened to a wider world: "But she was led to a very different way of thinking by a better understanding of what scholarship meant—of its untiring zeal and care for truth, and of its outlook beyond the fact to the including law."[20] And in another tale Esther, working for a doctorate, finds her "human" problems eased by her intellectual curiosity and her discovery that "there were tracts of knowledge infinite and unfathomable where one would never tire."[21] But overall these characters and situations are distinctly in the minority. Scholarly women faculty do not appear as role models, or perhaps it is more accurate to say that the kind of student who would choose an intellectual woman as a role model is excluded from the fiction for its own political purposes. Whatever the cause, the voice of the intellectual woman is indeed muted.

Even at Bryn Mawr, with its coveted European fellowship and the emphasis on scholarship, the fictional students who achieve academic distinction participate in other college activities. In "A Diplomatic Crusade" Marjorie's plan includes encouraging bright, studious young women to broaden their interests so that they will not fit the outsiders' stereotype of learned women. Cornelia Otis Skinner, attending Bryn Mawr in the early 1920s, remembered the "standard idea was to be athletic, studious (to a temperate degree), and splendidly clear-eyed. . . . [S]cholarship went hand in hand with hockey and chapel." [22] The intellectual young woman must not reject other parts of college life; if she does she is selfish and failing to contribute to the whole. "Grinds" and "digs" who study too much or too obtrusively, win notoriety perhaps but not admiration and are in danger of becoming "freaks." At the other extreme are the young women such as Arna and Eleanor, who cannot bear to be perceived as needing to study and violate ethical standards to preserve their self-image.

Brilliant, dedicated scholars who are happy in their work rarely appear in these pages, and, in fact, after the first books the academic side of college life, is minimized and all but ignored. Helen Dawes Brown assumed that the students had come to learn and she demonstrated that they could learn. Perhaps they are not to become scholars, but their primary reason for coming to college is to get that education equal to the men's colleges: Greek, Latin, literature, mathematics, science. Edna and her friends were part of the "handful of eager souls" that Smith's President Neilson would later remember longingly; they were the pioneers, they knew they were, and there was no questioning their primary purpose. [23] Brown's classroom scenes make the point clear; here are young women with good minds who are now being taught to think with those good minds. Like Edna, Anderson's Will stands high in academic rank and her studies are part of her life; Anderson too is concerned with proving that women can excel, even in a man's world. Though in reality the faculty would have named the "preparation of scholars" as part of their goal, the fiction writers all but ignore it. [24] In *College Girls*, however, Goodloe offers a brilliant woman professor who has made her mark in the scholarly world as a dry, desiccated being regretting her lack of "life," and the young mathematician of "An Acquarelle" is one of the few examples of an attractive woman who is also an intellectual, but it is her looks and charm that matter in the story.

Keeping up in one's studies is never ignored or downplayed; studying for exams is an accepted part of all the fiction, and earning respectable grades is part of the student life: Betty Wales, when she comes to college, takes all the new experiences with delight and almost forgets the academic purpose until she has an encounter that she describes to her friends, asking them to explain a "back-row reputation." When she stopped to pick up her history paper, she tells them,

> Miss Ellis looked hard at me when I went in and stammered out what I wanted. She hunted up the paper and gave it to me and then she said, "With which division do you recite, Miss Wales?" I told her at

ten, and she looked at me hard again and said, "You have been present in class twelve times and I've never noticed you. Don't get a back
row reputation, Miss Wales. Good-day," and I can tell you I backed
out in a hurry.   (F 78–79)

Betty needed the lesson, and she hastily incorporates studying into her
balanced life. The values are clear throughout the fiction: "At Vassar
there is a cold shoulder for both Miss Grind and Mademoiselle Fripon.
She who can stand high in her class and yet keep in with most of the fun
can 'have' the other girls" ( *Vassar,* 73). These are, we remember, the
"well-rounded girls" of President Taylor's time.

So intellectual achievement on its own is never a path to prominence,
perhaps because the authors wish to avoid frightening parents or trustees. The ideal is balance, the well-rounded student living a life of which
academics are a part. In fact the ideal of balance pervades the turn-of-
the-century stories. The perfect college woman is one who is good in
many things, but excels (dominates) in nothing intellectual. Like the
activist, the committed intellectual woman has no role in the fiction.

A figure who appears often in the college fiction is the outsider, the
young woman who is technically part of the green world, yet somehow
remains distant from it. Nearly every author presents this figure, and
there are several kinds. Helen Chase Adams works her way inside, but for
all her achieved prominence and happiness, she somehow retains a de-
tachment that characterizes one group of these women: "she never
seemed to herself to 'belong' to things as the other girls did. She was still
an outsider. An unexplainable something held her aloof from the famil-
iarities of the life around her, and made it inevitable that she should be,
as she had been from the first, an observer rather than an actor in the
drama of college life" (Sr 106–107). This sense of the self as outsider is
shared by many of the young women with literary talent or different
backgrounds, like Madeline Ayres in the Betty Wales books, who is an
outsider by choice, and the only one who knows she is. For them the
"outside" is a kind of vantage point that adds to the richness of their
experience.

Other outsiders, however, do not have so comfortable a situation. In
"Submerged," Charlotte, a factory worker discovered by a teacher and
sent to Wellesley, is all wrong. It is not her cheap clothes and dowdy hair-
style that separate her and make her a "freak," but that her life has
taught her a different and incompatible language. To her college is wonderful, "It's just like a story here, I think" (164), but it is never her story.
She is bright, but she cannot do the work because the college goals are
strange to her; in fact she does not know what they are. She has no quality—enthusiasm, charm, dramatic or athletic ability, or even the desire
to grow—which others can admire or which would contribute to the

college life. Though there seem to be socioeconomic class factors in her situation, the narrative insists that it is not money-based snobbery that excludes her, or even a different cultural background; she watches the new world, but she cannot put herself into it. She does not know there are codes to be learned and, more important, she neither claims the college nor offers anything to it. If a college education can provide an opportunity for upward class movement, it is an opportunity that Charlotte never perceives.

Different cultural backgrounds make separations, as all the authors admit, but the separations need not be permanent. Vassar's Lucretia, in "A Sense of Obligation," has an intellectually impoverished background like Charlotte's, but finds everything she wants in college. The extreme of potential exclusion, Webster's orphanage-bred Judy Abbott of *Daddy Long-Legs*, is able to see, articulate, and deal with the differences as Charlotte is not. For Judy all the commonplace acts like riding a train, seeing a farm, walking outside boundaries are new, and she sees and writes about, in letters to her guardian, the lacks that make her different from "most girls with a properly assorted family and a home and friends and a library" who know so much "by absorption":

> I never read "Mother Goose" or "David Copperfield" or "Ivanhoe" or "Cinderella" or "Bluebeard" or "Robinson Crusoe" or "Jane Eyre" or "Alice in Wonderland" or a word of Rudyard Kipling. I didn't know that Henry the Eighth was married more than once or that Shelley was a poet. I didn't know that people used to be monkeys or that the Garden of Eden was a beautiful myth. I didn't know that R. L. S. stood for Robert Louis Stevenson or that George Eliot was a lady. I had never seen a picture of the "Mona Lisa" and (it's true but you won't believe it) I had never heard of Sherlock Holmes. . . . I find that I am the only girl in college who wasn't brought up on "Little Women." I haven't told anybody, though (that *would* stamp me as queer). (46–48)

Judy is, to use a modern term, culturally illiterate, but she wants to belong and knows how to do it: she sets aside time each day to read the books that "eighteen blank years" had denied her. Charlotte, on the other hand, was an audience to college life and never saw a way or a need to make herself a player.

One of the most moving of the college stories is "A Family Affair" in the Smith collection (151–201). It is worth examining at some length because it brings together so many of the themes: ways to prominence, differences, living together, and the outsiders. It illustrates as well the refusal of the best of these writers to claim that the college world is perfect.

The story's protagonists share a name: Sue Jackson, the secure, happy, loved daughter of an old, wealthy Boston family, and Susan Jackson, whose father retreats into his small-town shop to avoid the rest of the family—a vulgar, insensitive, wife who spends her days reading cheap novels and two other daughters who value only clothes and boyfriends. Susan learns early to escape into books, but she is a brilliant, insecure, tortured young woman, and for her the presence of another student with the same name is threatening, while for Sue it is an interesting coincidence.

Sue's college career is marked by all the right things. She is freshman vice-president and later senior class president, her friends are the most interesting and prominent young women, she belongs to important societies, is active in athletics and dramatics, becomes an editor of the *Monthly*, and maintains a very high rank in her classes. Susan is too brilliant and talented to be ignored, but she is isolated. Never having known open affection, easy friendship, confident and careless social interchange, she does not know how to have these things now that they are available. The classmate with the same name but a different life haunts her and becomes the "visible expression of all the triumph and ease and distilled essence of the successful college girl" (165). When Susan sees Sue with her cultured, gracious family, "her heart swelled with angry regret and a sickening certainty that all the cleverness in the world could not make up for the youth she was cheated out of" (161). Susan's first poem, instantly recognized as being far better than even the best college writing, is assumed to be written by Sue, who quickly corrects the error but is flattered by the mistake; for Susan the error takes the joy from her success.

Yet the haunting is in Susan's mind, for she is making her own reputation, and her classmates, "the girls that she thought patronized her," far from disliking or ignoring her, view her as the outstanding young woman in the class: "They took her after-successes almost as a matter of course. 'Oh, yes! she was far and away the most brilliant girl in the college!' they said. But she never heard them" (181).

Although Sue is the symbol of all that Susan has missed, the latter's emotion is never jealousy, but rather a longing for what she knows she can never have, and she hides her "smarting sensitiveness" under a defensive "reserved disdain" (167). She makes friends, though she is never part of a crowd. She goes from one literary success to another; when *Twelfth Night* is forbidden because of the scandalous speeches of Sir Toby, she writes a version that not only parodies the play but includes "the trials of the committee, the squabbles of the principal actors, open hits at the Faculty, sly comments on the senior class . . . all these were interwoven with the farce; and this not in the clumsy, harmless fashion of most college grinds, but pointed by a keen wit, a merciless satire, an easy, brilliant style already well on to its now recognized maturity. . . . It was the most perfect success of her life—though the girls who thought she scorned her college triumphs would have laughed had she told them so, later" (189–190).

When money runs out before she can graduate, "a complete consciousness of how bitterly she loved the place came to her," along with awareness of how much she has done for herself. "Alone, unhelped, she had by sheer personality and natural power made herself not only respected, but respected to an unusual degree. . . . Whether they loved her or not, her class was proud of her" (196). Before she must leave, she is offered a position on a prestigious Boston magazine, so her departure is not to her deadly little town, but to the city and the start of a brilliant literary career. The story ends with a letter from Sue to her uncle, the publisher of the magazine: "I knew that when you saw that essay on the French and the English as short story writers, you'd want to give her the chance. And she was the very girl to leave college, too—it isn't everybody who would be so glad to go just before senior year. Not but I would, fast enough, if I had her future before me—Mon dieu! she's the only girl I ever thought I'd rather be—" (200).

Susan's separateness grew out of her own lacks and it is the presence of the like-named child of good fortune that drives them home. The irony of the story's ending lies not in the desire of each to be like the other, but in their inability to understand each other. For Sue college is a pleasant experience in a life of pleasant experiences; for Susan it is a bittersweet time that will always leave a scar even as it directs her toward all she values.

Both young women are admired and important, but they achieve their success in very different ways. Sue goes through the ranks, taking part in a variety of activities: "Her idea of the four years had been to do everything there was to be done as well as any one could do it, and she was not a person accustomed to failure" (154). The difficult, agonized Susan achieves recognition differently: with the publication of a poem, "In two days she was famous, for High Authority publicly placed the poem above anything yet done in the college" (169). Then "a Chaucer paper that became vaguely confounded in the matter of literary rank with the works of its famous subject" (173), other writing, and finally her version of *Twelfth Night* bring her as much if not more fame and respect as Sue; she is chosen for one of the two important societies and becomes editor-in-chief of the *Monthly*. So both through their different paths achieve prominence and the respect and admiration of their world, but it is well-rounded Sue who is comfortable and at ease in it while the gifted, driven Susan remains outside.

The realism of the women's college fiction is tempered by the "domestic" in the sense that, like much of women's writing in the nineteenth century, the narratives focus on human and social relationships, on understanding character, on acting for the good of the community rather than the self. Prominence and leadership are encouraged and rewarded, but are channeled; these young women may become clubwomen or heads of charities, but they will not lead corporations or make decisions that shake the world. Perhaps women are offered not a new role but an intensification of the old one in which education could claim to help women perform their traditional duties even more effectively. The outside world, with its reform movements to help the slum poor, its labor unrest and exploitation of women workers, the activity of the fighters for women's rights, is not allowed to intrude.[25] And perhaps the intellectual is ignored and the literary genius remains an outsider because their drives are masculine attributes that have no place in this balanced feminine world.

But there is another side to the message of this women's college fiction: as long as a young woman stayed within its limits, there is no doubt that the college world offered her opportunities that she was unlikely to find anywhere else. Compared with today, the opportunities seem narrow and restricted; compared to the world then, the opportunities were enormous. If women must serve community, they did not have to immolate or submerge themselves; they could act publicly and win the admiration of their peers. Even the balance of study and activity shown as desirable in so many of the stories was new to women, and could be achieved only in this small, private, feminine space which in fact became a woman's modification of man's world outside. If the advances seem small today, the subtext of gratitude and awareness of privilege found in the fiction indicates how important they seemed then. What readers saw were young women finding and using their abilities and talents, shaping their world, freeing themselves from at least some restrictions, and both enjoying themselves and winning approval as they did so.

Thomas Wentworth Higginson had said "Woman must be a subject or an equal; there is no middle ground." A popular magazine essay declared that woman had lowered herself to equality with man. The fiction reflects this still-present ambivalence, chiefly through its consistent refusal to discuss anything controversial or upsetting or to emphasize any connection with issues in the outside world to which these young women who are enjoying their opportunities must eventually return. Conservative and careful in dealings with that outside world, in the image presented to it, and in the celebration of vaguely defined womanliness, the turn-of-the-century fictional green world was nevertheless radical in offering women a space that could be lively, dramatic, fulfilling, and that gave more chance for self-realization than was available to them anywhere else.

# THE FAMOUS VASSAR GIRL SERIES.

## Three Vassar Girls in the Tyrol.

An entertaining description of the travels of our Vassar friends through this well-known country, giving an interesting account of the Passion Play at Ober Ammergau. Illustrated by " Champ" and others.

1 vol., small quarto, illuminated board covers and
linings, - - - - - - - - $1.50
1 vol., small quarto, cloth, beveled and gilt, - 2.00

Uniform in style and price with the above, the other volumes of the series can be had as follows:

## Three Vassar Girls in Switzerland.

By ELIZABETH W. CHAMPNEY. An exceedingly interesting story interwoven with bits of Swiss life, historic incidents, and accounts of happenings at Geneva, Lucerne, and the Great St. Bernard. Illustrated by " Champ" and others.

## Three Vassar Girls in Russia and Turkey.

During the exciting scenes and events of the late Turko-Russian war, with many adventures, both serious and comic. Profusely illustrated from original designs, by " CHAMP" and others.

## Three Vassar Girls in France.

A story of the siege of Paris. A thrilling account of adventures when Germany and France were engaged in their terrible struggle. Ninety-seven illustrations by " CHAMP," DETAILLE, and DE NEUVILLE.

## Three Vassar Girls at Home.

Travels through some of our own States and Territories,

## Three Vassar Girls in Italy.

Travels through the vineyards of Italy, visiting all the large cities, and passing some time in Rome, in the Vatican, the Catacombs, etc. 107 illustrations.

## Three Vassar Girls in South America.

A trip through the heart of South America, up the Amazon, across the Andes, and along the Pacific coast to Panama. 112 illustrations.

## Three Vassar Girls in England.

Sunny memories of a holiday excursion of three college girls in the mother country, with visits to historic scenes and notable places. Ninety-eight illustrations.

## Three Vassar Girls Abroad.

The vacation rambles of three college girls on a European trip for amusement and instruction, with their haps and mishaps. Ninety-two illustrations.

### THE NEW SERIES.

## Great Grandmother's Girls in New Mexico.

By ELIZABETH W. CHAMPNEY. This is the second volume of this delightful series describing incidents in the life of a quaint little maiden who lived in the time of the Spanish adventurers. Illustrated by " CHAMP."

1 vol., 8vo, chromo-lithographed board covers - $1.75
1 vol., 8vo, cloth, gilt - - - - - - 2.50

## Great Grandmother's Girls in France.

By ELIZABETH W. CHAMPNEY. A charming volume for girls, consisting of romantic stories of the heroines in the early colonial days—their privations and courage.

Advertisement, from Elizabeth Champney, *Three Vassar Girls in the Tyrol*, (Boston: Estes & Lauriat, 1891).

"The Freshman will be refreshed with lemonade, and entertained in the most polite way." Alice K. Fallows, "The Girl Freshman," *Munsey's Magazine* 25 (Sept. 1901): 823. Illustrator, "H.K."

Alice K. Fallows, "The Girl Freshman," *Munsey's Magazine* 25 (Sept. 1901): 820. Illustrator, "H.K."

# THE GIRL FRESHMAN.

## BY ALICE KATHERINE FALLOWS.

HOW SMITH, BRYN MAWR, VASSAR, AND WELLESLEY RECEIVE EACH YEAR'S NEW CLASS OF STUDENTS, AND INITIATE THEM INTO THE SOCIAL LIFE OF THEIR COLLEGE.

ONE hears and reads so much about the fidelity with which women's colleges are copying the methods of the universities and higher institutions for men, that those unfamiliar with the facts are likely to receive a totally wrong impression about the social side of the college woman's life. Parents who are thinking of sending their daughters, and the daughters themselves, often shrink from the idea of exchanging home life for the loneliness and the unknown dangers of a wholly new existence.

There is presented herewith an epitome of the "shaking down process," as it might be called, in four of the most famous women's colleges in this country, which shows "how the freshman becomes one of them," and incidentally proves that the gulf between the spirit of men's and women's colleges is still enormously wide.

### THE NEWCOMER AT "FAIR SMITH."

After a sub freshman has spent thirty five minutes in the leisurely local f r o m Springfield, looking out at a gray sheet of rain dropped between her and the fabled beauties of meadow and mountain, her enthusiasm for Smith College is likely to be at a low

THE SMITH COLLEGE FRESHMAN, WITH HER BANDBOX, UMBRELLA, AND GUITAR CASE.

ebb when the conductor calls out: "Next station Northampton. Do not leave any packages or other articles in the car!"

As she stands waiting for the train to stop, with a guitar case under her arm, a hand bag in one hand, a bandbox and umbrella in the other, holding up her new tailor skirt with a thumb and finger, she feels ready to barter all the uncertain joys of a college course to escape the lonely arrival in this strange town. But just as she dashes down the car steps and through the pelting rain to the shelter of the station, and, setting her teeth hard, determines to meet what comes like her father's daughter, some one in a short skirt and a "tam" steps up and says cordially:

"Do let me take your bandbox. You're a freshman, aren't you? And what house are you going to?"

If the sub freshman has quick intuitions, she will realize that this is one of the upper class welcoming committee come to meet her.

The new girl who arrives unattended is conducted safely to her boarding house; and her guide, before saying a cheerful good by, leaves her a passport into the college world, a little handbook with a map of the campus, and

"You cannot imagine how anxious the girls are to see you." Abbe Carter Goodloe, "Revenge," *College Girls* (New York: Scribner's, 1895), 174. Illustrator, Charles Dana Gibson.

"'Georgia Ames doesn't cut,' said Madeline." Margaret Warde, *Betty Wales, Junior* (Philadelphia: Penn Publishing, 1906), 112. Illustrator, Eva M. Nagel.

"I've passed off my entrance Latin." Margaret Warde, *Betty Wales Decides* (Philadelphia: Penn Publishing, 1911), 113. Illustrator, Eva M. Nagel.

End papers, Margaret Warde, *Betty Wales, Junior* (Philadelphia: Penn Publishing, 1906).

"I think I shall like it here." Frontispiece, Margaret Warde, *Betty Wales Decides* (Philadelphia: Penn Publishing, 1911), Illustrator, Eva M. Nagel.

Cover, Amanda M. Douglas, *Helen Grant, Senior* (Boston: Lothrop, Lee and Shepard, 1907).

"Lorraine, I love you very much." Amanda M. Douglas, *Helen Grant, Senior* (Boston: Lothrop, Lee and Shepard, 1907), 92. Illustrator, Amy Brooks.

" 'I think my trunk is on this train,' she said." Frontispiece, Nell Speed, *Molly Brown's Freshman Days* (New York: Hurst, 1912), Illustrator, Charles L. Wrenn.

" 'I wish you would tell me your receipt for making friends, Molly,' exclaimed Nance." Nell Speed, *Molly Brown's Freshman Days* (New York: Hurst, 1912), 51. Illustrator, Charles L. Wrenn.

"Good-bye to Wellington and the old happy days." Nell Speed, *Molly Brown's Senior Days* (New York: Hurst, 1913), 302. Illustrator, Charles L. Wrenn.

" 'You're right in the fashion, Miss Brown,' observed Adele." Nell Speed, *Molly Brown's Senior Days* (New York: Hurst, 1913), 25. Illustrator, Charles L. Wrenn.

"Grace Measured the Distance." Jessie Graham Flower, *Grace Harlowe's First Year at Overton College* (Philadelphia: Henry Altemus, 1914), 185.

"They Clustered About the Fireplace." Jessie Graham Flower, *Grace Harlowe's Second Year at Overton College* (Philadelphia: Henry Altemus, 1914), 141.

"The Four Friends Were Strolling Across the Campus." Jessie Graham Flower, *Grace Harlowe's Fourth Year at Overton College* (Philadelphia: Henry Altemus, 1914), 215.

"Over Tea and Cakes the Clouds Dispersed." Jessie Graham Flower, *Grace Harlowe's Second Year at Overton College* (Philadelphia: Henry Altemus, 1914), 235.

"I Am Sorry That We Have Failed to Come to an Understanding." Jessie Graham Flower, *Grace Harlowe's First Year at Overton College* (Philadelphia: Henry Altemus, 1914), 79.

"It Is My Theme." Jessie Graham Flower, *Grace Harlowe's Second Year at Overton College* (Philadelphia: Henry Altemus, 1914), 109.

"Listen my children and you shall roar
With the midnight deeds of the sophomore."
Frontispiece, Christina Catrevas, *That Freshman* (New York: D. Appleton,
1910). Illustrator, Howard Heath.

"Girls, I can't have this racket in this room!" Christina Catrevas, *That Freshman* (New York: D. Appleton, 1910), 68. Illustrator, Howard Heath.

"The next day's recitations hastily prepared, the Lookouts had gathered in Ronny's room for a spread." Pauline Lester, *Marjorie Dean, College Freshman* (New York: A. L. Burt, 1922), 207.

"Leila claimed the privilege of conveying the freshman to Silverton Hall, her destination." Pauline Lester, *Marjorie Dean, College Sophomore* (New York: A. L. Burt, 1922), 115.

"They merrily gathered about the greensward table, on which paper napkins formed the cloth." Frontispiece, Laura Lee Hope, *The Outdoor Girls of Deepdale* (New York: Grosset and Dunlap, 1913).

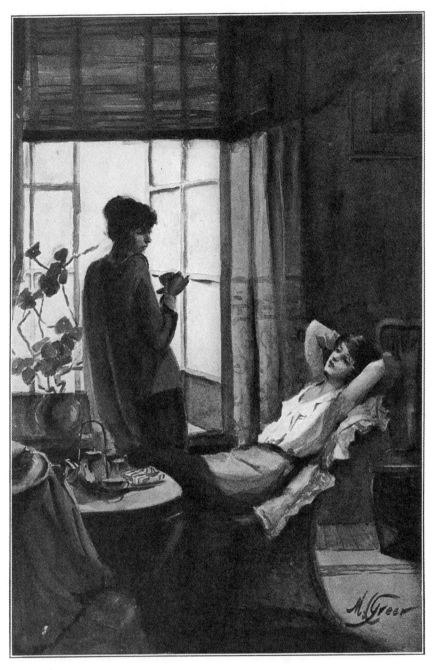

"Sometimes, over a cup of tea, Margaret and Caroline talked the matter over." Lela Horn Richards, *Caroline in College* (Boston: Little, Brown, 1922), 81. Illustrator, M. L. Greer.

"Many heads turned to watch the alert, slender figure as it passed." Lela Horn Richards, *Caroline in College* (Boston: Little, Brown, 1922), 46. Illustrator, M. L. Greer.

"The man they were chasing drove like a madman." Frontispiece, Clair
Blank, *Beverly Gray, Senior* (New York: Grosset and Dunlap, 1934).

## · FIVE ·

# Living Together: The Disintegration of Community

T he warm and magical women's community created in *Two College Girls* and intensified in the college collections and the Betty Wales books, characterized by maturing, joyousness, and love of the college, begins to fall apart, at least in the fiction, somewhere in the first twenty years of the new century. New elements enter the college stories, particularly money and romance, diminishing and in some cases destroying the integrity of the green world. In general, it is a group of juvenile series books that best reflect the changes.

Perhaps the earlier writers had done their job too well, for the women's colleges entered a period of growth that transformed them. As enrollments increased, the days when all the students, and especially members of the same class, knew each other disappeared into the past, and as numbers grew, so did fragmentation. Since sources give many different dates, it is difficult to pinpoint an exact time when general suspicion of the women's colleges eased and a different kind of student entered.[1] William A. Neilson, president of Smith from 1918 to 1939, saw and regretted the changes; according to his biographer, the "mother who had once been obliged to explain why she let her daughter go to college now felt constrained to apologize for her girl who stayed home. Going to college became suddenly, in the twenties, the thing to do and the women's colleges were flooded with applicants. . . . The trail the pioneers blazed had become a path and then a highway." In 1926, when Smith was fifty-one years old, Neilson compared the "handful of eager souls, brought into this place by their appetite for intellectual things" with the two thousand students now there "largely in obedience to a social convention" and he leaves no doubt that his comparison is much to the disadvantage of his own students.[2]

Neilsen places the change in the 1920s, but the fiction suggests that it began earlier. As the colleges survived and grew, they became respectable, then fashionable; wealthy young women came to college for something to do—perhaps, as in Goodloe's tales, to pass the time before marriage. Magazine commentary began to focus on the evils of snobbery, and the fiction displays sharply defined groups, often oppositional, with the sense of community diminished or fragmented. As a result, conflict moves from the internal, like Helen Chase Adams's attempt to find herself, to the external, so that introspection and the examined life give way to resistance or adventure.

Snobbery based on financial status does appear in the Betty Wales books, where what the girls themselves call "democracy" is more than the refusal to allow domination by a political clique; it is an assertion of the equality of all students regardless of financial background. When Dorothy King, the admired prominent senior who has been Betty's mentor, is about to graduate, she leaves her protégée with a charge: "I know I can trust you to work for the democratic, helpful spirit and to keep down cliques and snobbishness and to see that everybody has a fair chance and a good time" (S 345).

Betty first becomes aware of financial differences through the character of Emily Davis, a bright, talented young woman who is working her way through college. When Mary Brooks has overspent her generous allowance and needs more money, her friends help her make Valentine cards to sell until Betty discovers that they are cutting into the market of several scholarship students, including Emily, who sell their cards to earn living expenses. At the end of their first year, Emily is to work in the oceanside hotel where Betty and her family will spend the summer; Betty is pleased, but Emily cautions her, "Now, Betty, you must not expect your family to see me in the same light you do. Here those things don't make any difference, but outside they do; and it's perfectly right that they should, too" (F 358). Yet Emily is so talented and respected that she is among the "first four" to be chosen for an honor society; at that moment she contrasts her own "shabby coat, made from Babe's discarded golf cape" with Eleanor Watson's "irreproachable blue walking suit" and says, "Here all girls are really created free and equal, aren't they, Miss King?" (S 135).

Degrees of wealth show as well in various living accommodations. After their first year in off-campus houses, most sophomores go into the more expensive dormitories. A few, like painfully shy Roberta, hesitate to move away from familiar surroundings, but others, like Rachel, must choose less expensive housing that will physically separate them from the campus and students. When Rachel quietly tells her friends that she will be living off campus for financial reasons, they are careful to make no comment, and indeed the new location does not affect her: "Though Rachel was off the campus, her room was far and away the most popular meeting place for the Chapin house crowd. Perhaps it was because the quiet of the little white house around the corner was a relief after the noisy bustle of the big campus dormitories. But besides, there was something about Rachel that made her quite indispensible to all gatherings of the clan" (S 110–111). Rachel's first year on campus has established her identity and ability, but most students who live off campus are outside the green world. Like Rachel, who becomes class president, the talented Emily and a few others make their mark early and can never be excluded, but some live their college lives unnoticed and apart. They are not snubbed for lack of money; rather, lack of money isolates them from the special world.

At the end of junior year, when the commencement ushers are selected, Betty discovers that a few young women plan to resign the honor because they cannot afford clothes that do justice to the occasion. Choosing her target, Betty goes to Babbie, a close friend noted for her rich and tasteful way of dressing. (Babbie's mother, in fact, sends her money to hire a French maid; Babbie uses the money to keep a horse, to give spreads and dinners, and to make sure that Emily Davis has an income through sewing and mending jobs.) When Betty arrives, Babbie has just taken her ushering dress out of its box, and it lies on the bed, the "filmy, beruffled gown, with its rows upon rows of tucking and shirring, and its dainty trimmings of hand embroidery and real lace," as they talk. Betty explains her worries to the tight-lipped Babbie, ending with "Do you know, I think Rachel [the class president] is worrying about her own dress. She wouldn't admit it, but she brought it out to show me, and it's very plain and it's been washed a lot of times. . . . Rachel said she hoped the class wouldn't be ashamed of her" (J 312–313).[3] Babbie agrees to wear a simpler dress; in fact, she helps make a game rather than an obvious sacrifice out of the gesture by turning the whole thing into a bet: the junior who makes the prettiest dress for the least money gets a prize. "We certainly want to keep Harding College so that every girl, no matter who she is, can enjoy it," sums up Christy, one of the class leaders and herself from a wealthy family. "And the only way to do that is to keep clothes in the background and brains and real good times in front" (J 317).

The whole class accepts the idea, and their reward is more than good feeling; an elderly gentleman, impressed by the simplicity of the ushers and hearing a little of the story, donates fifty thousand dollars to the college. The class that inspired the gift can control part of it, and they decide to establish a fund for students who need financial help. As a topic, the concept of "democracy" becomes part of the ideal of college life, with Betty, who on her entrance was probably the kind of uncommitted young woman whom President Neilson deplored, as an unconscious force not just for good, but for the maintenance of high standards for the college.

Only a few years later a story by Margaret Warde in *St. Nicholas Magazine* exposed snobbishness to mockery.[4] First-year student Margaret is labeled a "freak" because of her "short hair and freckles, and the most awful clothes; and when Kitty asked about her family, she answered up as if she was proud of it, and said that her father was a machinist and her mother did fine embroidery . . . her clothes are frights." She makes a few friends who appreciate her skill at sports and her agreeable personality, but she is generally snubbed until it comes out that she appears as she does because of an elaborate bet with her brother. Her machinist father is a wealthy man who loves to tinker with his cars while her socially prominent mother does embroidery as a hobby and the brother who is "at college somewhere" goes to Yale. Suddenly Margaret has all the right qualifications for popularity. The classmates whose focus on wealth have blinded them to her good qualities are left looking foolish and petty.

While there are indications in even the most joyous fiction that the green world is a fragile place, the portrayal of its infiltration or undermining takes place chiefly in the later series books for girls. By the early years of the century, series books were well established. There had been the sentimental Elsie books, continuing works like the *Five Little Peppers*, boarding school stories, camping adventures, and many others. Boys and their sisters could read the adventures of Frank Merriwell, for example, featuring one athletic exploit after another. One would like to believe that Merriwell's years at Yale were not characteristic of that respected institution, or else that the hero was a supernatural being, since his trials and ordeals would have killed a normal man before his twenty-first birthday. However the books strike a reader today, with their unlikely adventures and emphasis on the physical, their popularity was enormous. One need only look at the success of the Stratemeyer Syndicate to know these books sold well, and regardless of their lack of quality, their wide circulation argues their success in carrying their message to a huge number of young readers.

The stable of writers who turned out volume after volume of children's and juvenile books under the direction of Edward Stratemeyer produced such titles as *The Rover Boys, The Hardy Boys, Tom Swift,* and, the women's champion, *Nancy Drew*. While Stratemeyer planned the stories and assigned the author's names, the actual work was done by a host of anonymous writers. "Carolyn Keene," the author of the Nancy Drew books, was first Stratemeyer himself, then his daughter, Harriet Stratemeyer Adams. Other series might have any number of authors.[5]

Series books about the women's colleges shift the focus of the earlier works, and the integrity of the green world suffers. Money-based snobbery and the battle for democracy eventually become the central themes, but there are other reasons for the erosion of the green world. Though Warde's Betty Wales and Amanda O. Douglas's Helen Grant series are separated by only two years and are therefore contemporary, no two visions of college life could be more different. Douglas, born in 1837, was long established as a minor popular writer for both adults and young people when in 1906 she sent one of her heroes to college. Helen Grant already has an existence in earlier books; her four college years, contained in two volumes, are stages along her road to maturity.[6] Douglas was elderly when she wrote the books, and her ideas and standards, her echoes of True Womanhood, are mid-nineteenth century. There are strong indications that since she did not go to college herself, she read and used both Helen Dawes Brown and the Wellesley collection as models.

As her heroine already has an identity established in earlier books, Douglas cannot change her character. Helen is a serious girl on the way to becoming a noble woman. She has come to college to prepare herself to teach, so the experience is chiefly a step on the way to her goal: a vocational interlude. Popular novelist though she might have been, Douglas is not, here, a very good writer. She insists that Helen is charming, witty, sparkling, full of fun, but what she shows the reader is an over-earnest, pompous, and boring young woman, incessantly examining each experience and possibility to see whether enjoying it is compatible with her duty. She does not grow and change, but simply intensifies her existing qualities.

Even more unfortunate, Helen Grant and her story are old-fashioned. For all Douglas's insistence that Helen is an up-to-date young woman ready to go into the world and make her way, the character remains the creation of a writer who lived most of her life in the nineteenth century and whose other novels portray girls learning painfully how to be True Women—by which the author meant learning Christian forbearance, rising above pain, insult, and victimization to become exemplars of Christian love, and finally taking their places in women's sphere. The most interesting aspect of the Helen Grant books is their ongoing discussion of womanly standards, and the relationship of college to those standards and to marriage. Though Douglas gives lip-service to the idea that women have choices, she does not convince.

Comparison with college stories written at the same time makes clear the missing element in Douglas's work. The other stories, written out of love and experience, are not simply more youthful, they celebrate a life that the authors lived. Try though she does, Douglas is not authentic;

she has done her research, but her work is full of echoes. She simply cannot convey the special quality of student life as the writers who had been there can. Though her college may be a separate space, it is no world of discovery, transformation, and delight, and any unique codes disappear under those Helen has brought with her. As nineteenth-century fiction, Helen Grant's adventures may be correct; as a guide for the early twentieth-century college woman, they are irrelevant, and Helen Grant's college has a campus, but not a green world.

Like the Betty Wales books, Nell Speed's Molly Brown series (1913) is well written, handsomely published, has interesting characters that carry out skillfully the various themes, and centers on a hero whose chief talents are natural charm and goodness. But although the series makes a positive portrayal of college life, it, too, suggests flaws in the integrity of the green world.

Unlike Betty Wales, Molly Brown is almost poor; her proud old Kentucky family has little more than its land. Molly ekes out her allowance by doing odd jobs, and at one point a lack of money threatens her college life. But Molly, though immature (she is fifteen when she enters college), has charm: she is described as a "tall girl with auburn hair and deep blue eyes . . . There was a kind of awkward grace about her, the grace which was hers by rights and the awkwardness which comes of growing too fast" (F 6). She mentions several times her lack of "shape," but although her friends think she gets prettier each year, her warm, loving personality, not her looks, defines her. Wealth and money-based snobbery, perhaps because Molly herself is poor, are much stronger elements here than in previous tales: "the sophomore class . . . had the reputation of being run by a clique of the most arrogant and snobbish set of girls Wellington College had ever known" (S 34). The dormitories, in which Molly, Judy, and Nance have a three-bedroom suite with a large living room, are for everyone, but the very rich might live in lavish apartments while those who are working or on scholarships live in the village, "over the post-office" or "at Mrs. O'Reilly's," a former small hotel. Molly's clothes are not new, and she does odd jobs to earn money until as a sophomore she becomes a tutor; the unpleasant Judith Blount, a vicious snob and the first dedicated "villain" in any of these books, frequently attacks her. But Molly is loved, and her gracious manner as well as her happiness in sharing her lavish food baskets from home create for her a circle of loyal friends.

The real difference, however, is that college was the heart and center of the Betty Wales books, as it was of the collections of short stories and *Two College Girls*, but, while there is a physical green world here, the center of the Molly Brown books is not the college but Molly, whose story plays out in the college world. The trouble with her is that she is perfect. Under her shy southern charm she does not so much adjust to the college as make it adjust to her, so that it is easier for the reader to identify with her two friends, Nance and Judy, both of whom seem more accessible. It is a subtle shift, but an important one. Added to the new emphasis is romance, in earlier books waiting in the wings, and the presence of men from a nearby college who move freely in and out of the green world, quietly undermining the strength and self-containment of the women's community.

Some of the fragmentation may come from a lack of authenticity in the college itself. The author, Emma Speed Sampson, a novelist under her own name and a writer of juveniles as Nell Speed, graduated from Hampton College in Louisville, but the college she portrays is supposed to be one of the eastern ones. She seems to borrow elements from all the colleges, or perhaps all the college stories, to create her composite version, so there are inconsistencies and contrivances that deny the kind of convincing reality found in other books. Too, the author suggests some provocative themes but fails to develop them. The real difference, however, is that neither Speed nor Douglas find that just being in college is enough to carry a story.

In 1911 Jeanette Marks, a professor at Wellesley, wrote *A Girl's Student Days and After*, a book that tells young women how they should behave in college, and whose thrust makes it clear they were not, in her eyes, behaving properly. She sounds as if she might have welcomed another Hannah Lyman, the autocratic Lady Principal of Vassar's early years who controlled everything outside the classroom. "A college," Marks says, "is no place for vocal soloists. Its life is the life of an orchestra, of many instruments playing together."[7]

The orchestra falling into disharmonious groups and snobbery as a reality show clearly in two very popular series that portray the college lives of Grace Harlowe (1914), by Jessie Graham Flower, and Marjorie Dean (1922), by Pauline Lester.[8] Change, lack of harmony, and the sense that the college experience in itself was no longer enough to carry a story are amply proved as these wonderfully simplistic series turn the green world into a battleground. The battles are not physical, like those of the men's arenas; rather they are battles for college standards and "democracy," the themes that here overshadow all others. Both focus on the resistance to cliques, snobbishness, the classification of students according to money, and power won through wealth—the perversion of the college spirit. Students fall neatly into three types: the snobs, the working girls, and the nice girls.

These two series are worth consideration because they were enormously popular and many times reprinted. One reason for their popularity is probably that there were so few books for girls compared to books for boys; publishers' listings in the backs of these juveniles show a significant difference in numbers. According to a more recent author, publishers believed that girls would read about boys, but boys would not read about girls.[9] Grace and Marjorie, therefore, were major sources of information and acceptable behavior, as well as entertainment, to a young, wide female audience that may or may not have planned on going to college. The two series are so similar in their events that one almost suspects a formula.[10]

Youthful readers already knew both heroes, having followed them through four years of high school (and four books), and neither author seems concerned with interpreting the college world for a general audience. Like Helen Grant, the protagonists intensify their characters rather than develop them, although they are more interesting than the older heroine. Both are opposed to injustice, but they differ in their personalities and reactions. Sweet Marjorie responds to rudeness with womanly pride and quivering lower lip, tomboy Grace with womanly pride and flashing eyes. Marjorie is a portrait of a girl gazing pensively at violets; Grace is a strong Gibson girl. Readers had shared their battles, for both dealt with enemies in high school: Grace converted her chief tormenter into a close friend, while Marjorie not so much converted as defanged hers. Both are experienced fighters by the time they get to college.

Grace's high school years show another new element, adventure, that had entered books for girls. The nineteenth-century emphasis in women's fiction on the social, civilizing role of women and the specialized situation in which these traits flowered was apparently no longer enough to make a story. Girls began to have things happen: they solved mysteries, found long-lost children, and were even exposed to violence. Grace Harlowe's freshman year in high school, for example, is enlivened not just with an enemy and class rivalry, but with a strike against an unfair teacher and a bobsledding accident, as well as opportunities to foil a burglar, to stop runaway horses (single-handed), and to be attacked by wolves. All this she takes calmly and capably, although the following year, when she is captured by a lunatic and imprisoned, tomboy Grace does give in to feminine weakness long enough to faint.

Both heroes have similar backgrounds. They are the only children of families of comfortable socioeconomic status, each close family equipped with a solid, protective father and a truly womanly mother. In their small city or large town the fathers are respected businessmen and the mothers, while maintaining happy homes, are leaders in community affairs. Both daughters are honorable: they have been taught to identify good and evil and given the strength to choose good at any cost. They are upheld even in their most discouraging moments by an inner confidence that they are doing the right thing, no matter what others may think, and that good will eventually triumph. Each is surrounded by loyal friends who share her upbringing and solid middle-class virtues.

Described as tall and gray-eyed, lithe and slender, loving nothing better than a run across campus when no one can see her, Grace Harlowe is a former tomboy—an All-American girl. She is wholesome, honorable, and strong; typically, on the train, to conquer her sadness over leaving home and parents, "she threw back her shoulders and sitting very straight in her seat glanced defiantly around her" (F 15). Her series inaugurates some friends from home who accompany the protagonist; hers are Anne, quiet, very bright, and already on the way to becoming a Shakespearean actress, and Miriam, brilliant and vivid, once Grace's enemy and now her loyal friend. Their first year starts well; they are properly met at the station by upperclass women, as college custom and etiquette by now demanded, and settle into their dormitory where they make friends with other students.[11] But at the same time trouble starts, establishing the pattern for a long succession of encounters: in trying to help others, Grace makes problems for herself.

On their train journey Grace and her friends had met Elfrieda, a crude, self-centered but humorous new student who almost immediately becomes the butt of a cruel sophomore joke. Far worse, she breaks the college codes by reporting the joke to the authorities, thereby putting herself outside college life. Grace, in trying to defend her, also becomes the target of sophomore anger.

Grace goes on to win the kind of popularity, affection, and respect that her friends expect for her. One of them, listening to her regret her lack of special talents, smiles to herself, for she knows "that Grace already possessed a talent for making friends and an ability to see not only her own way clearly, but to smooth the pathway of those weaker than herself. . . . She knew, too, that before the end of the school year Grace's remarkable personality was sure to make itself felt among her fellow students" (F 61). Grace is a star on the basketball court, and she organizes her friends into a society (called Semper Fidelis) whose purpose is to establish a fund to help women students who are poor, who live off campus, and who must work; above all, she is a nurturer.

Nevertheless, in spite of her popularity the major events of her four years are confrontations, one after another, as she straightens out young women who do not or cannot live up to what one of her friends articulates as the college ideal:

> Doesn't it seem wonderful to think that girls can be so splendidly impersonal and honorable? . . . College is the very place to cultivate that attitude. Living up to college traditions means being honorable in the highest sense of the word. There are plenty of girls who come here without realizing what being an Overton girl means, until they find themselves face to face with the fact that their standards are not high enough. That is why one hears so much about finding one's self. College is like a great mirror." (J 126–127)

Though Grace is concerned with "democracy," her difficulties do not come only from snobbery based on wealth: "Overton had a reputation

for democracy in spite of the fact that most of its students came from
homes where there was no lack of money" (F 104). Many of the problems she solves are caused by those who cannot find "that intangible and
yet wholly necessary principle, the college spirit" (Sr 40), particularly, as
she moves toward senior status, with new students who fall under bad
influences. Misunderstandings abound, friendships are broken and re-
paired, enmities develop; in between there is the occasional small mystery to solve and, probably, classes to attend, though these are mentioned
only in passing. Except for the constant guerilla warfare that Grace and
her friends must wage against those who would subvert the college ideal,
her life would be pleasant, and, of course, it would take up fewer pages,
because the author really has not much else to say.

There are pleasant moments when the friends talk and act together,
but with dramatics, sports, helping potential misfits, and one reforma-
tion task after another, Grace's four years are busy. At the end she is
honored as the outstanding example of the college spirit, and a benefactor, left over from the high school books, suddenly appears and decides
to build a campus dormitory for the poorer students, to be called Harlowe House.

If Grace's life is a series of sorties, Marjorie Dean's is a war against a
clearly defined enemy. Marjorie too has her satellite friends: her roommate, Jerry, a kind of stock humorous character, plump, slangy, and
quick-witted; Muriel, forthright and fearless; Lucy, who has a scholarship
and must work; and Veronica, wealthy, talented, and confident. These
five enter the "Country of College," Marjorie's name for this version of
the green world, together; although each is given individual traits and
the characterization, developed in the high school books, is fairly successful, all the focus is on Marjorie.

Their first year gets off to a bad start. College etiquette is breached
when no one meets them at the train and when, tired and bewildered,
they have found their rooms and are settling in, they are visited by the
sophomores who should have met them. The openly insincere apologies
of their visitors display a hostility that the newcomers cannot understand
and underline the snobbery that will be the dominant conflict through
the following years. The sophomore visitors went to a fashionable prep
school: "I really know nothing at all about high schools," one visitor says,
"I did not suppose you could enter college from one." Veronica points
out that they did not have to take entrance examinations, since their
diplomas "will admit us to any college in the United States." Leslie
Cairns, the leader, ends the conversation with the drawled comment that
she had heard high schools were "really excellent" but that they "turn
out a lot of digs and prigs . . . in fact, you are the first high school girls I
have ever met" (F 108–109). To add injury to insult, the visitors stay long
enough to make sure the tired, hungry new arrivals miss dinner.

Eventually the cause of the hostility is explained; the sophomores know one of Marjorie's old and defeated enemies. But the war is not simply personal. The friends have inadvertantly entered a house where there are few new students, and where the dominant sophomores are already engaged in a power struggle. Jerry says, "It wouldn't surprise me if that [snobbery] were the main issue . . . the snob proposition has become a grand nuisance here. Who knows? Before long we may be taking part in a regular fight against 'our crowd.' Maybe both sides are looking for recruits." When Marjorie points out that both Jerry and Veronica are eligible for the snob group on the grounds of family fortune, Jerry with her colorful language is emphatic: "Any time you catch me toddling along with that foolish aggregation you may discard me forever" (F 139).

At first isolated in their war-torn dormitory, Marjorie and her friends finally meet other students and discover that their house is not characteristic of the whole college and that they have allies. When Marjorie is maneuvered by one of the "good" sophomores into a beauty contest, she jumps into instant (and, to one of her modesty, unwelcome) prominence as the College Beauty. In response, Marjorie's enemy defines itself: eighteen very wealthy young women from a New York prep school who call themselves Sans Souci and intend to dominate and control campus life. They are undifferentiated except for their leader, Leslie Cairns, who for two volumes is simply the nastiest of a group of nasties. The reader has some difficulty taking the situation seriously because the motivation seems so slight.

The writer of this series is something less than skillful; her writing does, however, have a kind of energy and can create convincing scenes, especially when she presents interaction among the friends. The character for whom one must not just willingly but with some effort suspend disbelief is Marjorie, who is so sweet and good that she seems inhuman. One of her high school enemies called her an interfering busybody and a priggish goody-goody, and at times the epithets fit all too well. If the reader can accept Marjorie's perfection, the story flows logically: she gradually becomes the center of an ever-widening group who dislike the Sans and all that they stand for and want to preserve the college for everyone. The conflict thus generated continues for three years and affects every part of college life except the classroom. (The reader must assume that there are classrooms; aside from Marjorie's occasional need to write a theme or her complaint that she stained a favorite dress while doing an experiment in chemistry, academics hardly intrude.) Basketball, that staple of series books, becomes another battlefield, the senior committee and the teacher running the sport having been suborned by the Sans' wealth and influence.

But Marjorie and her friends work out their strategy: "Our best way to fight the Sans is by influence. Their influence, founded as it is on money values, is not beneficial to Hamilton College. Ours should be founded strictly on observing the traditions of Hamilton. . . . We can't lecture on the subject, of course. It will have to be a silent struggle for a nobler aim" (S 14). Later Marjorie, regretting that Hamilton is a "battle-ground," affirms, "I will fight for my rights, if I must, but I will ignore a worthless enemy as long as I can. . . . We must put them in the background by being true and kindly and honorable. Then their false standards will count for nothing" (S 35–36).

The strategy works and the message is clear. In spite of their scheming, the Sans consistently fail in everything they do. Earlier the author commented, "Under their false and petty ideas of life there was still so much of the eagerness of girlhood to be liked, to succeed, to be happy. Only they were obstinately traveling the wrong road in search of it" (S 271). When they haze Marjorie, they break one of the college's most stringent rules, and afraid that they will be found out before their imminent graduation, they become quiet and reclusive. But retribution is inevitable and there is no honor among thieves; with no external enemies, they turn on each other and finally one of them betrays the group. Only weeks before graduation they are expelled.

Peace and democracy reign on the campus. During Marjorie's senior year there are some mopping-up expeditions—a few underclass students who were influenced by the Sans are either reformed or removed—but the year ends with "the last really pernicious element" gone and virtue triumphant. As Marjorie and her friends receive awards as outstanding citizens of the college, the author comments, in sadly typical language, "The turn of the tide for democracy had occurred almost four years before when the ten seniors thus elevated to distinction and a few other loyal spirits had set their faces firmly against snobbery and false principles. Now they were to experience the full sweep of the waves of approbation on which their classmates proposed to launch them" (Sr 247).

Keeping the college up to standard is the dominant theme, but not the only one. Like Grace, Marjorie is concerned with working and scholarship students, and heads a movement to build and endow a campus dormitory for them. She rights a wrong and makes a major contribution when she heals the breach between the college and the founder's elderly niece, who controls the institutional endowments.

While here, as in the Grace Harlowe books, there are scenes in which the friends get together and simply enjoy the atmosphere, meet in each other's rooms, or, amazingly often, go to a favorite restaurant to celebrate some event or achievement or to get away from dormitory food, both series must evoke a mixed response to college life. Although Marjorie's sweetness is cloying, her friends are fairly well differentiated and the group has a pleasant liveliness. Grace is the more appealing character simply because she is allowed to have a fault: she has a temper, is not above the quick retort, though she may regret it later, and therefore seems more human. But there is nothing of what was in the Betty Wales series, where the growing maturity of the hero and her friends gave depth and substance to the text. Part of the problem may be that exploration of characters and relationships was done in the high school books; like Helen Grant, Grace and Marjorie and their friends come to college already full-blown and are therefore fairly static.[12] Nearly perfect to begin with, they cause others to change, but they do not change themselves. Another part of the problem results from the extreme polarization, which reduces differences to a simplistic good or bad. Rather than enjoying different kinds of people, Marjorie and Grace are forced to be busy turning other young women into copies of themselves.

The question of whether women can live and work together as part of a community seems to be answered here in the negative. Far from a display of bonding, these books present a world of malice. How, a young reader might wonder, does an ordinary student get along in college if she does not have a Marjorie Dean or a Grace Harlowe to protect her? And what does it say about this world when even those who recognize these heroes as perfect examples of the college spirit can be swayed and influenced by the slightest rumor or accusation?

Nevertheless, the narratives make some statements about women, their roles, and their lives that are significant because of the popularity and wide readership of these books. Womanliness is still a concept of value; these characters have freedom to move and act, but they themselves limit that freedom by accepting the codes of suitable behavior. And both heroes are, without doubt, nurturers. Far from seducing them from their womanly function, college gives them wider scope. Dainty Marjorie and tomboy Grace are exemplars and mother-figures, straightening out those who are heading in the wrong direction, solving problems for those in trouble, and consciously upholding a kind of semi-religious image of the college itself. And the message is clear: good triumphs, good women lead the way.

In performing their functions, both heroes are doing what has been recommended as the way to success in college: they have found their talent and are using it for the good of their institutions. The college life does not provide them with the opportunity to find themselves and enjoy, however briefly, a unique experience; their green world is more physical than spiritual and offers them another theater for taking care of others. Perhaps the product of education is to be a highly superior light of the home, splendidly performing women's classic role of establishing and upholding a place of high standards and morals. In one sense, then, the two heroes are fulfilling a woman's task of creating an orderly society that shares acceptable standards and values. Looking ahead, however, the continuations of both series show a curious irony, for both Grace and

Marjorie become spider women who symbolically devour—or castrate—their mates.

The struggle for and maintenance of democracy, the major theme in the Marjorie/Grace books, connects their college life with the outside world. Much critical and concerned writing about the women's colleges at this period shows that snobbery and divisiveness did exist. Given their dates, just before, during, and after World War I, it is possible to speculate that women fighting for democracy on a college campus might reflect the historical fact that men were fighting and had fought for that same cause in Europe. Women did take part in war work, driving ambulances, nursing, aiding refugees; Grace in fact later goes overseas and fights (literally) for her country. So college women, too, could "do their bit" for the same principles within their world and with their own weapons: sweetness, integrity, and all the womanly virtues. They could tackle the "big" issues, but in their own way and safely within their sphere.

None of Grace Harlowe's enemies are very interesting; they are simply young women heading in wrong directions who have to be taught the right way, and they are interchangeable. If they have internal conflicts, problems, backgrounds—or indeed, any motivation at all for their behavior—the reader does not know it. The same is not true of the Marjorie Dean books, where, it seems, the villain escaped the author's control; Leslie Cairns, just another nasty young woman in the beginning, becomes the most dynamic character in the series. Sweet good Marjorie is far less vivid than wicked Leslie, who has strength, humor, and wit, no matter how she misuses these qualities. Presented as power-hungry and something of a bully, she even has convincing motivation. Motherless, she idolizes her father, described as the "hardest-headed tyrant among a group of financiers who based all values on money" (F 226), and her goal is to be like him, to dominate and control, and thereby win his approval. She is a risk taker who enjoys battle but has not learned to accept the consequences of her acts. Brusque, ruthless, and forceful, she is frequently described as "mannish"; she wears clothes in her own style: "a sports suit of a white wooly material that was a marvel as to cut and finish. The white silk velour sports hat, the heavy white silk stockings and fine, stitched buckskin ties that completed her costume were the acme of distinctive expense" (F 104–105). But Leslie wants power; she cannot "sit back and see a bunch of muffs like those Sanford girls run Hamilton College" (S 99), and later "She was determined, this year, not only to win back and maintain her former leadership at Hamilton College, but also to crush the rising power of the girls she so greatly disliked" (S 103). Like others who consciously strive for prominence and power, she will fail, but there is no doubt that her efforts are really all that keep the story going and the reader reading.

By the junior year volume Leslie has stopped being merely the leader of the Sans and become a person. She has, in fact, as the strongest and most vividly drawn character, almost taken over the narrative, for half the book is about her. Even descriptions of her change and deepen:

> Gifted with a keen sense of humor, she had tricks of expression so original in themselves that she might easily have gained a reputation as the funniest girl in college. Had good humor radiated her peculiarly rugged features she would have been that rarity, an ugly beauty. Due to her proficiency at golf and tennis, she was of most symmetrical figure. She was particularly fastidious as to dress, and made a smart appearance. Having so much that was in her favor, she was hopelessly hampered by self. (J 39)

Toward the end of the year, Leslie and her friends are expelled from college. Readers might think the forces of evil have disappeared, but that is not so. Estranged from her father, at loose ends, and blaming Marjorie for her problems, Leslie haunts the town, waiting to see what damage she can do. In fact six more volumes are needed before Leslie is gathered into Marjorie's fold. Her ultimate conversion is surprisingly logical, since it is based on the same motivation that caused her villainy. In her attempts to hurt Marjorie, she goes too far—in a business deal, the territory she considered her own. Marjorie and her friends have raised money to buy land and build a dormitory for students who cannot afford to live on campus, and Leslie tries to stop the project several times, by what she thinks are her father's methods. Not only are her procedures unsuccessful, they are ridiculous; her father, who knows about everything she does, is angry and contemptuous. Alienated from the only person she cares about, she is lonely and vulnerable, and an unexpected act of kindness on Marjorie's part opens her eyes to her own futility. Since she changes as much to please her father as herself, and since in the later books the author has been at some pains to show her strength and her potential for good, her conversion is more consistent with her character than one would expect from this author.

Clearly Leslie represents one version of the "modern" young woman. She is part of the "roaring twenties," the time of flaming youth, flappers, bobbed hair, and short skirts, with all the dramatic changes in women's behavior. Though drinking, smoking, and sexual experimentation certainly do not appear in these pages, Leslie is in other ways the worst kind of New Woman, establishing an area, to borrow Carroll Smith-Rosenberg's title, of "disorderly conduct" around her.[13] Opposed to the modified True Womanhood and All-American heroes, Grace and Marjorie, who create order, Leslie must fail.

College administrators were among those who had to face the shocking changes in women's behavior. Smith's President Neilson, who might have welcomed a Grace Harlowe or Marjorie Dean on his campus, noted that drastic changes began immediately with the end of World War I. Young women experimented with "new manners and new morals," as

their mothers and older sisters at home were doing, and college administrators had new questions to answer: "Why shouldn't a lady smoke, or
drink, or bob her hair? Why must a girl be chaperoned? If women can
vote, why can't they—?" Administrators were forced to deal with totally
new situations while "parents and alumnae . . . were adapting themselves
to the new world at a rate a little different from their daughters' . . . the
campus was becoming less and less the center of undergraduate life. The
automobile, no longer a rarity, was making it easy to spend weekends at
home or at football games and proms, and the invasion from Dartmouth,
Princeton and Yale, which used to occur only on scheduled dates once
or twice a year, now took place every Sunday." As a result, the importance
of college activities diminished and the "'collegiate' attitude of the
1910's began to look a little old-fashioned and funny; the world was wider
now." [14]

Both series reflect this changing reality, and especially the effect of the
automobile. In the Marjorie Dean books, cars are everywhere. They are
not of themselves evil; several well-behaved students have them and use
them wisely. Contemporary with Marjorie are such series as *The Motor
Maids, The Motor Girls,* and *The Automobile Girls,* in all of which a group of
young women, chaperoned, travel about in their cars. [15] The Motor Maids
even take their car to Japan (where, ironically, a car is unfamiliar and
frightening to the "natives"). The young women drivers are all responsible and competent; Cora, the chief character in the Stratemeyer Syndicate's Automobile Girls series, does her own repairs and is a better
driver than her brother, who, in his car and with his friends, often joins
in their adventures. Reality went further: in 1913, *Harper's Bazar* carried
a short piece called "Women Who Achieve" about Alice E. Waxham, a
Wellesley graduate, who with four assistants, "college bred and of excellent social connections and training" owned and operated "automobiles
in New York under regular chauffeur's license." Her car-hire service
"cater[ed] to women patrons." [16]

The Marjorie Dean books reflect Neilson's concerns and an almost
symbolic use of the automobile. The students who misuse their cars are
the ones who break other codes; the nonconforming Sans treat their cars
with the same recklessness they apply to college rules and womanly standards. While Marjorie and her friends remain caught somewhere between the reality of their time and prewar values, the villains exhibit
"modern" behavior. Though they do not drink or smoke (at least within
the pages of these books for the young), they are slangy and brusque in
speech, extreme in dress, and generally disconnected from any aims
other than their own gratification.

Leslie Cairns moves the car to the level of symbol. She is a skillful
driver; when she drives too fast it is not from poor control but because
she wants to. And she spends a great deal of time in her car, often alone,

driving away from the campus, but always returning. When she has been expelled and alienated, she seems to haunt not the forbidden campus but the area around it, circling like a Peter Ruggles, near home but unable to get there. She is constantly in motion, unrooted. Although the term is never used, and might even have been out of date, Leslie and her friends are New Women, in the worst sense, outside the sphere and standards of womanliness, accepting no boundaries but their own will. And again the message is clear, for none of their plots is successful, nothing they do brings them happiness, and finally they are expelled from the world of which they were not good citizens. Only Leslie, misguided but strong, can, with considerable pain, redeem and change herself, becoming a contented, womanly nurturer.

Both Marjorie and Grace have mothers who are lovely, gracious, and home-centered, while Leslie, motherless, focuses all her love on her father. Her acts are imitations of his, as her ideal is to join him in his business. After her conversion she softens, dressing and behaving in a feminine way and modeling herself on Marjorie; the result is that all her good womanly qualities, so long suppressed, rise to the surface and direct her life. She and her father, who has also reformed (far less convincingly, but the plot needs it) become truly close, and by the end of the series, Leslie, courageously returning to complete her degree and completely aware of the irony, leads the battle to maintain democracy on the campus.

A near-contemporary series by Edith Bancroft, the Jane Allen books, starts off in an almost revolutionary manner, for the protagonist, far from being a paragon, has, to put it mildly, faults.[17] The motherless daughter of a rich Montana rancher, Jane grew up without restraints; though the reader is told she is really charming and lovable with the right instincts and principles, she has never interacted with peers and is spoiled, self-willed, and imperious, used to being given what she wants and unused to any criticism of her behavior. She agrees to go to college only because her dead mother wished it, and the stage seems set for a story of initiation, with Jane learning to control her will and temper, learning to live with other women, and developing all the qualities she lacks. But she arrives with the wrong attitude and in her first hours manages to alienate both her roommate and the housemother. Pride that will not let her explain or conciliate and that hides her deep loneliness and unhappiness makes her, at the end of a few weeks, disliked by everyone.

Jane has no Grace Harlowe to reform her, but an older student's comparison of college to a new land and students to pioneers makes her look at her own attitude. Gradually she makes a few friends, including Judith, her roommate, and some of her difficulties in adjustment are explained. "You see I've always lived in a man's world. Can you wonder that I don't care much for this world of girls I'm forced to live in?" she asks Judith

( *Sub-Team*, 266). "In the brief season she had been at Wellington she had discovered that girls could hate as fiercely as men. Among them sharp words became deadly bullets, sly innuendo the proverbial stab in the back, while scathing criticism could deal sledge-hammer blows." Judith, with a more normal background, is quick to contradict Jane's insistence that all girls and women are despicable and disloyal: "Oh, no, they aren't. It's just the other way. Ninety percent of them are true blue. It's the other ten percent that make loyal ones appear under false colors. I'm very fond of most of the girls I know. Some day you will feel the same about the girls here" ( *Sub-Team*, 176). Jane doubts it, but she is beginning to look around her and make a few friends, realizing that she herself is at fault and that if she is to make anything out of these years, she must learn to control her own pride, temper, and rebelliousness. Like motherless Leslie Cairns, Jane has had a male role model; she has no sense of a woman's community and sees nothing in it to respect or admire.

What effects the change is basketball. By the time these books were written, sports and athletics were well-established parts of college and high school. The days when women students were on their honor to walk an hour each day were long past; each college had its gymnasium, tennis courts, golf course, and playing fields. Team sports had been harder to accept: basketball, suitably modified for young ladies, was the first, and when it was introduced in schools it brought cries of outrage. It was physically dangerous, it forced women into that immodest garment, the bloomer, and, worst of all, it taught them to compete. A high school series produced by the Stratemeyer Syndicate, *The Girls of Central High* (1914), has as its major theme the coming of sports to girls in a small town, overcoming parental and conventional horror, and incorporating regulations, descriptions, controversy, advocacy, and even competition into its otherwise standard plots. Sports and sportsmanship make healthy, honorable girls who are on the way to becoming fine women, and basketball is described lovingly: "It was a pleasure to watch the lithe, vigorous young girls. They were untrammeled by any foolish fashions, or demands of dress. Their bodily movements were as free as Nature intended them to be. They jumped and ran, and threw, with a confidence that none but the well-trained athlete possesses." [18]

The importance of basketball to Jane Allen is indicated by the titles of the first three books in her series: *Jane Allen of the Sub-Team, Jane Allen, Right Guard,* and *Jane Allen, Center.* When she discovers and falls in love with the game, she teaches herself to play and, put into a game, becomes a star. For the first time her class can admire her; her own attitude softens as she discovers how pleasant it is to be liked and to like others. Unfortunately, after the promise of individual growth and maturity, the series degenerates, repeating over and over the attempts of Jane's enemies to hurt her and her friends, and their noble reactions to evil deeds. They

enact the now-standard business of starting a fund to help students without much money, but the rest of the series is simply one hostile encounter after another. Jane, like Grace and Marjorie, becomes an exemplar
of the college spirit.

The Stratemeyer Syndicate sent one of its popular heroes, Ruth Fielding, to college in the eleventh volume (1917) of her long series.[19] Carol
Billman's informative and readable study, *The Secret of the Stratemeyer Syndicate*, has a chapter called "Ruth Fielding, Orphan Turned Hollywood
Sleuth." Billman sees Ruth and her series as important and revealing,
arguing that "Ruth Fielding deserves to be rediscovered. She is one of
the best representatives of her many contemporary series heroines—
best because of her series' popularity and because of her own position as
a pivotal figure in fiction for American girls." She is an orphan, "a carry-
over from the nineteenth-century sentimental tradition, turned movie
star and sleuth, two new roles for fictional heroines in the 1900s. Further,
Ruth's development over the course of thirty books in a society that presents seemingly infinite possibilites is as fascinating as it is confusing in
its account of the tensions that arise when a smart girl with old-fashioned
values wants to enjoy the new possibilities open to her." Her problems
go beyond the external: "The choices she is allowed to, and must, make
regarding her personal life and her career are not easy ones, no matter
how decisive a character she is cooked up to be or how simply these di-
lemmas are sometimes written off" (59–60).

Billman classes the Ruth Fielding series as adventure stories, and the
volume that begins her college years certainly reinforces that point, without relegating college entirely to background. Ruth has already gained
fame as the "authoress" of a movie scenario when she and her "chum,"
Helen, arrive at Ardmore College. A few students, feeling she may be
conceited, are ready to make her life uncomfortable, but Ruth is calm:
"Now girls, we want to take what is handed us good-naturedly. . . . We are
freshmen. Next year we will be sophomores and can take it out on the
new girls then." She reminds her friends that they have been through
the same thing at boarding school (48).

There are some curious patches of explication, facts that seem thrown
in to establish the authenticity of Ardmore College: tuition costs one
hundred seventy-five dollars a year; room and board nine dollars a week.
Classes are held from nine to three-thirty, after which everyone takes
gymnastics of some kind. Seven to seven-thirty is free time, followed by
two hours of study and bed at ten. In actuality this uniform scheduling,
like the lights out at ten o'clock rule and compulsory chapel, had long
since passed.

Ruth's narrative combines a version of the outsider in need of help
with the problem of snobbery. A student who pretends to wealth has
trouble adjusting and making friends: "I didn't know just what college

was like. I never talked with a girl from college in my life. I thought this was a place where only rich girls were welcome" (136). Ruth tells her that the best of college life is "Friendship. Companionship. The rubbing of one mind against another" (133), but the student cannot believe it. Poor as she is, she refuses to take a job because others will scorn her. Ruth is sympathetic but wiser; she has already noticed that far from being scorned, the "girls who were waitresses, and did other work to help pay for their tuition or for their board were busy and happy and were respected by their mates. In addition, they were often the best students in their classes" (139).

The presentation of college life in these popular and widely read stories is a fairly sensible and pleasant one, balancing friendships, studies, and sports (Ruth and her friends go out for rowing, not basketball). Surprisingly, even with the intrusions of the mystery plot, there is a green world, perhaps because the characters spend so much time outdoors, or perhaps because the community of women, though neither celebrated nor emphasized, retains its separate integrity. Nevertheless, the focus is not on college: Ruth has an adventurous life behind her, so much of her first year is spent solving a mystery, whose theme winds in and out of daily life and, though dependent upon coincidence, is not too far-fetched to be believable. Ruth's difficult choices are not much influenced by her college years, which seem to be simply a normal part of her thirty-volume growth to maturity.

The college series written during the period from the turn of the century to the end of the twenties continued to be reissued, carrying their standards of suitable womanly behavior to a wide female audience. But the world in which that audience lived had changed: women could vote; during World War I they held necessary jobs and some, including many college graduates, went overseas to drive ambulances, nurse, or work with the Red Cross.[20] They had thrown off many restraints, including long hair and long skirts, and would throw off more. They drove cars and flew airplanes, and some planned careers as a matter of course. Newer fiction began to reflect those realities.

Beverly Gray, name character of her popular series (1934) by an author who signs herself Clair Blank, is a child of the thirties. She and her friend Anne, described as "young, intelligent, and actively modern," had wanted a "more modern college, co-ed preferred."[21] They are at Vernon College because their mothers, both alumnae, insisted; at first they are not favorably impressed, but they quickly learn to love the college and forget their desire for a different kind of school.

In the advertising these first four books are called The Beverly Gray College Mystery Series and the subtitle fits, for college life is balanced with Nancy Drew–like adventures that are often less than plausible. But in Beverly's first year most of the emphasis is on life on campus. As in other narratives, the reader meets the protagonist and her friend Anne as they arrive and make their way to the dormitory. There are rules to be learned and young women of all kinds to meet; gradually they make friends, especially with blonde, outgoing Lenora and quiet, artistic Lois, who will establish themselves as the "campus madcaps," and musical Rosalie. Beverly is almost unable to play in the big basketball game, not through machinations of evil enemies, but, far more logically, because her geometry grade is too low. She even breaks a rule or two. The chief conflict of her first year is also plausible: she has a difficult roommate. Shirley is a rich New Yorker sent to college by her socially prominent parents to break up an unsuitable romance. Hostile to everyone, she particularly dislikes her roommate. Beverly eventually prevents her from eloping with the fortune hunter, but it takes a rescue from a burning dormitory to establish friendship.

When the six friends form a "sorority" in their sophomore year, their aim is "anything that is fun." They are kind, but no one expects them to be nurturers, so any poor students who need to be helped through college remain invisible. Beverly's adventures begin in the second volume; as a reporter for the college paper she investigates a haunted house which happens to be the headquarters for international smugglers, though the reader may wonder at their choice of location. She joins forces with a handsome young aviator, Larry, who turns out to be a Secret Service man infiltrating the smugglers and therefore, fortunately, available to teach her to fly and to rescue her as needed. In her junior year Beverly is kidnapped by Gypsies, and as a senior she is elected class president and foils the plot of criminals who are trying to ruin the movie being filmed on the campus.

While the literary quality of these books is not high (they may hold the record for number of clichés per page), the characters, events, and interactions of college life, excepting always the adventure elements, seem far more believable and normal than, for example, the world of Marjorie Dean, whose volumes were still being reissued. Like many of the girls' adventure stories of the time, the events are fairly predictable: if the hero goes ice skating, there will be a hole in the ice; if she flies, the plane will crash; if she takes a winter hike, there will be bears or wolves. Criminals are bunglers, easily overcome, and local police welcome the help of young girls. All the adventures barely dent the composed and confident surface of the heroine; in fact, Beverly shares Nancy Drew's "infallible ability to judge character and reduce crooks to jelly." [22] But in this series there is a healthy balance between these activities and the life of college itself.

Studying, for example, is taken very seriously, and while the stories do not enter the classroom, academics are a fairly constant presence and implicitly the reason for being in college. Students worry about some courses and enjoy others, comment on professors, and are pleased with good grades. Sports are important, though not so crucial as they were in the Marjorie/Grace books. Making friends, adjusting to new situations, respect for differences, learning to live together, becoming prominent through service and ability: all these concepts, once so new and challenging for women, are present as givens, as if the author knew and expected her audience to know that they are all part of college life, which, though still not the usual pattern for the majority of women, was no longer unusual enough to be the center of the story.

It is still, however, significant. Beverly and her friends take for granted their right to be there—they are, after all, second-generation students and have heard their mothers' reminiscences—and know what to expect. Commencement day brings mixed emotions: "With a swelling of pride and sinking of heart the girls had come finally to their goal—the last of many college days" (Sr 234). But Beverly places college within life:

> She had been living in a world of girlish dreams and troubles, but now that was all past. Her girlhood was almost over, and she was going out into the road of life to seek her place. She had to find her work and do it gladly and wholeheartedly . . . she would take with her memories of the girls and the scenes she had known. She would take with her the high ideals, good sportsmanship, clear thinking and the courage that had grown to be a part of her daily life here at Vernon. . . . Now she could devote herself to her ambition until it had been realized. She was going to forge ahead to success and make her parents and friends proud of her. She was determined to play her part in the great scheme of life to the best of her ability. (Sr 237)

The passage underscores a real change in focus and underlying assumptions about women's lives in its complete acceptance of the idea that college prepares a woman for a career. Beverly found her "ambition" early: at first she knew only that she wanted something to give her "freedom. Freedom to travel to China, Bermuda, France, London—I want to see new places, meet new people" (F 71–72). Later she realizes what she wants, so the "second year of their college life meant the beginning of the fulfillment of their careers, if careers they desired. For Beverly it meant a chance to launch herself definitely on the literary sea. She wanted to be a writer, and the next term would see if she was successful in winning a place on the staff of the college newspaper" (F 242–243). Her friends, too, are planning active futures in different directions: Lois wants to paint, Shirley has found her talent for acting, and happy-go-lucky Lenora wants to enter the business world. Rosalie will study music, and Beverly's hometown friend Anne will marry the boy next door.

Beverly is not quite the first series hero to think in terms of a career. Helen Grant's college education was primarily vocational, training for teaching, a job commonplace and acceptable for women. Grace Harlowe (1914) is concerned with finding her work, whatever it might be, and for all its haziness, her desire marks the first indication since *Two College Girls* (1886) of young women trying to discover, through college, what they will do with their developed abilities and how they will use their educations. Grace's work comes to her; she will take charge of the new dormitory and the fund for needy students in the books that continue her adventures. But Beverly, like the characters in *Two College Girls*, never doubts her right to search for and chose her "ambition" and then follow it. Both the men in Beverly's life—Jim, the faithful friend from home, and Larry, the dashing Secret Serviceman-aviator—propose marriage, but she is not ready to think about it. Perhaps the chief difference between this and much of the earlier fiction, aside from the mystery-adventure elements, is precisely this assumption that college is preparing students to be active participants in life and that they no longer need argue their right to the work they want. The attitude is in line with much girls' fiction of the period, for the 1930s brought a spate of "career" books, stories that took a young woman through the steps involved in becoming whatever the topic was: department store buyer, bookkeeper, airline stewardess (in those days a job requiring brains and nurse's training), reporter. Probably the best and best-known of these career stories were the widely read Sue Barton books, which presented well-drawn characters, portrayed nursing as a calling, and certainly benefited from the superior writing ability of the author, Helen Doré Boylston.[23] In the girls' books of this period there are few limits on what women can do if they choose, and that fact is reflected in the Beverly Gray books. College prepares Beverly and her friends not simply by making them practiced in interpersonal relationships and confident of their abilities, but by assuming the right to a career if that is what they want.

There is still a green world at Vernon College; it is separate, beautiful, and a place of growth and change. But there is much traffic in and out of it. Men come and go in the green world; so do Gypsies, thieves, and international criminals. The boundaries are weak—or the once isolated green world has changed from another part of the forest to another part of reality.

Josephine Daskam Bacon, the author of *Smith College Stories* (1900), sent young women to college again in 1934. Her juvenile novel, *The Luck of Lowry*, introduced three girls, and in its sequel, *Kathy*, all three go to Smith.[24] Both books have family mysteries to unravel, and both have a depth provided by the author's interest in young women growing up and by her ability to write well. Differences in personality are strong: Barbara, reared by an uncle, is a bookish, bright, but undisciplined tomboy; Kathy, whose identity was established in the first book, is a hardworking, conscientious, all-around girl; Sally is a frivolous butterfly who goes to college only because she has nothing else to do and some of her friends have told her she will have a good time there. Barbara and Kathy, both academically gifted, chose Smith for its English faculty and its academic reputation.

Smith is as lovely and welcoming as it was for Bacon's young women thirty years earlier, or for Betty Wales and her friends. But differences show how far both college women and the fiction that portrayed them had come since 1900. Active and involved in college affairs though they are, both Kathy and Barbara have commitments outside and goals for the future that temper their emotional attachment to the college and the present. With a nice irony Bacon has Barbara, disgusted with Sally's pregraduation sentimentalizing, say, "She's acting like that book of *Smith College Stories* I used to read, Freshman year. As far as I can see, those girls used to spend Spring term lying around in hammocks, under the apple trees—where'd they get the time?" (260). Of the three only the lightweight, superficial Sally has time for the commencement melancholy of earlier days; Kathy and Barbara are simply too busy and too forward-looking to enjoy romanticized sadness. The emphasis now, at least for Kathy and Barbara, is on college as preparation for the future. The job of the women's community is to enable women to function in the outside world.

All the fiction examined in this chapter was written for a younger audience, and it must have brought them ambivalent messages. Helen Grant carries the nineteenth century into the twentieth. Marjorie and Grace inspire and nurture amid hostile forces and triumph in the end, but community has narrowed to "our crowd" or to proof of a moral statement: young women who act the right way will have a good time and those who do not, will not. The good characters are easily identified; they are honest, have high standards, and for all their increased freedoms, still represent the moral virtues associated with earlier ideals. For them college is a stage on which a feminine morality play acts itself out. Ruth Fielding, Beverly Gray, Kathy and her friends get on with their lives, of which their college years make a pleasant and useful part.

The desire to see a progression here is somewhat complicated because these series books were reissued many times (as were the Betty Wales books, last reissued in 1932, and *Daddy Long-Legs*, still in print), so all the messages from different sources were available at the same time. Within the bounds of this study, however, there is consistency in movement: the green world, so strong and magical in the turn-of-the-century fiction, recedes in importance; it loses its inviolability and its transformational power, becoming interesting background. Illyria, the magic country, has lost, if not its existence, its power. There is still a pleasant and important women's space, but by the 1930s it is simply to be taken for granted.

# · SIX ·

# *Worlds Not So Green*

The passage of time and changes in social attitudes brought about cracks in the walls of the fictional green world communities, as the juvenile series books have shown. By the 1920s and 1930s the few novels about women in college offer visions of a world in which that self-contained, magical women's space either never existed or is so marginalized as to be nearly unattainable. In the novels with coeducational settings, attempts to create a woman's space are distorted by the dominant male ambiance. Those set in the women's colleges, unlike the earlier idyllic fiction and even the still attractive if disintegrating communities of most of the series books, present what can only be described as "exposés" of their institutions.

Higher education for women was common enough by this time so that it could appear not as a center or goal, but as a stage of growth in the developmental novel, fiction that traces a young woman's journey from childhood to maturity.[1] In this kind of fiction emphasis on the time in college varies according to the needs of the narrative; what matters is not the experience itself, but its effect on the hero. Within the boundaries of this study, such novels serve as commentary on those that do focus on the experience.

The reason why, until after World War II, few stories are set in coeducational colleges is probably connected to history and reality. Women began entering Michigan, Cornell, and the other large state and public universities in the early 1870s; supported by taxes, these institutions could not legally exclude the daughter of a taxpayer while admitting the son, but it is fairly clear that they tried. Studies of women's entry into Michigan (1870) and Cornell (1875) show a real contrast between the welcome young women found at the women's colleges and the cold reception given the "coeds."[2]

At Michigan the entering women students, like Will Elliott, lived in boardinghouses, occupied by men and women, and townspeople often stood still to stare as they walked by. Not until 1896 were there dormitories for women, and these resulted from a reactionary desire, shared by many of the now coeducational institutions, to segregate the women they could not get rid of. Wisconsin held separate classes; Stanford had strict quotas; Chicago and others aimed at an "annex" like Harvard's or Brown's. Cornell did not admit a class of women until Sage College, a self-contained, Mount Holyoke-style building, was completed.[3] Then the women's dormitory was compulsory, a "warden" was appointed, and the number of "female beds" became a de facto quota.

Accounts from the early days suggest that the lot of the college woman was less than pleasant. The articulated fears were that women attending classes with men would be coarsened; worse, men attending classes with women might be feminized. Furthermore, the presence of women would make impossible the creation of a true (male-defined) academic atmosphere, like that of Harvard or Yale. Socially their position was even worse; at Cornell, "By unwritten law, the women . . . were definitely out of place. While campus organizations discouraged the participation of women, the fraternities categorically excluded women from social events. Fraternities would not allow their members to speak to women on the campus, to invite them to parties, or to consider giving a Cornell woman a fraternity pin."[4]

In *An American Girl* Anderson at one point stops her narrative for a passage of explanatory direct address to the reader:

> A freshman year in college is full of trials for a boy, but for a girl, who enters an institution where boys have held undoubted sway for generations, every day brings persecutions which he never feels. He enters a field which has been his without dispute from time immemorial, for his father and grandfather were there before him; while for her every step costs a battle; and every innocent action is the subject of unkind criticism. She is presupposed to be loud, masculine, and aggressive, until she proves herself different.   (55)

Why did women go where they were clearly not wanted? One reason was financial; tuition and living costs were low. There were academic reasons as well: the established universities had faculties of important teachers and scholars already in place, while the infant women's colleges had to search for qualified faculty. Vassar had the internationally famous astronomer, Maria Mitchell, but there were few women of her status and achievement anywhere at that time.[5] Many men were reluctant to teach at the women's colleges: some shared the prevailing disapproval; some saw the colleges as experiments that might fail; and undoubtedly some saw the environment as a threat to their manly self-images. Coeducational faculties had no places for women and therefore no female role models, although many of the great names of the women's colleges came from the coeducational institutions: Cornell educated the dynamic M. Carey Thomas, president of Bryn Mawr, while from Michigan came Alice Freeman (Palmer), who became the first woman college president when she headed Wellesley, and Lucy Maynard Salmon, distinguished and widely respected scholar who for years taught at Vassar and influenced its growth.[6] Graduates of the women's colleges who wanted advanced degrees usually went to Europe for them and frequently came back and taught in their own colleges.

The atmosphere at the coeducational colleges was never warm and welcoming for women, and it seems logical that few fictional works could celebrate the experience. And although the women's college stories show a gradual disintegration of community over time, the few set in coeducational institutions do not, simply because there was never a real community to disintegrate. Rather, the coeducational fiction that did appear in the late 1920s shows a flawed and almost pitiful attempt to create an artificial women's community within an overwhelmingly male world. This does not mean that there was no fondness for the institution, or achievements and joys, but where these positive elements occur, they are individual rather than shared. Will Elliott and her friends at Michigan were a small enclave, intruders in a man's world, and the later fiction tacitly suggests that the development of sororities was an attempt to institutionalize or legitimize these enclaves. Protagonists are obsessed with the desire to join a sorority, as if that were the only territory they could legitimately claim. It is understandable, perhaps, that these fictional treatments display a subworld in which all the perceived negative elements of women's character, like backbiting and disloyalty, are dominant. Far from bonding, these young women learn each other's weaknesses to use as weapons.

Other than Will Elliott's account, early coeducational life can be glimpsed briefly in the turn-of-the-century collection of short stories set at Stanford by Charles K. Field and Will H. Irwin.[7] Women are present, though chiefly as decorative objects; they are characters but not protagonists, and the point of view is firmly masculine. Sitting on sorority house verandahs, dressed in floating chiffons, young women admire the exploits of men or wait to be called for. But at least they are included; nothing in the comparable volume set at Cornell indicates that that institution was coeducational at all, for there are no women characters except those who come from other places as dates on big weekends.[8] That their attitude toward women classmates remained in force fifteen years later is indicated by Dorothy Canfield Fisher in her developmental novel, *The Bent Twig*, when she explains a sorority's reluctance to pledge someone with an unconventional background at her midwestern state university. Part of the group's unwillingness comes from fears for their own status, which depends on male acceptance:

> These young men, under the influence of reports of what was done at Cornell and other more eastern co-educational institutions, were already strongly inclined to ignore the co-eds as much as possible. The tradition was growing rapidly that the proper thing was to invite the "town-girls" to the college proms and dances, and to sit beside them in the grandstand at football games.[9]

As a result young women from recognized sororities, while still acceptable, felt their status endangered. In a rather incoherent juvenile series, written around 1930 and set in a coeducational institution, a male character arrives at his university having sworn to show his disapproval of coeducation by never speaking to a female classmate.[10] It should be added that although Cornell seems to figure as the prototypical villain, coeducation as a whole was frequently attacked on the grounds of unfair treatment of women, and the tones range from humorous to bitter.[11]

Commentary on women in coeducational institutions had two main approaches: comparison of their status and educational opportunities measured against the women's colleges, and the question of "secret societies": sororities. Articles about them range from gushing description of the life and the houses to such serious examinations as Edith Rickert's "The Fraternity Idea among College Women," a thorough look at the good and bad of sororities. Rickert searches for balance, but does not find it. Fraternities, she begins, using the term generically, "are admitted to be groups in which like seeks like, and the whole flock aims to induce still greater likeness to the pattern of the group. The girl with a streak of genius cannot easily find her like, so she flocks not at all; the poor, proud girl fears patronage, and will not; the awkward, ill-bred country girl can't; the dig dare not for fear of missing some intellectual good thing. All these must develop more or less as individuals." She sums up by wondering whether the sorority system is not "rather like a crystallization of an immature stage of development."[12]

The view Rickert expresses colors three fictional accounts of life in coeducational colleges that are close in time, if not in approach. The novels are *Co-ed* (1926) by Olive Hormel, a narrative of growth and change; *I Lived This Story* (1930) by Betty White, a bitter, painful account that might be a parody of Hormel's tale; and a four-volume series by Elizabeth Corbett, *The Graper Girls* (1931–1935), a sunny, well-written story of husband hunting at Wisconsin.[13] Different in tone and perspective as they are, and regardless of what the authors think they are saying, all present women as intruders into male space.

White sets her novel at Colossus U., which originally had had chiefly women students, but,

> Gradually the masculine side of the university developed. More boys took the chance of having their manhood suspected, and came to Colossus. The university wisely saw the advantage of this, and offered inducements to athletes and red-blooded men who would prove magnets to other men, red-blooded or otherwise. Last year there had been evidences of a football team. Enough to warrant building a mammoth concrete stadium. Colossus was not going to be tight in her method to get the men. They were coming. Get more at any price. Never mind the girls. There would always be plenty of them. Fine brick fraternity houses were built facing the lake. A beautiful gymnasium and swimming pool. Every possible advantage. (46–47)

By the time Dorinda, the hero, gets there, the college has achieved both large enrollment and a wholly masculine orientation, although women students came in numbers: "The prettiest girls in the country went to Colossus; and if the intelligent ones went to Smith or Vassar—what matter? Beauty has its place, even in a university" (46).

Both White and Hormel have a hero who is perceptive, intelligent, and a seeker after knowledge, but who arrives at college wanting nothing so much as to be chosen by a sorority. She succeeds, and eventually finds it is not the great thing she thought it would be. The sorority makes an enormous, clearly identifiable gulf between insiders and outsiders, a gulf that first shows itself in living conditions. Rushing takes place before the semester begins, and women who are chosen can move into the comfortable sorority houses. The others must live in boardinghouses like the one Dorinda stays in briefly; it is infested with bedbugs.

White's tone and approach are bitter, but her novel has the same elements as the less-harsh versions by Hormel and Corbett. Even the most positive coeducational narrative tacitly admits that sororities as women's spaces are artificial, have false boundaries, and in a sense exist as service areas to the masculine majority. While sororities give women identity and power, these qualities are defined by a male elite and depend on the exclusion and rejection characteristic of oppressed groups who strengthen themselves by diminishing others. Obviously this situation will affect the theme of living together, but as it occurs in this fiction it is hardly a theme and never a positive element: each book, for example, shows the sisters discussing possible pledges, and for lighthearted brutality, these scenes are hard to beat.

The effort the protagonist makes to get into the sorority blinds her for a while to its superficiality. But not long after joining, Dorinda is embarrassed and horrified when their oldest alumna scolds the members who do not seem to appreciate their privilege: " 'Some of you who take it so lightly! You ought to be non-sorority girls for awhile,' she told them fiercely. 'Then you'd appreciate what you have. Watching all the other girls happy together, and you alone and cold on the outside—then you'd see what it means.' " As she goes on to tell what the sorority meant to her, she is moved to tears. "Dorinda looked at the floor. There was something indecent in watching the tears run down lined cheeks. Sixty years old and this woman could weep over her sorority" (85).

Dorinda finds the intellectual stimulus and growth she wants only in a few classes and in the home of her English professor (who despises the college and finally leaves it). Her mentor in the sorority house gives her advice for academic success: "Tact is what counts. . . . You must be tactful to your profs. They're such earnest, unsuspecting folks. Be wide-eyed and subdued and they'll love to fall for it. . . . Just remember the virtues of flattery, dear. If you're skillful you won't need much else" (68). But conning the faculty is not what Dorinda wants: "There were men to teach the marvelous things she wanted to learn, men to appease this burning fever, men to show her beauty—to bring her wisdom" (70).

She does not find these men (women professors do not exist) except in her English courses, and eventually she rebels against the university and especially her sorority and all it stands for: "A houseful of girls— drugged with sleep and complacency. Clothes and pocket money and dirty stories. Why couldn't she be a healthy little moron and enjoy herself with the others?" (205). In protest she smokes in public, drinks, and gets mixed up with unacceptable intellectuals, and she insists on trying to learn. After the first glow fades, she lives out her college years in opposition to the university and its codes. Finally she is all but drummed out of the sorority and leaves the college in disgust before her graduation. The courses that she thought would satisfy her hunger to learn have been worthless: "College, as college, was a failure, of course. But wasn't it almost worth the four years to discover that? After all, one must learn, sometime, that life is not rose petals and pansy beds. College could at least teach one that" (303).

White is writing fiction and aiming at an effect, but Margaret Mead remembered her first year at a midwestern university that sounds rather like Colossus: "a college to which students had come for fraternity life, for football games, and for establishing the kind of rapport with other people that would make them good Rotarians and their wives good members of the garden club." Arriving with what she calls "the snobberies of the east," she was confronted with "the snobbery and cruelty of the sorority system at its worst. . . . This was my first and only experience of discrimination—mild enough in all conscience." She notes that the experiences of discrimination "make the victims ache with bitterness and rage, with compassion for fellow sufferers or with blind determination to escape even on the backs of fellow sufferers."[14] Mead transferred to Barnard after her first year.

Preceding White's novel by a few years is Hormel's *Co-ed* (1926), a far more pleasant and friendly account of coeducation. Nevertheless, it tells the same story; one could read the second novel as a negative revision of the first. Like Dorinda, Lucia is an intelligent, sensitive young woman who finally discovers that she wants more from college than the social and superficial ambiance that first attracts her and, with some effort, finds it. She is trying to mature, to find out who she is and what her strengths are, so there is depth to her experience, and she is ultimately successful when she learns not to accept the college as it first presents itself but to search through all it offers and select what she wants. In some degree Lucia's quest resembles the women's college stories, for there is a green world, although it is not there waiting and welcoming; Lucia must seek it and must herself find and define its boundaries.

John O. Lyons dismisses this novel as "an ecstatic story of big games, big dates, and various academic crises which cause flurries of excitement in the dormitories."[15] While there is superficial truth in the comment, it suggests that he may not have read the whole book, or that he could not fit the exploration of a woman's growth into his thesis. For all its pleasant atmosphere, this is a fairly serious study, not so much of the way young ladies should behave at college as of a bright young woman attempting to find out who she is. The novel merges, rather successfully, going to college and coming to maturity, so that there are distant relationships to *Two College Girls* or *Daddy Long-Legs*. The titles of the five sections, Enchantment, Disillusion, Readjustment, Romance, Realization, signify the stages of Lucia's growth. Since she wanted to go to Vassar, the hero does not plunge delightedly into a new world or a joyous new experience; after the first dazzling months, she is clear-eyed and unenchanted about what she finds, and gradually grows selective enough to make choices beyond the conventional and superficial. As she matures and grows strong in herself, Lucia becomes interested in her studies and finds friends and satisfactions outside the sorority, which was her identity base at first.

The Graper Girls books, aimed at older girls rather than adults, tell the story of three sisters and their pleasant family in a midwestern town, first in high school, and then at "the U"—the University of Wisconsin. These are well-written books; their author, Elizabeth Corbett, was already an established novelist. Her technique is to allow each sister to be the narrative voice of a chapter, advancing her own story and commenting on her sisters, so that the picture is created from three different perspectives. That her characters lead fairly superficial lives is hardly noticeable at first, perhaps because she has simplified life for a younger audience.

The college community depicted in this series has the kind of shiny surface that dazzles the hero of Anzia Yezierska's developmental novel, *Bread Givers* (1925). When Sara escapes from her New York tenement to a college town, she sees a world of beauty peopled by magnificent beings with "the settled look of those who belong to the world in which they were born." [16] This daughter of immigrants has fought her way out of the ghetto to an education, and looking at her classmates she is aware of "their difference from me, their youth, their shiny freshness, their care-freeness, they pulled me out of my senses to them. And they didn't even know I was there."

Her description fits the Graper sisters, who go to college because, in the world in which they were born, that is what one does after high school. The oldest, Marian, is ravishingly pretty and very stupid; barely able to finish high school, she enters college conditioned in several subjects, is immediately chosen by a sorority, and enters at once into a world of clothes and dates. She learns to study just enough to pass because she wants to stay where she is having such a good time. Her younger sisters, Ernestine and Beth, both very bright, follow her to the school and into the sorority; again, it is the thing to do.

The focus in these books is on life within this women's community, a place where, although the tone is cheerful and pleasant, all the charges that women cannot get along together seem to be both justified and taken for granted. It is a given that they will attack each other; Beth comments, without heat or dismay, about one of her friends, "I should have known better than to tell Clara anything. Her principal amusement was doing an Indian war-dance on other people's weak points." [17]

The three sisters are strongly differentiated, and each achieves her own kind of prominence, but clearly the popular Marian is the star, and intellectual Ernestine and tennis-playing Beth are acceptable because they too are popular with men. There is neither attack nor disapproval in Corbett's presentation of college life. These are nice young women, and this is the way nice young women are expected to behave. A certain amount of involvement with the town and with family dilutes the effect of the campus and sorority life, and in several cases characters with problems are straightened out, but none of the sisters is a Grace Harlowe-type crusader upholding the standards of the college; their whole emphasis is on having a good time.

For the most part sorority women become prominent through their ability to attract men rather than by developing individual and varied talents. Their worth is based on that ability; they must be pretty, well dressed, and socially adept. Predictably, in this atmosphere there is no celebration of intellectual ability or talent, nor is the emphasis on growth and maturity. Ernestine Graper writes well; she and a few of her friends become prominent by taking part in college activities, but these activities are given little emphasis, for the story is concerned with the social elements and the often malicious interaction among girls. When Ernestine makes Phi Beta Kappa, her reaction is chiefly embarrassment: "I was already thinking that I'd have to spend my Senior year living down Phi Beta Kappa. Nobody knows how good your marks are, though they may tease you by saying, 'I suppose you get Ex in everything.' But once you're labeled 'Shark' for everyone to see, it makes you self-conscious." [18]

In all three representations life within the small enclosed group is narrow and constrained. Brought together by looks, money, and connections, the young women have no basis for bonding other than loyalty to their sorority. Far from celebrating differences, members are encouraged to conform to an image, and are in trouble if they will not or cannot. Transgression against the codes is unforgivable, even though the codes themselves are superficial and unexamined. Though the students form individual friendships, there is no celebration of community and no shared attitudes and goals. While the women's colleges, according to the early fiction, encouraged young women to stretch themselves, the coeds were encouraged to display themselves most attractively to the community of men surrounding them.

Both White and Hormel create a character who is rejected by the sororities, and later achieves prominence through her work on the college newspaper; each author handles the situation in her own way. White's outsider, Sally, is cynical, intense and has fought her way to her position. Dorinda, contemptuous and superior at first, comes to value Sally as her own dislike for the college and the sorority ambiance grows. Theirs is not a strong friendship, however, for Sally is chiefly focused on her studies and her future career in journalism, and like Dorinda's English professor and James, the brilliant engineer she will eventually marry, Sally is scornful of the "collegiate." When she achieves prominence as the first woman editor of the paper, the sorority she did not make "almost considered pledging her till Sally curtly refused their generous invitation to tea" (187).

Hormel handles her similar situation without anger. Lucia and Eva had stayed in the same boardinghouse, made friends, and gone through rushing together. The night the sorority bids are made, Lucia was overjoyed to be chosen, but "as she passed Eva Marshall's door she was suddenly frozen by the sound of muffled sobs—slow wrenching sobs that it troubled one's soul to hear" (53). Three years later, Eva (like Sally, a journalism major) has become the most prominent woman on campus, and the sorority that once rejected her now wants her. There is no bitterness in her refusal: "I don't mind telling you that it's what I wanted more than anything on earth three years ago . . . But to tell you the truth . . . it's an anti-climax now . . . I honestly couldn't think of it." Lucia returns to explode to her "sisters": "Ye gods, Bea!—I'd like to shake the cock-

eyed Gamma chapter that passed up Eva Marshall when we were frosh—
and shake it till its cock-eyed teeth rattle! How did you ever happen to
pull such a boner?" Bea lamely points out that "rushing is an awful
gamble" (302–303).

In *The Bent Twig* Fisher begins her chapter on her hero's college life
with this statement:

> To anyone who is familiar with State University life, the color of
> Sylvia's Freshman year will be vividly conveyed by the simple state-
> ment that she was not invited to join a fraternity. To anyone who
> does not know State University life, no description can convey any-
> thing approaching an adequate notion of the terribly determinative
> significance of that fact.   (145)

Sylvia Marshall is an attractive young woman, an obvious choice for a
sorority, but she is rejected by the most prestigious ones because her cultured, intelligent family leads what seems to the conventional a Bohemian life. The important sororities have made up their minds in advance
about Sylvia; she is painfully snubbed by all of them, so that she is "stung
into a speechless rage by her impotence to do anything to regain the
decent minimum of personal dignity which she felt was stripped from
her" (150) by both the decision and the publicity surrounding it.

By contrast, in Bess Streeter Aldrich's novel, *A White Bird Flying*, the
sorority the hero joins at the University of Nebraska has almost no effect.
The author uses the situation chiefly to characterize Laura's loving but
manipulative mother, who wants the prestige of the best sorority for her
daughter. Aldrich's novel concerns the awakening of this granddaughter
of Nebraska settlers to the meaning of her own country and roots; although her college years occupy a large part of the novel, they are mixed
up with family, the land, and a growing romance. The sorority provides
a pleasant place to live and Laura makes a few close friends there; otherwise it is treated in the novel as tolerantly as one treats something that
does not much matter. Laura did feel, at the beginning, that joining a
sorority was vital, but the feeling passed:

> Yes, Laura went Alpha Beta. But some did not. One girl was not
> taken on account of her freckles, one had been tabulated a crock
> the moment she stepped inside the door, and another had made
> the fatal error of eating a bite or two of the garnishing on her salad.
> In the four years of their schooling, Laura saw the tan spots miracu-
> lously fade into the background of a pink and white complexion,
> the crock become the May Queen, and the lotus eater—no, lettuce
> eater—earn the Phi Beta Kappa key. But it's a wise sorority that
> knows its own child, and no fraternity can read all there is in the
> stars and the crystal ball in one mad week of rushing.[19]

Except in Aldrich's novel, the fiction presents a world in which competition, however vicious, is perfectly acceptable. That is, of course, competition for men—for approval and admiration in the tangible form of dates and admirers. Women can be as ruthless in achieving these goals as they choose; the fiction in varying degrees approves any behavior that finds the right man and "catches" him. In a juvenile developmental novel called *Caroline at College*, the hero attends Berkeley where, after some doubts about elitism, she joins a sorority. She is bright, charming, and popular, and on the whole her sorority experience is good. Nevertheless, Caroline's only crisis occurs when she is falsely accused of cheating; the arranger of the trumped-up charge is a sorority sister who thinks Caroline is trying to steal her boyfriend.[20] No one approves of the false accusation, of course, but there is tolerance for the motivation.

In a 1927 *Harper's* article that attacks the women's colleges on the grounds that they create "unnatural" conditions for young women, Edna Yost condemns in passing the large state universities, which offer a woman student "an environment in which she is not wanted, in which she is disgracefully treated and inadequately cared for." She recommends "one of a small number of coeducational colleges . . . whose standards are high and whose atmosphere is one of cordial fellowship between students of the two sexes"; Swarthmore is one example she gives.[21]

Her thesis is borne out, not in the college fiction, but in Gladys Hasty Carroll's autobiography, *To Remember Forever* (1963); subtitled *The Journal of a College Girl, 1922–23*, it looks back on her years at Bates.[22] To some extent her account is fictionalized autobiography, since she selects rather than records, and it makes a useful comment on the coeducational fictions. Bates was small, academically oriented, and without sororities. As Carroll, herself bright and with a future as a highly acclaimed novelist ahead of her, tells her story, learning was prized, and women made friends and were active without needing to conform to an image. There were still limits: she became an associate editor of the newspaper, and it seems clear that the editor was always male. But the portrayal is one of individual growth and pleasant, normal male-female friendships, with dating as part of these comfortable relationships. Smallness is partly responsible, and location may be as well, since the majority of the students came from Maine or New Hampshire and understood and shared similar backgrounds.[23] Like the women's college students of the early fiction, the young Gladys feels joy in being there and regards her college with respect and love.

Something very similar happens when L. M. Montgomery's Anne Shirley leaves Green Gables for college in *Anne of the Island*.[24] Redmond is a good, small liberal arts college where everyone can know everyone else; there are no sororities, and learning, at least for Anne and her friends, is respected. The small-town formality of the time separates men and women students in their living arrangements, but otherwise they interact in the same friendly manner. There are college activities and loyalties, but for students like Anne and the friends she has chosen, these are simply pleasant adjuncts to the purpose of learning. Since all the Anne books together certainly constitute the equivalent of a developmental novel, the hero's character has already been established, but her college years continue her growth to maturity. College is an extension of the learning she loves and the means of gaining the academic credentials she needs to earn her living. Carroll in reality and Anne in fiction find community and self-expansion in the academic and social space their colleges provide.

Generally in the coeducational fiction, however, academic goals and values women may have are simply not important. Dorinda has to fight to learn, and is eventually defeated. In Helen Hull's *Quest* (1922) another kind of obstacle appears. This developmental novel so strongly emphasizes family, friends, and community that though Jean's college years are important to her, they are presented only in occasional scenes. She is intelligent and loves learning. She commutes to a nearby university, and when she registers, the dean suggests the "course for women, leading to a certificate in domestic science and art." Jean wants to teach "Latin or English or anything with thinking in it," but the dean flatly repeats that domestic science is "peculiarly fitted to women." Finally Jean has to insist, in order to avoid being placed in a niche labeled "women," and she thereby earns official disapproval.[25] The refusal to take women, and especially any academic goals they might have, seriously and with respect seems characteristic of the few fictional accounts of women attending coeducational colleges.

When Will Elliott went to Michigan, she and her friends claimed a small and undefined space within alien territory, a space filled with idealism, courage, learning, and the search for identity and growth. Only traces of those attitudes remain, and what is left for the later books may indeed represent a sad attempt to hold on to a women's space. Tones differ, but the authors who focus on sororities present them without redeeming virtues other than their providing more comfortable and pleasant places to live than the boardinghouses which are the nonsorority woman's fate. Otherwise the fictional sorority is a distortion of women's space as a place of power: in a masculine world, the only power women have comes through winning the approval of the dominant group and then by extension to exclude, to strengthen themselves by weakening others. These enclaves of women reject compassion and empathy if either quality threatens what they have been forced to see as their territory.

In a 1931 novel set at a woman's college, there is a scene in which one character explains why she chose to go there. While they are dancing her escort asks, "Why did you go to a woman's college? I can't somehow visualize you here; you're too distinctly feminine." Betty answers that she wanted an education and rejected coeducational schools because "I wanted the real thing, not the concentrated essence of a small town: sororities, frat dances, dates every night. No, thanks. But that doesn't mean I don't enjoy a date when I get one." [26]

She and other characters who seek the uncluttered education and the movement toward maturity portrayed in the early fiction will not find either in the women's college novels of the late 1920s and early 1930s. If the coeducational novels present a world in which women find success only through social graces and male admiration, narratives of the women's colleges published around 1930 present an even worse picture—one which inverts all the strengths portrayed in earlier fiction and turns them into agents of destruction.

Martha Gellhorn published her first novel, *What Mad Pursuit?*, in 1934. Only the first two chapters of this developmental novel are set at Marlborough College, where its hero, Charis, is a student. Charis is socially aware and capable of "impersonal angers" over issues. When another student misses a train after a dance and stays in her escort's room overnight, she is expelled, even though the situation was totally innocent. The dean thinks it is sad to expel her, but "she knew what her own Board of Trustees was like and Sue Fethergill was forthwith expelled from the College of Marlborough, on the grounds of indecent and immoral behavior, unfitting to a lady and to an undergraduate." Charis hardly knows and does not particularly like Sue, but is outraged at hearing that she was never allowed to speak in her own behalf; indignant, Charis threatens to leave, as a matter of principle and to make a statement. But no one listens to her statement; the dean feels mild regret at losing her, "but being a Dean, she knew that one is helpless against the young, especially if they have a motto." [27]

The impersonality of administration and the importance of the institutional image over individual need displayed briefly in Gellhorn's opening chapters are major accusations made by two contemporary novels, Kathleen Millay's *Against the Wall* (1929) and Mary Lapsley's *The Parable of the Virgins* (1931), in which the women's colleges, once havens of delight, are the targets for negative exposure.[28] Even Betty White's unfavorable portrayal of coeducation is mild indeed compared to the vicious attack these novels make on the women's colleges.

Millay's *Against the Wall* is told in a feverish, staccato interior monologue clearly designed to jolt the reader, as it does, though perhaps not in the way intended. Rebecca, a small-town girl who works part time in a butcher's shop and seems to have no future other than marriage to the son of the shop's owner, wins a scholarship to Matthew College, a prestigious woman's college that declares itself to be democratic. Intellectually gifted, well read, sensitive, she is in love with learning and longs for new and wider chances. When the opportunity is offered her, she knows it will change her life. On campus, however, she learns at once to hide the fact of her scholarship; she would not be treated badly, just differently from those whose names were down for entry years in advance. The students, says the author, knew how to act properly toward those less fortunate; such behavior had become an easily learned pattern, a noblesse oblige, which signified a kind of political correctness rather than equality or inclusion.

The falseness of "democracy" is only the beginning. The college is a prison; administrators are smooth, cold warders; the faculty is tired and uninspired. Thrilled at the beginning to think of herself as a "Matthew Girl," Rebecca discovers that the term means a mindless conformist, "just a well-bred, well-meaning, well-educated imbecile like all the other girls at Matthew" (417). Perceiving the artificiality of the image, Rebecca refuses to let it shape her. At one point she accuses an administrator: "You have to want all kinds of girls because you must be democratic. And then you make it impossible for them to stay. You kill them. It's a nice distinction" (220).

The early fiction had celebrated difference and insisted that the college had something to offer every young woman. By this time, however, popular wisdom, and perhaps the colleges themselves, had made "*the* college girl" image even more specific. A 1920 feature in a popular magazine defines each:

> Smith College turns out the doer; Wellesley, the student; Vassar, the adventurer; Bryn Mawr, the social philosopher; Mount Holyoke, the conservative. . . . There is a standard joke to the effect that "If you give a piece of work to graduates of the women's colleges, the Vassar girl will sit down and talk about it, the Bryn Mawr girl will philosophize over it, Mount Holyoke will pray over it, Wellesley will go down to the library and read all about it, and Smith will go out and do it . . ."[29]

Like the earlier insistence on *the* college girl, this is another attempt to label, define, and therefore limit and control, and suggests both that the idea of educated women was still troublesome and that these college women were still targets for opportunistic journalism. Millay's and Lapsley's novels reinforce their colleges' insistence on the importance of image and conformity.

Other than the fine library, Matthew College has literally nothing for a bright girl who wants to stretch her brain. When she offends one teacher by "bringing too much outside information to class" (325), the intellectually curious Rebecca discovers that the way to get good grades is to give back what the teachers have said. When she stays at the college over a vacation to catch up on work missed through illness and to read in the magnificent library that for her is now the center and meaning of the college, a faculty member who meets her coming happily away with an armload of books is shocked to find that many of them are not on any required reading list. Edna Howe in *Two College Girls* could learn facts and her professors taught her how to think with them; here learning is held within tight bonds. Facts are acceptable, but thinking is dangerous.

Friendships are watched closely lest they become "perverse," and most of the students are nervous and tense, or silly and "collegiate." All suffer from sexual ignorance; Rebecca, with a less-sheltered background, has to explain what homosexuality means when classmates are bewildered by the administrative attitude to their friendships. Knowledge of all kinds is kept within rigid limits.

Only the physical campus is familiar to readers of the earlier books, but Millay detaches the green world and uses its beauty and natural life as contrast to the stultifying, unnatural world of college itself. Rebecca can escape momentarily into natural beauty: "What was more important than wild flowers in the springtime—what *could* be more important?" (296). Now the physical campus seems remote from the enclosed space that had once nurtured eager young women.

Rebecca's college career and her attempts to learn, think, and question produce a series of confrontations, for as a perceptive and intelligent young woman she is in constant opposition to the image-driven administration. Within months the place has become hateful: "The deadly monotony of classes and study—study and classes—chapel, classes and study. . . . And Rebecca studied all night long. Night after night—night after night—and wondered how many ages she could stand it. Machines they were—worn out and unalive" (285). The education she longed for has become a bitter joke. She achieves her own kind of prominence in an inversion of the old standards; she is stunned when she is told that she is "one of the most famous girls in college! Everybody's talking about you!" Further explanation reveals the reason: "Everybody knows you're the only one that's lasted over a year and isn't collegiate." The speaker is distressed because she finds herself beginning to conform, and Rebecca is horrified: "It was only a place for girls whose wealthy parents wanted a diploma to exhibit to the world. . . . It was no place for a student, that was sure" (411–412).

Causes for unhappiness range from the forced reading of "a lot of old New England mossbacks—like—oh, well, whoever they are—The Rise of Silas Lapham and that stuff—and The Wreck of the Hesperus . . ." (207–208) to the lack of intellectual freedom and the insistence on preservation of the Matthew Girl image. Finally Rebecca decides she must leave before the college destroys her, as she perceives it has destroyed so many others. Her physics professor, one of the few interested in students, tells her "It's no place for you. You may do us a lot of good, but I doubt if you get much out of it" (349).

More interesting, though hardly more positive, is Mary Lapsley's novel, *The Parable of the Virgins.* Its focus on several young women, each with a separate story, whose lives touch each other at Walton College, allows for shifting and often contradictory points of view, so that the overall effect is meant to be kaleidoscopic, but is more often confusing; the reader can easily lose track of just whose interior monologue she is reading. These characters are certainly not the Betty Wales crowd, who find each other compatible and create their own small subcommunity within a larger friendly space; the narrative asserts a solopsistic universe within which these unconnected young women grow from innocence to cynicism and disillusion.

The novel has elements of reality: dramatic Crosby O'Connor, the published poet, is supposedly based on Edna St. Vincent Millay. She smokes, drinks, and sleeps around, her actions driven by her need to defy the college's rigid moral views and regulations; part of the pleasure her sexual activity brings is the knowledge that she is offending the image of the Walton Girl. The administration, symbolized by the weak, petty, fussy president, whose whole being is dedicated to preserving the conventional image, hates her, but her fame makes her a public relations asset and expelling her would bring bad publicity.

The president's policies are not so much his own as a reflection of society's definition of an "educated woman" with whom it can be comfortable. This college, too, is a kind of prison, with lesser administrators as warders. The faculty is a mix; their star is Dr. Clive Austin (modeled on Vassar's internationally known scholar, Lucy Maynard Salmon), one of the few sane, intelligent characters, who sees what the college is doing to the students and intervenes when she can. The president would like to get rid of her, a point possibly based on fact: Dr. Taylor, the champion of the "well-rounded girls," did not like Salmon.[30] There is a scientist, a dedicated teacher who provides a sterile, clinical haven for a few students who glorify facts. But in contrast are faculty members such as Miss Allison, an incompetent, uncaring English instructor, whose careless grading of exam papers and refusal to admit she has made a mistake cause one talented potential writer (who in earlier fictions would have won admiration for her ability) to leave, and who justifies her role as teacher by being the confidant of the priggish, complacent head of student government. The latter is typical of student leaders, all hearty, shallow souls who conform to the administration's vision.

Free thought is discouraged because it is frightening. After Lee, a bright young woman with an inquiring mind, discusses religion with a less-intelligent acquaintance, she is called in to the head matron, who reproves her and states, "Religion, Lee, is a thing which had best not be discussed in college." To Lee's shocked response: "Where can one discuss it then? I thought college was where one had 'freedom to investigate many beliefs.' President Madison said so at Convocation," the matron calls her impertinent and dismisses her.

Both Lee and the editor of the paper, Helen, are helpless when the president censors Lee's article on college economics and the outrageously low wages of college servants. Both young women were already in trouble because Lee had investigated the reasons for students' choice of Walton College and found an unacceptable answer: they came to Walton because their parents forced them—a point made and emphasized by both Millay and Lapsley. The desire of both young women for truth wavers and collapses under the threat of expulsion.

As at Matthew College, young women suffer from virginity, or perhaps lack of clear sexual knowledge. This administration too is fanatically obsessed with potential lesbianism, and when an "extreme" friendship occurs, the matron, and most particularly the doctor, a woman, step in with such expressions of disgust and such heavy hints of abnormality that they hound one student into suicide.

Many of the minor players are presented unattractively. Nasty Jane lives by toadying to the rich. Mae, disturbed by ideas, wants "social prestige plus education; she hoped that college wasn't going to be like this, and she was reassured by a hundred tales like *Daddy Long-Legs* and the Patty books" (21). Phi Beta Kappas are narrow, smug memorizers of facts, and student government leaders are mindlessly complacent conformists.

Though there is no main character in the novel, Crosby the poet is a kind of central point; the lives of the others swirl around her. In the context she is a tragic figure. The perceptive outsider, Sophie, says that Crosby is being hardened: "defiance takes from her reverie, philosophic thought, spontaneous sympathy" (334). And Helen, a friend since their first year, "remembered the poet's early gaity, sweet and light. . . . And Crosby's gift of poetry. Would they wish to make her conform even at the risk of taking that power from her?" (353). Young women who bring originality and difference are not prized but seen as disruptive because they refuse to be molded into the pattern. When one student tries to straighten out a misunderstanding about another, her explanation is called insubordination and she is told that Walton decisions are always just: "The justice of the steam roller, levelling all, stamping everyone who submitted with the inevitable flatness of acquiescence. Let anyone be different: a day-dreamer or rebel; and the steam roller was put into motion. How estimate the whole from the broken fragments?" (212).

The seniors who know the way the college operates and have long since decided they will stay and get their degrees, whatever it costs them, share an enormous cynicism. And the younger students learn, painfully. When first-year Hilda, totally and naïvely honest, forces a classmate to report herself for cheating because the handbook tells her that is the right thing to do, she finds that no one wants to know. The student government representative shrugs it off, and the violator of the honor code has no idea what cheating is.

Lapsley introduces an outside observer who is indeed an outsider: Sophie, a Russian Jew, older, sophisticated, and intellectual, completely uninterested in clothes and appearance, transferred from the Sorbonne to complete her education at Walton so that she could work with Clive Austin (the students are astonished to learn that Austin has an international reputation). A few find her interesting, but most students regard Sophie as so far from the norm that she could never be one of them, unaware that she would never want to be. She wanders in and out of situations: "I watch. I observe. Already I see society in miniature, its pettiness, perhaps its tragedy, always its comedy" (54). Her reflections are, in a sense, authorial comment. She is appalled at the young women she meets because they are "without knowledge or curiosity. 'It isn't that they know nothing,' she told herself once, 'but that they desire to know nothing. It is that that makes them so—so like sawdust' " (111).

Because of her sophistication and knowledge, Sophie has power, and toward the end of the novel, when the president is going to expel her for working with strikers, she defeats him because she knows his weak spots. She calmly tells him that if he expels her, she will "make Walton's name the talk of the newspapers" (356). Since his fear of publicity is far stronger than any principles he may have, he gives in. That night he is sleepless after his defeat, and as he lies awake, tries to justify himself, deciding he has done his "duty according to his lights":

> Twenty-five years he had been president of that college. When he began they were still humble, eager to learn, thankful for the opportunity. He had watched the college grow in wealth, in importance, in social importance. He had been largely responsible for that growth, had pulled wires and got things for Walton. He wasn't a young man now. And they were always young. They were arrogant now, sure of themselves. They demanded things that ten years ago they would never have thought of. They were always talking about student rights nowadays. . . . As if the students had any real rights. He believed in paternal care, protection.

While he tosses sleeplessly and counts his own successes, he cannot free himself from the echo of Sophie's words: "I can never relinquish to expediency my conscience; you must not, President Madison, ask me that" (358).

Although this novel contains a character hounded into suicide and extremes of uncompassionate, rigid behavior, it is slightly less hopeless than Millay's. Some students will resist, will put to one side the despicable administration and the Matthew Girl image to get the education they want; some friendships will survive. But both Lapsley and Millay present a college world that has changed drastically in twenty to thirty years from the richly productive one celebrated earlier.

One of the Bryn Mawr stories talks of "all the joyous innocent froth of amusement that danced over the current of the real, serious life of the college."[31] There is no trace of either innocent froth or serious life in the two exposés; all the positives have turned negative and the green world has become a kind of Rappacini's garden, poisonous to the touch. Friendships and the art of living together are suspect. Prominence is won by prigs who can get along with administration. There is none of the rich and rewarding loyalty that informed the collections, nor any sense of the need to return something to the college that was giving so much.

Learning has been channeled into getting a degree, another major accusation in these two novels, as it is for Dorinda at Colossus U. Like Helen Dawes Brown's young women, Rebecca, Dorinda, and others have come to college for an education; unlike Brown's characters, they will have to fight the college to get it. Critical thinkers, explorers of ideas, and anyone who wants to go beyond a conventional body of knowledge, represented by the "New England mossbacks," have a hard time finding what they want. Two of them give up the struggle.

Vassar is the target of both these fictional attacks, as the name Matthew College in one case and the thinly disguised Edna St. Vincent Millay and Lucy Maynard Salmon characters in the other indicate; both authors went to Vassar, graduating around 1920. Whether the failures they portray were unique to their institution or whether all the women's colleges had grown the same way, as generalized commentary about them suggests, is impossible to determine from the fiction. Probably readers interpreted the novels as typical of all women's colleges, and certainly critics and reviewers did.

It is, of course, difficult to separate reality and fiction. Four of the novels discussed here were reviewed as serious works, and all the reviewers, whatever their judgments of literary value, treated the content as realistic. The *New York Times* thought *Co-ed* a "pretty good" college novel, while the *Boston Transcript*, with eastern superiority, declared that "in its way this story of the mid-Western state university is as important an addition to the story of the Middle West as was 'Main Street,'" though the reviewer does admit it is not so well written.[32] Critics were less friendly to *I Lived This Story*; one found in it "a pleasant manner, lively incident," a judgment that seems, at the very least, questionable, and the *Times*, after calling the prize-winning novel "the autobiography of thousands of co-eds," noted that White "may have sacrificed something in the way of popularity by her disavowal of the traditional color of college life, but her book may be earnestly recommended to anyone anxious to know what a girl's adventures at a co-educational university are really like." [33]

Except for the *Times*, which saw *Against the Wall* as a "bitter and thorough indictment of the women's colleges" but found it "remarkably skillful" with "racy and exciting" prose, most of Millay's reviews are negative. *Outlook* comments that "the times are out of joint in the women's colleges. But Miss Millay was not born to set them right," and E. W. H. in the *New Republic* called it a "bad novel—tasteless, flamboyant, dull" but noted that it could not be ignored because it was "being ballyhooed as a true and scathing indictment of the women's colleges . . ." [34] Lapsley fares somewhat better, though there is no enthusiasm either way in the reviews; the *Times* found her novel "readable, intelligent, informative. It gives one a quite accurate and well-rounded picture of life in an up to date woman's college." [35] The reviewers accepted all the novels as true, almost reportorial, accounts, inside looks at women going to college. None finds much significance in the fact that three of the novels portray the experience as negative and painful, while the one positive account rejects the standard college trimmings.

Although the validity of the comparison may be questionable, since the authors had different intentions and wrote for different audiences, Josephine Daskam Bacon's presentation of Smith in her juvenile novel *Kathy* (1934) differs from both her earlier version of her college and the contemporary exposés. Her Smith of the 1930s is a bigger, less-personal college with young women as busy off campus as on, but her characters are happy, productive, and moving toward maturity, and they are getting the fine education that was the tradition of the women's colleges. Millay and Lapsley show a dysfunctional environment and insist that even learning was confined to narrow channels that did not permit critical thinking or exploration of ideas.

In both these non-idyllic novels the separate women's world is no longer a place to stretch the self, but a restricted space controlled by partisans of a superimposed image of womanly women, with success defined by the ability to conform. The focus has moved from experience to product: the image. The ideals of the Matthew Girl and the Walton Girl, dominating behavior and crystallized as a desired standard, completely reverse earlier dreams and ideals of students and faculty. Constant in the earlier fictions was dislike of "*the* college girl" image; those fictions promoted desire for individuality, the celebration of difference shared by Brown, Bacon, and their contemporaries, and Betty Wales's articulated discovery that the way to happiness was to find one's individual talent and use it. The 1898 article by Alice K. Fallows in *Scribner's* firmly rejected "a brand of girl, put through the mill and turned loose upon the world, stamped and labelled 'Smith' " and declared that "any honest attempt to cultivate one talent or ten meets with encouragement. . . . The college which can comprehend the manifold interests of Smith students must be tolerant and broad of mind, and the bond which unites these different elements elastic." [36] Even more telling is the Vassar story of Lucretia (1900), with her tremendous gratitude for her college: "Its great gift was respect for herself, the assurance that she had a right to her own individuality, though it differed from that of every other human being." [37]

Thirty years later, however, the labels for each college's product seem to suggest that those shaping the images have won the battle. More even than sexual ignorance, it is this pattern of cloning that the two later writers are attacking. All the adventure and uniqueness and sense of purpose that characterized the early fiction have disappeared, and both authors present the college experience as hostile and unnatural. The women's communities, once special and rewarding, are now perverse and threatening. Though conformity to an image that would please the outside world was the goal, the colleges themselves seem to have little awareness of the changes in women's lives off their campuses. They are trying to hold back the tide, and the students caught between college and the world must suffer while the colleges do their best to negate the advances women had made.

In the earlier fiction, students moved from a narrow world into a magical and widening one, but Rebecca and her contemporaries are modern young women who move from freedom into confinement and restriction in a college that has institutionalized itself into rigidity and cares more about its image than its students, an institution that instead of being in the vanguard is now dragging its feet. The world had changed for women, but the colleges attempted to keep the vision and standards of the past. Time had, at least in the eyes of these writers, passed the women's colleges by, and they remained frozen in attitudes and procedures that had nothing to do with reality.

Different though the problems are for characters at the coeducational institutions and the women's colleges, there are parallels. In one case the green world as symbol for positive women's community does not exist, or the enclave that Will Elliott and her friends tried to create has been completely reshaped by masculine values; in the other, the magical world that offered so much has been undermined or badly distorted by the desire for a publicly acceptable image. Both have lost the urgent demand for women to develop their individual talents and needs, and both insist that women conform to an imposed image.

The earlier fiction was informed by love, loyalty, and desire to give something back to the beloved college. In the later works, only the cheerful, pleasant, shallow Graper sisters have "college spirit," and that is chiefly enthusiasm displayed at football games. The characters created by Millay and Lapsley, as well as White in her presentation of Colossus

U., show no such feelings and perhaps the reason is that their colleges do not give them very much. Clearly by this time "womanly" behavior is no longer definable; it has been subsumed into the college image and there are no other guidelines or role models. Logically, given the aims of the writers, the happy characters are unpleasant, and the focus is on troubled, dissatisfied young women who want something the college refuses to give them. The magical green world communities of women, once so rich and rewarding in their encouragement of students to discover and value themselves, no longer exist; they have become processors of raw material into something that may or may not have any relationship to individual needs and talents, but fits within socially acceptable boundaries.

# · SEVEN ·

# *Men and Other Loves*

In the arrangement and activity of these fictionalized women's spaces, where are men? The fictions that glorify the college experience present men in their authoritative roles as administrators or professors, but either exclude men as signifiers of romance, love, and marriage, or minimize their importance, making them occasional figures in a feminine landscape. Fiction that portrays the college years as part of a larger life may have strong male characters, since typically in the woman's developmental novel marriage brings closure, but in most of the women's college stories, men and consciousness of what they represent do not belong. As the outside world changed and the separate green world lost its integrity, however, men become more important in the women's college fiction and seem almost symbols, if not agents, of the green world's disintegration. Where the gender boundaries remain, affection is channeled into friendships, crushes, and in later works lesbian relationships. In the coeducational schools, men and masculine values control the women's spaces.

The young women in these stories are of marriageable age, in a culture that emphatically saw marriage as the only suitable goal for women. The earliest stories say little about men, romance, love, and marriage, although these vital elements of real life are acknowledged to exist and to matter. Especially in the fiction written at the turn of the century, men in their roles as suitors and potential husbands are present on the periphery, but they have no real place in the values of the colleges and remain outside the green world. When they appear, it is as visitors rather than those entering their rightful space.

The importance of men is downplayed in all the early fictions with the exception of Goodloe's *College Girls* (1895), where so many tales can be classed as love stories with a college background. More, Goodloe implies the unreality of the college world, presenting it as a diversion from life. In one story, "As Told by Her," a visiting minister tells the young women in his audience that "until woman rediscovers that life is everything, that all she can learn here in a hundred times the four years of her college course is the least part of what life and nature can teach her, until then I shall not be satisfied with the modern education of women" (77). His tactless words are smoothed over, but the story, which contrasts the woman who has "lived" with the professor who has had only a life of the mind, makes his point for him: the real world is outside and life is separate from learning. Men, in fact, become the symbols of reality.

Goodloe's Eva Hungerford, who appears in three stories, thinks of herself as a scholar and writer with a brilliant career ahead of her; when her friend Violet betrays their plan "never to marry, but to devote themselves to serious study as a life-work," Eva contemptuously ends the friendship.[1] After college she goes to Europe to study, but when she comes home, prepared to reconstruct the American theater through the plays she will write, she finds the New York theatrical establishment curiously indifferent and eventually drifts into marriage with a handsome, suitable, and completely unintellectual young man. The significance lies in the gently mocking tone in which Eva's story is presented: her image of herself as scholar and writer is a source of mild amusement as the patronizing authorial voice smiles at her pretensions and her idea that there could be any other life for a woman but marriage. When she does marry, still half reluctant, the author's tone suggests relief that the silly young thing is now settled. In "A Short Career" a young woman comes to college when she quarrels with her fiancé, but her expectations are unrealistic and she finds the life there disappointing: the president doesn't meet her at the train, and her plans to study mathematical astronomy are shattered when she learns she must study mathematics before she can get to the stars. When she and the young man accidentally meet, it is only minutes before they are setting the date for their wedding, and she leaves college to get her trousseau ready, again with the amused approval of the author. Even in "La Belle Hélène," which mocks the stereotype of the college woman as overearnest student and frump, Helen's revealed value is that she is beautiful, dresses well, and attracts men, just as the point of the mathematics professor's story in "An Aquarelle" is that she too is young and pretty.

In *An American Girl and Her Four Years in a Boy's College*, Anderson uses Will's romance to make a statement. The point of view, naturally enough, is very different here. Talented Will has choices; if she marries Guilford Randolf, not very appealingly presented as the normal educated man, she must relinquish her dreams and the use of her abilities by submerging her life into his. The novel does not rule out marriage; in fact, it has an open ending, in which romantic direction is neither indicated nor denied. But within the story this marriage would be an obvious disaster for strong, talented Will, and, indeed, for the young man, since for both sexual attraction has temporarily overcome drastically different values. Other young women do have romances, but Will notes sadly what happens when they get engaged: "that always seems to be the end of them, they settle right down and lose their individuality, and are as good as dead and buried" (112).

*Two College Girls*, with its thread of romance in the story of Edna and her gradually deepening friendship with her roommate's brother, puts men, marriage, and romance in the place that most of the women's college stories will echo: the future. Love and marriage are not rejected, but there is no suggestion that they are of such overwhelming importance that they should push aside Edna's college career. Their force is further diffused by the emphasis Brown places on choices and possibilities for the group of seniors, each with her own destiny but armed with the ability to have some control over a future. As pioneers, it was important for Brown and her contemporaries to insist that education did not make women unfit for marriage, but it was equally important to assert the availability of choices. The young women hope they will marry someday, but all are prepared to manage life if they do not, and while they are in school, their energies belong there. Even Rosamund, as she grows from a shallow butterfly to a woman dedicated to becoming a doctor and rejects popularity and the callow admirers of younger days, has marriage in her future. At her graduation a distant cousin, an intelligent young doctor, applauds her speech; that they find each other attractive and that there is a rapport between them is clearly established. Unlike Guilford Randolf, he admires her ambition, and the reader can envision a life of shared work and partnership as they marry and practice medicine together.[2] Elizabeth Stuart Phelps's "A Brave Girl" (1884), too, ends with the hint of marriage for Loto in the future, again with her roommate's brother. Like Edna's suitor, he sees what Loto has done with her life and is perceptive enough to credit and admire her courage and intelligence. Though the point is never emphasized, the fiction quietly insists that these are special women, and they deserve and will find special men who can appreciate what they are.

Of all the fictions, the turn-of-the-century narratives most clearly set marriage and men in the future, postponed until the unique experience of college is over. Men appear at the proper time and place, a fact which suits the lives of these busy young women. A Vassar student is described as having entered "a world of such absorbing interest that nothing outside of it could touch her" (9–10). Later, saying goodbye to a friend's brother and promising him dances at an upcoming reception, she thinks, " 'he's the last man-body I shall see in weeks,' but without sorrow, for Vassar's all-sufficiency was working within her" (13). A Wellesley student observes that it is "impossible to manage college and a love affair at the same time; she had seen friends fail in the attempt" (303). And a Bryn Mawr student, distracted from the arrangements for May Day festivities, grumbles about the "nuisance of having men mixed up with college functions" (113).

Men can indeed be a nuisance; at a basketball game at Vassar, a character pities a friend: "Poor Ruth! behold her skirting the edge of things with a man. He is only the second most interesting, and she has struggled to foist him off on somebody, anybody. Men are dear and desireable beasties, but, oh! not at Vassar. If they would only be more 'chirk,' and pluck up a bit more spirit while there; but they wear such an oh-for-a-man-and-a-brother expression" (225). Men are not excluded from the green world, but their entrances and exits are carefully controlled, and not simply by administrative authority.[3]

"Catherine's Career," though it is one of the few love stories in the collections, offers amusing and concrete evidence that young men are out of place in this world.[4] When an unknown young man, sent by her father, comes to call on Catherine at Bryn Mawr, she meets him in the reception room; he is sitting in the "least brilliantly lighted corner of the room" because he "had shrunk there from pursuing pairs of eyes!" Since they have not met before, and Catherine has no idea why he is there, their conversation is awkward, and their efforts at civility are constantly interrupted by "the top of a head and two eyes [which] rose perpendicularly above the window-sill in front of them, remained stationary for a few seconds, and then sank slowly, followed by a suppressed giggle and the sound of fleeing footsteps" as students passing by pause to stare in at the couple. Catherine counts twenty-seven sets of eyes, emphasizing the uncomfortable conversation, the situation, and the fact that the young masculine visitor is out of place.

The women who have pushed men aside for the moment are not desiccated and bespectacled frumps reacting to their inability to attract a man. They are appealing, interesting young women who enjoy the concerts and dances to which men are invited. They laugh among themselves at the unwillingness of their male friends to visit a woman's college, and they have second and third strings in case the first choice cannot come. They sometimes invite too many men, and then must persuade friends to take care of the extras. In "Her Fiancé," one of Bacon's later Smith stories, Evelyn is trying frantically to find someone willing to take care of a visiting man:

> "He's Emily Thayer's *fiancé* and he's never been up here before, and she's got the grippe and she can't see him at all, and I promised her I'd look out for him, and at the last minute my second and third men telegraphed that they found they *could* come after all, and the fourth accepted long ago, and they've all sent flowers, so I can't very well refuse, and the cards are all mixed up dreadfully, and Emily feels so disgusted and blue!"[5]

Once the men are there, however, they are treated courteously. The dances have a clear, structured format that encourages variety rather than concentration; one does not dance with one's man all evening, but rather arranges for him to meet as many friends as possible. The same conditions prevail at men's college proms; dance cards are made out ahead of time, and it is the duty of the escort, whether male or female, to make sure that his or her date has a good time. Brothers make acceptable escorts, and women who do not invite men are under no stigma; they may agree to dance with friends of friends or they may choose to watch from the galleries. Nor is there any indication that popularity with men is a factor in popularity or prominence on the campus. Dances do enable young men and women to meet each other and learn correct social behavior, but as the dances are presented in this fiction, their purpose is fun and they become part of the total experience.

Just how close this is to reality is hard to say, but the similarities in all the fiction seem to suggest that at least this was the accepted attitude and behavior. The stronger the sense of the unique and satisfying green world, the more peripheral the role of men in it. If indeed women without "dates" could watch or join dances without embarrassment or unhappiness or resulting loss of face, the contrast with the coeducational setting is a strong one: there those without dates find excuses or hide themselves away. But in these women's worlds, and whatever individual cases may be, men are not important factors.

Romantic commitment, then, is not rejected but is simply postponed until the absorbing life of college has ended; the underlying assumption in all the stories is that these young women are headed for heterosexual romance and marriage, but not yet. Emily, whose fiancé needed a date, has been engaged to him almost since childhood, but, as she has told him, "Smith girls never paraded their engagements. . . . Most people didn't announce them till their junior year and kept quiet about them after that. College wasn't the place for that sort of thing; if you wanted a lot of that, you were a fool to come. . . . Cornelia Burt had said, somewhat successfully, that at college it was perfectly legitimate to be interested in *men*, but very foolish to become attached to *a man*" (33–34).

In a continuation of the Betty Wales books, the friends, now graduates visiting the campus, discuss a younger sister who refuses college because she is "man-crazy" and "doesn't think you can have a good time with just girls."

> "Foolish young Constance!" said Mary scornfully. "The idea of thinking that Harding girls are less fun than boarding-school girls."
> "The idea of thinking that there isn't time enough later on for men," sniffed Babbie, playing with her engagement ring.
> "The idea of thinking that she won't change her mind about men and most other things, while she's here," added little Helen Adams, with a comical air of vast experience.[6]

Babbie's words as she plays with her engagement ring sum up the attitude toward men, romance, and marriage in these stories: there will be time afterward for these to become the most important elements of a young woman's life. But the present unique experience is too special to be diluted. Even the series books of Grace Harlowe and Marjorie Dean, while they have male characters—the "boys" safely and unobtrusively back home, who were part of the high school crowd—firmly reject any thought of romance, even, in both cases, for a long while after college days are over.

One feature of life in the women's colleges, mentioned in most of the fiction but most important in the Grace and Marjorie books, is what sophisticated Madeline Ayres calls, scornfully, "girl dances." These are very formal occasions, calling for one's best gowns, jewelry, and hair styles, but to them young women escort one another. As the rules loosened and men became more visible in campus life, the "Promenade and Concert" became the dance; one writer notes that somewhere in the first decade of the new century, "Smith College at a pre-arranged signal broke into a two-step and smashed forever their time-honored rule."[7] But the "girl dances" apparently did not immediately disappear, even when Havelock Ellis's psychology made them suspect; *Babs at College*, a juvenile celebration of traditional Wellesley festivities published in 1920, chronicles the students' delight in the first "Man-Dance" ever held there.[8] Even in the 1930s, Beverly Gray's class holds a "girl dance" in costume, perhaps so the author can bring the handsome aviator, illegally and in disguise, for a dance with Beverly.

The behavior patterns connected with these dances act out both masculine and feminine conventional courtship roles. The sophomore dance for the first-year students, a tradition occurring in many fictional accounts, meant that older students invited younger ones and assumed male roles: sending their "dates" flowers, calling for and escorting them to the dance, making sure they had partners, then taking them home afterward. Failure to perform these acts correctly was either insulting or disgraceful.

Women dancing together today are suspect, but there is not the faintest encouragement for lesbian interpretations of these scenes. Dancing is a pleasant activity and the dances are part of the learning experience; Betty Wales, in fact, holds dancing lessons for some of her first-year friends, because dancing and dance behavior are needed social skills. The pattern of these all-women dances is so exactly that of male-female social behavior that the whole performance can be interpreted as practice for the outside world: this is the way one behaves and the way one expects one's escort to behave at dances. As with the crush, there is a sexual innocence about the "girl dances," and their significance in some of the fiction, notably the Grace and Marjorie series, tends to be more political than romantic. Their existence as practice does suggest awareness of an outside world that will demand socially acceptable knowledge and behavior and underlines the need for making young women suitable for marriage by providing them with the required social graces.

The Betty Wales and Molly Brown series are alike in their pleasing presentation of life at the women's colleges, but there are major differences between them. One is, of course, the vision of college life in the Betty Wales books, with several stories that emphasize the move to maturity. Molly Brown's world, unlike the earliest fiction and many of the girls' series, but like the Helen Grant books, emphasizes men. Though Helen is a contemporary of Betty Wales, and Molly only a few years younger, they differ from her sharply, not only for their lack of interest in growth to maturity and self-realization, but in their handling of men and marriage. Helen Grant's college years are really an extended discussion of marriage; though Molly Brown and her friends do not discuss the subject, their green world is full of men.

Molly Brown's green world never quite coheres for several reasons. One is that Molly, not college life, dominates; another is that all her problems are external rather than internal; another, that Wellington College itself is not convincing. But most important, Molly's world, though it contains campus, dorms, and women students, apparently a women's community and space, is, in fact, male-dominated; men do not just intrude, they take over the space. The author has added another advantage to a college education: romance.

On her first day, Molly is accidentally locked in the college cloisters and rescued by a professor. Edwin Green is in his late twenties, the star of the Wellington faculty. To Molly he seems very nice though old, but he apparently falls in love with her at first sight. Of course he must hide his feelings—Molly is not only a student, she is fifteen years old—but the reader knows and so, by the end of four years, do all her friends. Though innocent Molly does not recognize his feelings or her own, he is the person to whom she turns with any serious problems, and he dominates her thoughts. A great deal of space is given to meetings between Molly and Professor Green, all of which strengthen the friendship between them. There are misunderstandings and jealousies that hurt both; in short, the relationship is so typical of romantic fiction that the reader finds Molly's lack of awareness hard to credit. Green even secretly buys the family apple orchard so that Molly can stay in school; when he falls seriously ill, she is so unhappy, she cannot concentrate on anything.

Nor is the professor the only male character. A few miles away from Wellington is Exmoor, a men's college. Early in the series the three central characters meet some young men from there, and after that there is constant movement back and forth. Nance develops a romance with Andy, whose father is the local doctor and a close friend of Green. The interaction among young women, the Exmoor men, the doctor's family, the professor (as well as some of his family and several young women who want to marry him) in the form of dinners, parties, and dances, weakens and almost destroys any sense of the boundaries for a separate green world. Marriage may be postponed, but its eventuality is clear to the reader. For this writer, the college experience alone, however rich it might be, does not provide enough interest to carry the narrative and must be enhanced with a love story.

Molly Brown herself is not preoccupied with marriage, but the opposite is true of Helen Grant. On Helen's train trip to college, a "fine-looking old gentleman" who sits beside her identifies college students in the car and says that he would never allow a girl to go to college: "Girls are meant to be daughters, then mothers. They're better off married, more content."[9] Later his place is taken by a fussy overdressed woman who, though his social opposite, shares his ideas: "Them girls down there is goin' to college. . . . They're a silly lot. . . . I have five girls, and I'm bringing 'em up to be good housekeepers and to get married. Marriage is honorable and old maids are abominable, and the college girls that go through are mostly old maids. Two of my girls have stiddy company" (8–9). Helen does not pursue the conversation, but Douglas pursues the theme; her portrayal of Helen's college years is a study of the points made by the two travelers, who, regardless of their different educational and social levels, represent a shared and prevailing attitude. One way or another, the issue of marriage, or of womanliness, which the author sees as preparation for marriage, dominates Helen Grant's story.

Helen is a serious student preparing herself to teach, though not for a career in teaching. Other characters are almost defined in terms of homemaker and nurturer—a friend, Juliet, has decided not to come to college; her past makes her value a home above all else, and she uses her inherited fortune to create one: "She is making a generous and noble woman, and is being interested in many of the higher matters of life" (273). Helen's roommate, Grace, is bright, and her highly educated aunt, who teaches in an English college, is paying for her education. But Grace wanted to go to a training school, then teach while she saved money so that she and her fiancé could marry, and after one year she rejects both college and the cold, unloving professorial aunt who has turned her back on the role of nurturer and homemaker. Helen and her friends do not condemn Juliet and Grace, but rather admire both young women for knowing their own minds.

After a dismal first year, Helen finds compatible friends, joins several societies, and has more interaction with other students. The real events of her life, however, take place off the campus and continue the already established pattern and relationships. She has a suitor, a childhood friend who now wants to marry her. Because his parents had been kind to her when she was a lonely child, she spends much time agonizing over whether it is her duty to show her gratitude by marrying their son. Deciding finally that she cannot, she tells him that she will not consider marriage at this time: "It would disturb me very much to give it [marriage] any prominence now. I want to go on in a girl's life, studying, enjoying, shaping my character to true womanhood, and learning, understanding what I would best like to be and have—" The young man interrupts her, "As if love wasn't the best thing that women could have" (347).

Helen and her friends are extraordinarily conscious of self and issues, and much of their discussion comes eventually to their own—or Douglas's—definition of the purpose and meaning of higher education for women: "Girls are generally effusive, and college training helps them to discriminate, to find true values, to decide between fancies and friendships" (48). College is not "Greek and Latin and ancient history and dried-up literature," but the "advantages that fit girls for society, general culture, correct judgment, and taste and attainments" (85). In college, says a woman faculty member, "girls . . . are tided over the most sentimental years, they understand true values better and know that love alone will not support a family" (117) and later she adds that going to college "keeps some of them from imprudent marriages" (322). The conclusions are neither new nor interesting; one can imagine the reaction of Helen Dawes Brown's pioneers to the philosophy that makes college into a finishing school keeping young women busy and out of trouble until they can marry wisely. The failures in Helen Grant's world are women like the flamboyant Carol who, doubting or fearing her ability to support herself, runs off and marries a rich widower with children older than she is.[10]

The distance between Helen's story and Betty Wales's, for example, is immense; one wonders if Helen's young readers would feel much interest in going to college except for job preparation. Helen learns about living with others by finding friends who are compatible with what she already is, and the nonvocational aim of Matthew Vassar and the other founders is lost in the training school ambiance and the preaching of a position. Though Douglas tries to insist that women have choices, she sounds like a weak and unconvincing imitation of Helen Dawes Brown's characters, and she adds her own dimension by insisting that to succeed, a girl must be womanly. Her attempt to reconcile what she clearly perceives as a conflict between education and true womanhood fails to convince.

Though still on the periphery, men in the abstract have stronger roles in the narratives that balance the aim of stretching women's minds and opportunities with that of better preparing women for a life that includes marriage. Jean Webster's *Daddy Long-Legs* is almost equally college fiction and romantic novel. Judy Abbott's Cinderella story does more than provide her with worlds that she has missed and help her develop her writing talents. She ends her college years ready to accept her new role in what

is clearly suggested to be a marriage partnership with the wealthy philan-
thropist (and handsome young man) who has been her benefactor. Like
Edna Howe, she has been made into a woman capable of taking on any
challenge.

Grace and Marjorie firmly marginalize men, keeping them back home
or at their own colleges and restricting meetings to vacations. Both these
series heroes seem not just unromantic, but sexless. As with the "girl
dances," innocence moves to asexuality; it is all but impossible to contemplate these two managers in a sexual relationship, even though the
presence of "the boys back home" indicates that eventual destiny. The
Beverly Gray books, however, nicely balance men with college by incorporating them into the adventure elements. Beverly has two suitors, the
boy back home and the dashing aviator, but in her senior year she rejects
both of them because she is more interested in the career she has chosen
for herself and for which the college has prepared her. She is enjoying
her life and she is neither in love nor ready for marriage; none of her
friends are involved in romances, though there are occasional indications of men in the background. For most of the early fiction, men belong to the future, but readers would find no evidence or suggestion that
the women's colleges present any barrier to marriage and the conventional happy ending, if that is what young women want.[11]

Since the coeducational novels tell of enclaves of women within a masculine world, it is logical to find that in them men are considerably more
obvious, though they seldom appear as fully developed characters. More
important than any participation, they set the standards. Interaction
among the young women concerns men, dating, jealousies, and the kind
of behavior associated with women whose society approves and even applauds their right to compete for men.

White's Dorinda has a series of romances, none of which work out, and
even before she turns away from the college, she has rejected the typical
college hero: "Flip fraternity men with slogan-writer minds roused from
their inertia to be witty with the personable coeds" (81). In the end she
marries the brilliant but eccentric engineer she has always liked, but
whom she avoided for a while because he was not acceptable to her sorority. Lucia, the hero of *Co-ed*, spends her first year in a whirl of popularity. She particularly likes dancing and temporarily seems to have lost
any other reason for being in college; men are valued as dancing partners. But toward the end of the year she reacts against her own behavior:
"In her brief career as a college butterfly, she had come to recognize
that as far as co-eds were concerned, college society-with-a-capital-letter
was made up of a very limited personnel" (111). The realization makes
her look more closely at the life around her, and she finally voices her
dissatisfaction to her father, who comments, "But when you sit there and
solemnly tell me you've got all the university can give you—in one giddy

year—I rather despair of your fitness. . . . Fact is, my girl, you don't know anything about the real university. You've been too busy frisking around in that little imitation society world—which is about as real a part of the university as the froth on top of new milk" (174).

Lucia changes, but the froth on the top of the milk is what delights Marian Graper, who was barely able to meet college entrance standards, but who is a complete success there. She is described at one point as walking in with "one of the seventy or eighty young men in the U who crowded each other for dates with her" (52). Later she comments that she does not yet want to settle down with one man:

> Anyhow I'd have had a hard time settling, I guess; if men get the idea that other men like a girl, that makes them want to be seen with her too. And of course pretty clothes and playing the piano are just as helpful in college as they are in high school.
>
> Being a "popular girl" isn't such a great career as some others. It seemed to be the thing I could do, though; and of course when you're labeled, you have to live up to the label. So in the U I accumulated a long "string of scalps," as Ernie called it. (176)

Her chief difficulty, besides doing enough studying to stay in college, is balancing her men, and her greatest triumph is being prom queen, an occasion that the author describes in great and loving detail. Even the comparatively intellectual Ernestine has her admirers, chiefly graduate students, though her reaction is different; when her phone calls become nearly as frequent as Marian's, "It only increased my wonder how she ever stands the strain of being a 'popular girl.' Fun is one thing; but having every minute jammed, and usually with men you don't care two whoops about, is just a particularly painful way of killing time" (106). Ernestine is happier with her childhood friend, Bob, who is always available.

White's novel attacks sororities and Hormel's portrays them as childish things, something the hero will grow out of with maturity. Corbett's presentation, in a way, is the most damning commentary on these societies because it cheerfully takes for granted that this is the way women behave as they compete for male attention and it reinforces the stereotyped misogynistic view of women as unable to live and work together. The areas of women's space in these masculine universes derive their values from male attitudes and approvals.

Although there is no doubt that the young woman who graduates with a diamond on her ring finger has found success, few leave college to marry; they, too, in their own way, hold off commitment until college is over, perhaps because there might be a more eligible man over the horizon. Dorinda leaves college and marries, but in reality she is rejecting the university, and marriage gives her a way out. Lucia's small and unimportant romances are merely part of her growing up; the man she will marry is offstage for most of the novel. Marian Graper marries immediately after graduation, as she was bound to do, and her sisters stay clear of serious romantic entanglements while they are in school. So in a sense they share with other women students the feeling that college is a unique experience and marriage should wait.

Noticeably and surprisingly, there is less romance in the coeducational stories than one would expect—less than in the Molly Brown books, for example. And other than the sorority member who gets pregnant and is immediately and scornfully labeled a "bad girl" and rejected by the college and her sisters, there is no emphasis on or discussion of sex. The taboo against premarital sex for "good girls" is fully operative; no important female character is sexually active. The immediate goal is popularity, which establishes value and strengthens the ability to choose a mate from a wider field.

Generally, then, men and the steps leading to marriage come after college rather than with it; in all the fiction there are very few examples of women leaving to marry. Within the women's spaces it is relationships with other young women that are emphasized as a positive feature of the college experience. In that world, focused on women, friendships are obviously important; making friends is part of learning how to live and work together. Again with the exception of *College Girls*, in which friendship is given slight emphasis, the early stories show relationships based chiefly on compatibility and shared interests. Variety in friends is stressed; young women like to study with certain classmates, go walking with others, discuss philosophical questions with still others. Or, most often, they draw together a group which makes a secure home base and to which the members feel a strong loyalty, although even those groups do not encourage exclusivity.

Crushes are a different matter. Nearly every author touches on them, usually as an amusing but acceptable part of the life. In a juvenile called *That Freshman*, set at Mount Holyoke, the restless, impulsive hero, constantly in trouble from thoughtless pranks, is encouraged by her friends to find a prominent upperclass student to worship, since then she would have to behave better. The author quotes:

> *Here freshmen fall madly in love twice a week*
> *With a Senior, you know, with a Senior, you know!*
> *They load her with flowers but never dare speak,*
> *At Holyoke, Mount Holyoke, you know!*[12]

When Helen, the hero, sends flowers to the senior she admires, the florist comments to his wife, "There's another one, Mother. But if they didn't do that, they'd be gettin' homesick, or spoilin' their stomicks with fudge an' the like" (92). The crush here is amusing, typical of the silly behavior of the young, but there is also the suggestion that the object of admiration is a role model, and it is worth learning suitable behavior to make a good impression.

As long as they are not silly, annoying, or overdone, crushes are perfectly acceptable, and most of the fiction, without making a strong point of it, defines right behavior. Admiration for achievement, particularly admiration from younger students, can generate such traditionally masculine acts as sending flowers, taking the object of adoration out to dinner, gazing sentimentally at her window, or finding strategies for spending time with her, always within the boundaries of the class codes. Crushes are often presented as mentorial; in the last of the *Smith College Stories*, as Theo thinks back over the four years and remembers her first-year adoration of Ursula, then a junior, Bacon steps out of her authorial anonymity to comment:

> There are those, I understand, who disapprove strongly of this attitude of Theodora's happy year: dogmatic young women who have not learned much about life and soured, middle-aged women who have forgotten. I am told that they would consider Theodora's adoration morbid and use long words about her—long words about a freshman! I have always been sorry for these unfortunate people; their chances for reconstructing Human Nature seem to me so relatively slight.
>
> When Theo had gone home that summer with hands almost as well cared for as Ursula's, sleek, gathered-in locks, and a gratifying hold on the irregular verbs (Ursula spoke beautiful French), her mother had whimsically inquired if Miss Wyckoff could not be induced to remain in Northampton indefinitely and continue her unscheduled courses! But perhaps she was a morbid mother. (328)

Where crushes exist in the turn-of-the-century fiction, this is the attitude toward them: Theo wanted to be like her model, and her behavior earned the approval of her mother. Betty Wales's admiration for Dorothy, the junior who met her on her arrival and who served as a guide, friend, and source of wisdom, awakens the heedless Betty to problems of too little money or too much snobbery. The friendship is wholly constructive, and many stories suggest this kind of healthful influence, with the admired one acting as a role model as well as advisor. When the adored figure is unworthy, as in "Clorinda" or "The Evolution of Evangeline," crushes are deplored, and in general young women who display them are mocked.[13]

Part of the clear but implicit definition of the acceptable crush in these stories is that it occurs over distance, never between equals. It is one-sided; the adorer is younger, full of admiration, and respectful in her approach, while the admired one is older, more poised, and always gracious to the adorer. Theo, remembering her crush on Ursula, notes with gentle amusement that she herself, as she gained prominence, became the object of well-mannered crushes from younger students. Series heroes Marjorie and Grace do not themselves have crushes, though they respect some upperclass women who are helpers and friends, but as they grow older they, too, are objects of admiration. In one of the Grace Harlowe books, a student is chided for her ungracious, in fact, contemptuous, treatment of a younger worshiper, and the inference is that those who are recipients of this admiration should appreciate the compliment and behave accordingly (Sr, 49–50).

An 1860s book called *The Friendships of Women* claimed that these were the most perfect earthly shadows of divine friendship. Carroll Smith-Rosenberg has defined these friendships further, showing that the separateness of men's and women's spheres forced both to find closeness and affection within their own sex, and that the language available for the expression of affection was what we today identify as the language of heterosexual love.[14] Phelps's "A Brave Girl" displays such a relationship; the close friendship between Loto and Fern, admired by their friends, is described as real love and involves much touching, although Phelps sets limits. Their affection "did not sentimentalize or mope. . . . In fact, it would have been difficult *to* sentimentalize with Loto. . . . What Fern might have been capable of in this direction if she had fallen into different hands . . . is not so easy to define" (28). But Phelps is chiefly amused and comments, "Why one girl shall select another out of all the world, be ready to die for her for two years, and equally ready to die for another one in two more—who shall tell us?" (27). And, as Loto matures, she outgrows her friend, finding her, at a later encounter, trivial and shallow. The friendship, the close contact, and the approval and admiration of their friends are presented as all very normal.

As Nancy Sahli shows in her essay "Smashing," not until the later nineteenth century, as awareness of sexuality grew, were intense friendship and its physical expression through touching, once taken for granted, seen as something to be avoided:

> In the late nineteenth century a very definite change was occurring in definitions of normal patterns of women's relationships. There was a great deal of pressure against the intense, emotional, sensual, even sexual commitment between women that had existed without censure during the earlier part of the century, and we can reasonably expect that many women adjusted their behavior to conform to the new standards. Those who refused to conform, for whatever reason, were risking the disapproval, condemnation, and persecution of both society and their own potentially divided selves.[15]

Clearly Josephine Daskam Bacon's authorial interruption in defense of the crush was impelled by the new interest in sexuality presented by Havelock Ellis and others. Even the popular magazines like the *Ladies' Home Journal* warned against too-close friendships between girls, although they sidestepped specific reasons.[16]

Read chronologically, the fiction supports a major point made by Lillian Faderman in her study *Surpassing the Love of Men*.[17] She argues that before the early years of the twentieth century strong friendships between women were acceptable and probably sexually innocent. She points out the idealization of women's—in fact, same-sex—friendships and reminds us that love and sex were perceived as separate: "In our century the sex drive was identified, perhaps for the first time in history, as being the foremost instinct—in women as well as men—inescapable and all but uncontrollable, and invariably permanently intertwined with real love" (311). But before that time, "sex was considered an activity in which virtuous women were not interested and did not indulge" (152). Women were thought of, and, more important, thought of themselves, as beings above sexual drives. Friendships between women were approved because a "woman who is not capable of the tenderest feelings and deepest intimacy toward her friend is lacking in an essential human component" (153).

Faderman's work suggests another point related to the strong female bonding in the fiction: in the women's communities, particularly while going to college remained a different kind of adventure for women, support was a necessity: "During the second half of the nineteenth century, when women slowly began to enter the world that men had built, their ties to each other became even more important. . . . Thus if they needed emotional understanding and support, they turned to other women" (160). Certainly the early fiction shows that young women entering this strange and perhaps frightening new world relied heavily on each other for comfort and support.

As one of her examples of the essential innocence of the crush, Faderman cites Josephine Daskam Bacon's "The Evolution of Evangeline," noting that when the students are getting ready for a "girl-dance," Biscuits is disappointed that she must take the uninteresting Evangeline when she wanted to ask an interesting first-year student she knows and likes. The language is almost that of male-female relationships, but it is "assumed in Daskam's universe, just as it generally was in nineteenth-century novels, that these loves would be superseded by heterosexual attachments. But while Daskam's characters are at Smith College, their passions are primarily for each other" (300). Passion is, in fact, too strong a word for the character of Biscuits, the context of this story, and indeed, for nearly all relationships displayed in this fiction. There are very few "twosomes"—pairs whose preference for each other excludes others. Probably the most intense friendship occurs in one of the Vassar stories, "At the First Game," in which the routine arguments of a pair of affectionate roommates escalate into a savage quarrel, so that they are left with passionate hatred. It takes the physical action of a basketball game to release the stored-up anger and restore the two to their usual relationship. When Janet is in danger of serious injury, Betty reacts and "something older than her hatred, older than that dreary Sunday, older even than her class spirit, hurled her in sideways between the bench and girls," taking the damage herself. As she is carried off, anger completely gone, "Janet smiled lovingly. She didn't look deep into Betty's eyes nor press her hand, because she wasn't someone in a book" (236). She just got on with the game.

Friendships are important and crushes are characterized by their own decorum and a sense of fun. They are acceptable, even valuable, as long as they are not excessive, which means they do not annoy or embarrass. But crushes that break the codes become offensive. In "Letters of a Wellesley Girl," a series that ran in *New England Magazine* (1907–1908), Edna writes home to her father about all her college experiences. In one of the letters, titled "Goo," she defines this popular bit of slang: "all sorts of affection are called goo, particularly those demonstrations which are rather embarrassing—the idea of stickiness, you see, connoting the notion of molasses." She gives several examples, generally classing crushes as goo, then describes her own reaction to "a girl here who has fallen desperately in love with me!" The situation is "ridiculous" and "pathetic," but when her polite efforts to end the attachment fail and the admirer refuses to take her hints, Edna can no longer stand it: "But it would not have been so bad, I could have stood the epistolary effusions and the flowers and being followed as by a sleuth, if she had only kept her hands off me. But she always wanted to sit in my lap and kiss me and put her arms around me. Ooh! it made me sick!" She loses her temper and angrily frees herself from the incubus, but the experience has marked her: "It makes me feel all crawly when I catch sight of her little pig-eyes fixed upon me with the 'eloquence of despair.' . . . What's the matter with love sometimes, that it is so disgusting? . . . When I get married, I hope he won't be too awfully fond of me." [18]

This crush is an embarrassing extreme that breaks the codes and drives its victim to disgust; in most of the fiction, however, crushes are youthful vagaries and young women will grow past them to the valuable friendships that are part of the rich tapestry of college life. The happiest students are portrayed as having many, and many different kinds, of friends. All the relationships in a sense must remain light, in balance, and part of the delightful game that these young women are playing for a time.

The charge that the women's colleges encouraged homosexual relationships, hinted at in the women's magazines, is overt in a 1927 article in *Harper's*.[19] The author, Edna Yost, a graduate of a coeducational school, begins by noting that nearly all her classmates, male and female, are married, and many to partners they met in college; therefore, coeducation does not make women unfit for marriage. But the women's colleges are "unnatural" in removing women from the world, making them "misfits in life." Although there is "no conscious effort at our women's colleges to close the minds of their students to marriage," this is the effect. "For they take a girl at eighteen and, during those years when she is emotionally ready to fall in love, when it is easier to accept young men for what they are than it will ever be again, she is being consciously molded and led into good habits, one of which is to be happy and satisfied for four years without the real companionship of men" (195).

There are, to put it mildly, some curious contradictions here, and perhaps an underlying cynicism that the author herself may not realize when she says that it is easier for a woman to accept men as they are when she is very young and unworldly than it will be when she is more experienced. The passage echoes earlier unsettling suspicions that women with options might choose not to marry, and it reverses the positive judgment of Helen Grant's creator that the best thing about four years in college was the prevention of early and imprudent marriages. It contradicts too those who, for a variety of reasons, wanted women held separately in a kind of limbo until they were ready to be given in marriage.

Probably the most vivid part of Yost's article was her insistence that women were sexual beings; while admitting the higher standards and academic superiority of the women's colleges, she saw dangers:

> For women at least, it is dangerous to go through a lengthy period of intellectual development when removed from this contact with men which is absolutely necessary for her normal emotional growth. To the young woman placed in this biologically unnatural position one of two things is likely to happen: The development of her emotional nature may halt while her intellectual development leaps ahead; or she may find in other girls the substitute which forms an outlet for her emotions. And as we are beginning to face the beautiful warm facts instead of the placid myths about woman's emotional nature, we are finding that substitution not so good. (196)

She goes on to charge that "intense homosexual friendships of an undesirable nature form a problem that is admittedly disturbing some of our best women's colleges and unadmittedly disturbing the others" (196). Her solution is to send girls to coeducational colleges, though not, she warns, to the large state universities where they are not wanted. She ends by pointing out that such contact is advantageous to men, too:

"the co-educated man, far oftener than his men's college brother, possessed a genuine respect for and understanding of women which increased his possibilities for lifelong happiness" (201). Indeed, everyone
would be better off, for in a nicely (and perhaps unconsciously) ironic
passage she concludes that "men too often take for granted that intelligent women respect their mental powers, when as a matter of fact they
do not." Although men assume a "mental superiority . . . modern educated women" may not agree with the assumption; "when a young college woman's contact with men of her own age is limited to social affairs
while her contact with other young women is both social and intellectual,
her respect for the masculine mentality is bound to dwindle on account
of her ignorance of it" (201). In other words, the women's colleges not
only promote a climate in which lesbianism may flourish, they teach
women an objectivity that allows them to see men all too clearly without
the coloring of romance.

The charges Yost brings in her 1927 essay are the core of the two exposés of the women's colleges which appeared at roughly the same time.
Kathleen Millay in *Against the Wall* deplores sexual ignorance, lack of
understanding of those "beautiful warm facts . . . of women's emotional
nature" being discovered by the outside world but rigorously suppressed
within the college boundaries. Millay castigates not so much the attitude
that forbids sex, but an atmosphere determined to perpetuate sexual ignorance, an enforced innocence guarded by those in charge. As a result,
young women are bewildered and uneasy, unsure of what changes in
their bodies and hormones mean or how they should react. But if for the
guardians heterosexuality is a sin, homosexuality is far worse, and their
attitude toward even the possibility is obsessive.

Rebecca's friendship with a troubled classmate brings her a warning—
not a direct statement, but a message full of innuendo. Although Rebecca
is strong enough to respond by direct attack, others are more vulnerable.
One young woman, trying to fight her terrible homesickness ("I'd never
slept away from Mama in my life, you see") seeks help from her faculty
advisor but gets only bracing, useless advice. Then she finds an older
student who looks like her mother, and "I just worshipped the ground
she walked on! I'd have done anything to make her like me more." But
"You just bet it didn't take us long to get talked about! Of course, I hadn't
the faintest idea what they were getting at for a long time" (336). When
the comforting friendship is forbidden, she defiantly turns to other older
students, and the text may suggest that she finds a kind of lesbian sub-
culture, although here the author is as indirect as the administrators she
is attacking.

Later a group of students, reduced to embarrassed silliness by their
honest bewilderment and discomfort, seek out Rebecca after a hygiene

lecture: " 'Well, she was talking about—well, you know, friendships at college and things like that. And she said they were all right—in their way, you know. But, well'—giggle, giggle—and the rest took up the refrain—giggle giggle giggle giggle—'Then she said, well, what do you suppose she meant by this? . . . She said it was all right to be friends, of course—but— *to draw the chalk line at the bedroom door!*' They held their breath in chorus" (341).

A shocked Rebecca realizes that her questioners are not teasing or testing her, but honestly do not know what the hygiene teacher was talking about. She tries to explain: "Only sometimes—since we're all so dependent on other girls here at college—for companionship, I mean—sometimes one thing leads to another until we begin to think we can care as much for another girl as we might care for a man sometime—and that isn't very natural."

When her audience demands to know what happens on the other side of the chalk line, Rebecca is brusque: "How should I know? All you have to do is use your imagination. After all, you know how people are made, don't you? Men and women? Well, there are just so many things you can do with geometric figures—that's all. Sounds sort of dumb, if you ask me" (342). They react with "Is that all?" and go away, leaving Rebecca furious at the policies of ignorance that have forced this awkward explanation on her and that build mystery, making the forbidden more interesting.

Lack of sexual knowledge extends to heterosexual relationships as well. On a date Rebecca is tempted almost past control by her escort's passionate kisses. But she stops the lovemaking, and her outburst is as much explanation and analysis for herself as for him: "I know damn well why I'm interested in you. It's because I've been rottenly cooped up for a year. That's why. And you're the first man I've seen since." It is not just her "damned upbringing and that cussed nunnery I've been living in . . . folks in this country are so afraid girls won't get married and have children they're almost crazy. So, when girls show a tendency to study and learn a little something, they're sent to a coop" where they can be guarded: "So when they come out for a breath of fresh air they get nervous like this at the very first man they see. . . . And they get kissed by that first man, as you tried to kiss me just now, and they think they must be in love with him because they go hot all over and think they're going to faint and their bodies get beyond their control—and— . . . They marry that man. And have a lot of kids. And their education didn't do them any harm after all!" (384).

Rebecca's large disgust with Matthew College includes the enforced ignorance about sex as part of what she sees as a policy to retain and perpetuate ignorance in all areas—the refusal to allow students to think.

Administrators and even faculty cannot act otherwise, given the societal trap they themselves are caught in:

> After all, just what *was* their job? To teach girls and to keep them from knowing anything at the same time. A simple task, that. Let 'em learn Psychology Physiology Family History Astronomy Biology *Any*-thing—but never let them *think!* Never let them apply their learning to their own brains. To their own bodies. Let them praise God and get married—to the only man they've ever kissed—and hate him, maybe, but have lots of babies. And keep his house clean. And be a faithful idiot. But know everything just the same. (412–413)

Millay rather labors the point that the college holds up marriage and children as the ultimate success. Faderman notes, "In 1895, just as education for women was really coming into its own, there was a great public outcry when a survey revealed that more than half of the graduates of women's colleges remained spinsters. There had been at that time a general agreement that every married couple in America needed to produce at least three children for the Republic to survive, and higher education for women . . . was now held accountable for these women's escape from their patriotic duty." [20] Curiously, while the contemporary turn-of-the-century fiction is untroubled by these statistics, Millay's college seems obsessed by them.

Though their styles and approaches differ, Millay and Mary Lapsley share and project a sense of the hypocrisy of the women's colleges that profess learning but reserve the right to restrict it to what they consider suitable. As her title, *The Parable of the Virgins*, suggests, most of the lives that Lapsley interweaves to make her novel are variously affected by sex, lack of sex, or sexual ignorance. Crosby, the poet, entering as a talented, idealistic lover of beauty, reacts to the college's attempts to mold her by becoming sexually promiscuous. Other characters fear, evade, or sublimate their instincts into college-approved heartiness.

Peg, who becomes pregnant and secretly has an abortion, reflects that young women like her suffer because their "knowledge of contraceptives is so slight" (132). She and her fiancé plan to marry, but not until they both finish college, and she does not want either of them to be forced into marriage. She contrasts her own situation with that of a friend whose pregnancy is discovered after her fiancé is permanently crippled in an automobile accident, but whose parents, with the college's blessing, will force her to marry him anyway. Peg had listened to women talking about sex and betraying their ignorance and fear, and from her own point of view, "it was natural these girls should be curious; had she not been so, this time last year? Thank God that was over! no more unhappy brooding about simple facts" (109). Significantly, Lapsley makes Peg, with her sexual experience, one of the few sane, balanced characters in the novel;

discussing the abortion with Clive Austin, who had lent her some of the
money to pay for it, she shows no remorse or shame, only sadness for
others. "Miss Austen, if you saw the other girls, if you knew the way they
talk and think, trying to find out, restless because they don't know. It
would be disgusting, if it weren't so pathetic. I'm glad I'm not like
them" (348).

Sophie, the sophisticated European observer, also discusses the students and their need for information with Clive Austen. "I suggested that
they get from the library a book on sex life—since the hygiene lectures
tell nothing. They reported to me it is forbidden." Later in the conversation she comments that "they do not even know the names of any of
the female reproductive organs" and asks: "Why does not the college
instruct these children about matters of sex? Why do they have a course
in hygiene which tells them to keep their bowels open and not to dance
too close to their partners at the promenade? That is not instruction
worthy of Walton" (238–239).

But Sophie's disgust at the college's failure to inform is clearly not
shared by those in power. When Crosby is caught in an escapade that
could lead to her expulsion, some of the faculty discuss her over their
teacups. The professor of Bible exclaims, "Oh, these terrible modern
girls! . . . they have forgotten all honor and all decency. The fear of God
is not in them. I don't know what we are coming to. It seems as if only a
few of us held the fort against the world" (309). And the head matron
adds: "These sex cases . . . are something I find particularly disgusting. I
think any refined woman must find them so" (351).

Sex and knowledge of sex are the two major areas from which the students need to be guarded. A main theme in Lapsley's novel, as it was for
Millay, is the harm that sexual ignorance does to young women, and the
point is made in conversation and in elements of plot. But again, as in
Millay's novel, if heterosexual knowledge and experimentation are to be
repressed, homosexuality is so terrifying to those in charge that fear of it
becomes obsessive. The crush, harmless, mentorial, amusing in earlier
eyes, is now immediately cause for suspicion. Students are warned and
warn each other; one senior advisor tells her first year advisee, "Don't get
a crush. You can admire some girls a lot, but don't get slushy about it. It
makes a girl conspicuous, and the college authorities don't approve. Do
you understand what I mean?" When the younger student clearly does
not, her mentor says she will understand "when you hear the freshman
hygiene lectures. Why, there are some girls in this college who actually
hug and kiss each other as if they meant it" (32).

Such advice comes too late for Mary and Jessica, whose love affair
makes one of the main strands of Lapsley's novel. They have been roommates, and their relationship is long established and intense, particularly
on Mary's part; there is certainly the implicit suggestion that it includes

genital contact. Whatever the degree of closeness, the relationship is not presented as happy and secure. When they are alone after a "girl-dance," Mary's jealousy because Jessica danced with another girl leads to a tortured, unpleasant scene, with Jessica weakly defending herself against Mary's frantic accusations. The quarrel is resolved finally, as much out of exhaustion as anything else, and the scene ends as the two kiss "lingeringly" (95).

Doctor Royal, whose advice to students to "Keep their hearts wrapped in cotton batting till the right man comes along" echoes that of the doctor in Millay's novel, is a woman obsessed by sex, probably because of her own repressive virginity, and particularly by what she reads as any sign of homosexuality. She is unpleasantly busy in her efforts to root out such sin: "Clive [Austen] had a swift image of the physician trotting about, probing, questioning the girl; and then trotting busily across the campus with her hard-reaped harvest of information" (350).

When the president, head matron, and doctor decide that something must be done about the Mary-Jessica relationship, the doctor attacks the weaker member, the less-committed Jessica, who has indeed grown uncomfortable with her roommate's intensity. The doctor's attitude is unsympathetic; to her these young women were either silly or evil when they "got themselves entangled and insisted on their right to their own emotions. The thing to do was to frighten them a little, and then to be frank with them, frank always within certain limits." Her words, vague but threatening, are effective:

> The hint of some powerful knowledge made Jessica shiver. Older people knew so much that one could only guess at; and behind those tortoiseshell eyes lay all the strange magic wisdom of the physician. How did she know what Dr. Royal had in store for her, what Nature might not be willing to assist Dr. Royal in doing? Dim suggestions of awful illnesses brought on by dissipation, half-recollection of tales of madness that might arise shook her heart. She felt empty and blindingly sick . . . (215–216)

Jessica caves in under the pressure and agrees that she wants the relationship to end, giving the doctor ammunition for her next interview. Speaking to Mary with disgust and contempt she makes no attempt to hide, she separates the two and makes Mary believe that Jessica fears and hates her. For Mary, it is the end: "If this was true, there was no use fighting. If Jessica could expose her to these torments, then her love was certainly dead" (255). The doctor wins, and Mary, left isolated and despairing, with the future seemingly intolerable, hangs herself.

Jessica, who finds her, lashes out, accusing Dr. Royal, but the doctor denies responsibility and is unmoved by the charge; she seems almost relieved that Mary's suicide has cleared up the problem. The college covers up the situation efficiently, its first concern for itself and its reputation. Jessica, distraught and hysterical, cannot even have psychiatric help lest the news get out to damage the college image. Finally a worried student goes to Clive Austin for help. The professor listens and understands more than the specific situation:

> [T]hey swung together, these children, without thought, crowded into an abnormal environment; then all at once the Administration was upon them, raising shocked hands and clamoring of sin. If the college only started its campaign against crushes before they got so intense,—or, better still, if it treated them in less breathless a fashion. . . . If the Administration didn't talk in hushed whispers and avoid the word homosexual; or if they even differentiated between the environmental and the genuine Lesbian, one could hope for some results. (315)

The college creates an "unnatural" environment for girls but does not know how to treat or help them within the framework that it must maintain. The result is pain, confusion, and in this case, tragedy.

Notably, the attitude, even as Lapsley compassionately chronicles the progress of the lesbian affair that ends in suicide, is not today's acceptance of variety in sexual preference or nature. Though the weak, vacillating Jessica and the tragic Mary, whose love is the most important thing in her life, are both sympathetically portrayed, no one, not even the understanding Clive Austin, finds the behavior other than aberrant. Austin can differentiate what she calls "environmental lesbianism," implying that it is the result of the confined space, the rigid control, the young women's developing sexuality and their ignorance of their own feelings and bodies, from "genuine" lesbianism. She can feel the pain involved, but she cannot approve, and her condemnation of the administration is that they do not help the students understand their situation and the potential dangers it holds. Mary herself accepts guilt; earlier, talking to Crosby, she exclaims, "I can't help it. You don't suppose I haven't tried not to care for Jessica—not to find in her everything I'd find in a man?" Crosby says, "Then you do think it's wrong!" and Mary responds, " 'I suppose so. Everyone else seems to.' She took the teacup with both hands, which were trembling" (124).

Faderman comments on the kind of situation Lapsley depicts. By the early twentieth century, European popular literature, influenced largely by sexologists, was referring to "thousands of unhappy beings" who "experience the tragedy of inversion in their lives" and to passions that "end in madness or suicide." As a result "love between women was becoming identified with disease, insanity, and tragedy. It soon became a condition for which women were advised to visit a doctor and have both a physical and mental examination." [21] But the doctors Lapsley and Millay depict are incapable of offering help, since they can see the situation only in terms of good and evil, or healthy versus sick, and their chief reaction is disgust.

In the early women's college stories, sexuality, however directed, is simply not a factor. The students are young, and women were not thought of as sexual beings. (Though sex outside marriage is never a topic, it is safe to assume that the fiction before Lapsley's novel would uphold the taboos against it.) Marriage is important, but the earliest stories show young women too busy and having too good a time in their unique world to live anywhere but in the present. Romance is minimally important; it is part of what the future holds but out of place in this absorbing new adventure with its emphasis on knowledge that comes from books and knowledge that comes from interaction. Men and marriage are perhaps the next great adventure, but in the meantime there is so much to learn and enjoy. The fact of choice is certainly stressed, and the idea that men, romance, and marriage should be postponed prevails in all the early fiction and in the series books, and even, in its own way, in the coeducational novels. None of the fiction rejects marriage as the suitable end for women.

In the balanced life celebrated in the early fiction, and even, to some extent, in the series books, friendships and variety of friends are important parts of the rich experience, but they, too, like relationships with men, are never all-consuming. There is a lightness in their handling, regardless of who the author is, that does not mean insincerity, but rather places them as one part of a rich life. The focus is on the present, on the unique experience that, as the young women involved in it know, will never come again.

Since Millay's and Lapsley's exposés turn all the strengths of the women's colleges into agents of pain, it is not surprising that what had been so easily and pleasantly dealt with earlier becomes part of the negative experience. Uptight administrators watching with fanatical vigilance the behavior of young women confined to a rigid mental space rule the worlds that the two authors depict. Sexual innocence equals sexual ignorance which, bottled up, is ready to explode with destructive force.

Obviously there is connection between the disintegration or lack of community discussed in earlier chapters and the contrast in attitudes about friendships, men, and sex examined here. European writings about sexuality, appearing late in the century, provided a weapon that could and did shatter the female bonding that was at the core of the best and happiest women's college communities—a weapon wielded not only by outsiders, but inside, by inept administrators who did not know how to use it and were not even sure what they were aiming at.

# · EIGHT ·

# *Afterward*

W hat happens to the young women who have gained an education, learned how to live together, enjoyed prominence and admiration, have, in short, had the unique experience of the green world and then must leave it? The bittersweet tone of so many commencement chapters in the early fiction indicates that the students themselves know that life will never again be like this, that they are ending something that can never be repeated. For heroes of developmental novels, graduation signifies a logical move from one part of life to another, but aside from the series continuations, most writers of college-focused narratives have chosen to ignore what happens next.

The question of what to do with educated women surfaces early in critical commentary and by 1885, twenty years after the establishment of Vassar, is a frequent topic for newspapers and magazines. Careers and jobs for women were limited: there was teaching, of course, and college graduates could command the best teaching jobs; there was eventually a growing field for secretaries (many Oxford and Cambridge women, who could get the education but not the degree, found jobs as executive secretaries to powerful men).[1] For women who did not have to support themselves, the arts and charitable organizations found uses for their talents. The intellectual young women ignored by the fiction found positions at their own or the other women's colleges, usually after several years' study abroad. Those who found jobs or made careers other than teaching were not the majority.

In 1913 a *New York Times* feature, headlined "When the College Girl Comes Home to Stay," written in a style guaranteed to bring a tear to the driest or most misogynistic eye, presents the plight of both the young woman and her parents: "The dear daughter upon whom has been lavished so much love and care comes home from her college experience unable to fit into the little attic room she left at the age of 16 or thereabout, and more often than not she is equally unable to fit into her mother's and father's existence."[2] Ignoring the implications of the "little attic room," the article continues with the worst possible scenario, although it does offer its own version of hope: a picture of a science laboratory is captioned "Laboratory Work Prepares for Duties in the Kitchen." The feature page is headed "A New Kind of Page for a New Kind of Woman," but it is clear that the new kind of woman had better be prepared to take up the old kind of duty. The solution offered is that the parents and the colleges must change their goals so that they prepare the young woman to find satisfaction in bringing what she has learned to her home. Many colleges, especially the coeducational ones, had developed a home economics curriculum which was an attempt to bring scientific methods and knowledge to homemaking; in the universities, the "women's course" had the further advantage of isolating women students, creating a sphere in which they could be confined.

Generally the thesis of those attacking women's education is that the educated woman is a misfit; she cannot return happily to her home, nor is there a place for her in the world of work. One critic mourns "The Passing of the Home Daughter," "such a winsome thing to eye and to heart; her mission in the home was so plainly ordained by God; her companionship so clearly the lawful recompense of the mother's weary waiting and willing sacrifices of personal interest and desire—that we mourn her passing with hearts hotly resentful of the new order which relegates the old to the rubbish heap of effete traditions."[3] The graduate does not marry, either because no one wants her or because she is no longer interested in that commitment, but she has no role if she does not wish to wait at home, "gracefully passive," in hopes that someone will appear to marry her.

Even the defenders cannot deny the existence of a problem. A 1913 *Harper's Bazar* article points out that all young people, not just women college graduates, cause difficulties for their parents, and it deplores the influence of those who sensationalize the issue.[4] An earlier piece in the same magazine asks reasonably why parents should be surprised to find a daughter changed by such a different experience, but defends the result:

> The world is still old-fashioned enough to think that a woman's highest and happiest lot is as a much-loved wife and mother. College girls marry in spite of the predictions to the contrary of a generation ago. They not only marry, but they marry well; indeed, as a class, they carry off the real prizes in the matrimonial market: the young professional men—doctors, lawyers, college instructors—and men engaged in running the big machinery of the industrial world. The college girl marries discriminatingly, and she marries late. Perhaps these are the reasons why the college women so seldom figure in the divorce court.[5]

Educators and sociologists made their contributions to the discussion. In a hopeful but not very precise early study, "Occupations and Professions for College-Bred Women" (1885), Jane M. Bancroft surveyed the job market and found it meager but improving.[6] Most women, she says, will marry; those who teach will eventually find their salaries equal to those of men doing the same work; medicine is a suitable and available field. Opportunities are beginning to come, and it is up to educated women to widen these opportunities. Charles F. Thwing, president of Western Reserve and an advocate of women's education, wrote his "What Becomes of College Women?" after the twenty-fifth anniversary of Vassar's founding.[7] He supplies figures, although he is imprecise about their sources: 55 percent of all college women marry; 20 percent do not; 40 percent of recent graduates have not as yet. He says there are at present 8,000 graduates from all institutions, 5,000 of whom are or will be married. He uses 1890 census figures, but his work is flawed by the inability to distinguish college graduates from nongraduates: "Out of 4,000 women who are physicians it is probable that not more than 200 have had college training" (549). Finally he laments that no major literary talent has emerged "in the same class with the works of Miss Wilkins [Freeman], Miss Murfree [Craddock], or Miss Phelps" (551), and others.

Roughly parallel but far better controlled is Frances M. Abbott's "A Generation of College Women."[8] Abbott used Vassar alumnae records for her small but representative study, and her facts are based on 1,082 graduates since the first class. She is properly cautious about the figures, reminding her readers, for example, that since women càn marry at any age, estimates of college graduates who do or do not marry must be fluid. In the four earliest classes, 63 percent of graduates married, 18.33 percent taught. Of all graduates, 37.6 percent have taught, and one-ninth went on for advanced degrees. A count of the remainder shows that 47 are writers; 16 teach informally (music, art); 12 are scientists, 6 librarians, 5 artists, 5 farmers, 3 missionaries, 3 philanthropists, 3 astronomers. Many serve on school boards (to which women could be elected) or are trustees, or are active in clubs or charitable organizations.

These articles are samplings; the subject was of considerable interest and remained so. But the methods used in the studies were so vague that either side could probably find support for a position, and no matter how objective authors tried to be, there is a hint of defensiveness in their arguments. Whether they state their point directly or not, most of them seem at some level to be insisting that higher education does not really prevent women from marrying.

The popular magazines were less equivocal; they presented educated women as displaced persons and offered a subtext that advised putting them back, undoing their educations, and teaching them to be womanly again. In 1909 the *Ladies' Home Journal* serialized a story called "When

She Came Home from College," which fictionalizes prevailing attitudes.[9] Barbara Grafton returns to Auburn, a small prairie town, after graduating from one of the "great Eastern Colleges for women," later identified as Vassar. Her father is a doctor and the family is presented as close and loving. The town is "sleepy" and conservative; Barbara's mother says, "The things that keep a town awake are usually sent away to college." Barbara wants to write and was badly disappointed when she missed out on a fellowship by a fraction of a point, but she has determined to make the best of her situation and comes home ready to apply system to the household. In her efforts to reform management, parents, and siblings, she misses the signs of her mother's exhaustion. When her mother collapses with a nervous breakdown, Barbara is left in charge.

Her efficiency alienates everyone, including the cook-maid, who leaves. Her father says affectionately, "She's taking herself so very seriously these days. She feels that she must gush forth a stream of living water for thirsty mankind, forgetting, dear little lass, that she is not a spring yet, but only a rain-barrel." A procession of cooks create one disaster after another, then leave; a neighbor advises Barbara to learn to accommodate herself to circumstances. Finally Barbara asks herself, "Was it possible that housekeeping was a science, instead of merely an occupation—to be learned by study, and experiment, and experience?"

At this point she is offered the fellowship she had wanted, but her little brother falls seriously ill and needs careful nursing. The importance of what she is doing becomes clear to her, and she refuses the fellowship. Her father suggests that she leave the "collegiate summit"; "We must come down into the plain and struggle and help to raise it [the world] by our individual effort." Lizzie Borden's father may have said the same kind of thing, but Barbara is finally able to understand and find happiness in her tasks.

Running through her story is her desire to write. When she first comes home she puts aside a certain time each day to work on her "psychological studies," which, though she considers them her art, are gently mocked by the authorial voice. Her mother shows Barbara's lively letters from college to an editor she knows, however, and he advises the prospective writer to use them as her model and write such stories or sketches of everyday life. So the tale ends with a hopeful compromise: Barbara has learned the importance of keeping a home, and it is clear that her writing will be successful, if somewhat less grand than her dreams.

Obviously the *Journal*'s policy, lukewarm approval of college provided it does not keep a woman from her divinely appointed tasks, is a guideline for the development of the story. Barbara must learn practical wisdom and womanly values; when she does, she finds satisfaction and her life has purpose. Her education and talent must come second, and in fact the story is not about her realization, but her humiliation. A modern reader might point out the stunningly illogical but unnoted fact that it is Mrs. Grafton, that fine wife and mother whose life is totally shaped by domesticity, who has the nervous breakdown, and no one, including her doctor-husband, shows surprise or guilt.

What the story presents is not a very attractive future, especially when contrasted with the magical green world with its space in which women were invited to stretch themselves and grow and be appreciated for precisely that. If these college stories are classed as tales of initiation—and they do contain elements of the initiation process: separation from family, tests and ordeals, the teaching of tribal lore, ending in the ceremony that returns the initiate to her society as a responsible citizen—the problem is that the society to which the initiates are returned does not want them. Elaine Ginsberg gives her reason for what she sees as a lack of female initiation fiction: "Given these restrictions on the roles of women in fiction, it is obvious why the female initiation story is rare in American literature: there has been no adult female world for the young girl to be initiated into. The woman who was to be a redeemer, spiritualizer, and ennobler could never be an initiate because she had to remain pure and innocent, forever a child, even after (and despite) marriage." [10]

But the fiction and the reality are initiatory, if only in their structure, and perhaps the problem is that the women's colleges initiated young women into a world that was confused in its expectations for them and therefore had as yet no real place for them, either economically or socially, other than the traditional role of wife and mother. Education does end their innocence—not sexually, of course, but in other ways: they have been taught to question, to go past the obvious, to reason and behave accordingly. And they have lived with the concepts of ethics and honor, another way of destroying innocence according to a story by Abbe Carter Goodloe in the *Ladies' Home Journal* (1898) entitled "Was It Her Duty?" [11] Her college woman hero has met a young man and their compatibility and attraction to each other is clear and promising. But his younger sister is being courted by her brother, whom she knows to be immoral and dissolute. She hesitates, but finally her sense of honor impels her to tell the young man the truth; while he is grateful for the information that allows him to protect his sister, he cannot stand the discovery that the woman he admires knows such behavior exists or that she could talk to him, a man, on a subject about which women should know nothing. As she had feared, her honesty destroys his interest in her.

The expectation that young women could go through four years of a wholly different, stimulating experience and return home to the "little attic room" unchanged is irrational. Yet the tone of Barbara Grafton's story is affectionately patronizing, as what she has learned is discounted and what she has not learned is held up as the highest good. The laboratory must prepare her for the kitchen.

Commentators assumed that women who returned to cities would find more stimulation and adjust better than would those who returned to the country. A minister writing for the *Ladies' Home Journal* about "The College Girl in the Country Town" suggests that she will find opportunities to reform the town; she must start by joining an already existing group like the "Sewing Society of the parish church." At the end of six months she might have "earned the right to make a modest suggestion" for improvement.[12] Seventy years earlier, the Lowell Mills girls, who had embarked on a venture almost as revolutionary as women's higher education, went home to their villages and small towns after their three or four years of work to become active citizens; many of them plunged into the task of establishing town libraries. They, according to one of their chroniclers, Harriet Hanson Robinson, were admired for their ideas, became community leaders, and made good marriages.[13] Perhaps the difference was that their sophistication came from work experience which, even occurring in a comparatively cosmopolitan environment, was easier for their communities to understand and accept than was a woman with a bachelor's degree.

*Rebellion* (1927), by Mateel Howe Farnham, is a developmental novel that shows the emptiness to which many graduates returned.[14] The protagonist, Jacqueline, is in conflict with small town mores and chiefly with her father; it is that relationship and her escape from it which the novel examines. Her college years are not chronicled, but she "was happy at college, proved an eager student, was popular with both the teachers and students" (111–112). When she graduates and comes home to her small midwestern town, she finds nothing to engage her mind and energy. Her desire to leave brings the smouldering conflict with her father to the surface; he rages at her statement that she has nothing to do, suggesting that she take up church work or help with the Junior League. "Father, don't you *realize* that this town is overrun with women and girls who are bored to death because they have so much time on their hands and nothing interesting or constructive to do? Why, they fairly go out of their way to make work for themselves" (121). But reason cannot get past his inability to view her, a young woman, in any but the conventional situation.

To her older relatives, who love her but do not understand, she is even more forthright: "Cousin Julia, do you think it's such a shocking, unholy, God-awful thing for me to want to make some use of my education and what brain I have instead of settling down and twiddling my thumbs?" (126). But for them, "naturally she will marry when the time comes and in the meantime she ought to enjoy herself like any other young girl" (127). They are sure that "young ladies [are] deliberately unfitted for marriage by being sent to college." Education might be "necessary for teachers and other unfortunately plain members of the fair sex" but "their worst suspicions were confirmed of what college did to sweet pure young girls" (127).

The compromise is that Jacqueline will stay home for two years and take a secretarial course, although it is clear that there will be nothing for her to apply that learning to, either, and that her elders want to keep her busy until someone comes along to marry her. Jacqueline's story differs from Barbara Grafton's, particularly in its tone, since Farnham is clearly on her hero's side, but both narratives present a barren landscape for intelligent female college graduates, a place where all that they have learned is useless and unappreciated.

Fictional portrayals of college life do not have to account for their characters after they leave, but many of them do suggest futures. The early *Two College Girls* remains the most radical and encouraging; the scene near the end in which the seniors discuss their futures shows that each one has both a "sense of obligation," a need to do something worthwhile with her education, and a thought-out plan for a useful life. Equally important is their shared confidence that even if their plans change or are changed, they are ready for whatever happens. They have been educated, they have ideas, abilities, and the belief that they can make something out of whatever life presents to them. Marriage is not ruled out; it is one option—the preferred option—but not the only one. Undoubtedly their attitude reflects that early generation of college-educated women and their creator; Helen Dawes Brown was among the pioneers and made a successful academic career of her own. The end of her novel is very much a celebration of rites of passage, with the initiates ready to enter a world for which they believe they are prepared.

Will Elliott's future, too, is definite and planned: she is going to teach so that she can earn money for medical school. Although the ending has a hint of irresolution because her suitor has not given up, nothing suggests that he will succeed. And there is even less doubt about the future of most of the characters in *College Girls*: they will marry. Dominant throughout that collection is the insistence on the marriageability of the young women, though that may not be the theme of all the separate stories. Finding mates, being attractive, giving up career plans for matrimony are all important features. As the favorable review pointed out, *College Girls* proves that no mother need be afraid her daughter will become a pedant and therefore unsuitable for marriage.

Although the logical heir of Helen Dawes Brown's novel, the women's college fiction that follows a few years later does not support her positive conclusions, or, rather, it avoids any conclusions at all. *Smith College Stories*, *Vassar Stories*, and *Wellesley Stories*, with their focus on the unique and satisfying present, have no need to predict futures. To do so, in fact, would weaken the emphasis the writers want: the glorification of the experience itself. All three end with the bittersweet graduation ceremony that marks the exit from the green world and the joy and pride of achievement mingled with the awareness that something lovely and irreplaceable is over. There are few indications of futures, except for the exceptionally gifted—Susan Jackson, Madeline Ayres, and others like them will become famous and honored writers—but generally life after college is seen as something different, the next phase, and perhaps one that will never duplicate the kind of pleasure they have known. But if the future is a blank, it is not negative. The implicit message is that these women will use what they have in ways that will bring them happiness and that they are the better for the college experience. A kind of self-containment is implied here, a sense of boundaries in time as well as space, so that the fiction, for all its joyousness, does not promise more than these unique four years. After that time, they will be "dignified, sensible women of the outside world, in a little house in a little corner of that world somewhere; and gone forever would be the dear old tribal life." [15] Perhaps this explains why none of the stories reflect the statement that Margaret Emerson Bailey gives to M. Carey Thomas, that if the college has done its job well, the students should be ready to leave it. These young women must seize the day; it will not come again, and the outside world has different goals and purposes for them.

The writers of popular series books were in a different situation, one that invited continuance of their stories. Series like the Helen Grant or Ruth Fielding books, in which going to college is a phase of the heroine's total story, simply allow the character to get on with her life. Ruth Fielding, who becomes a Hollywood director, marries, has a child, and finally gives up her career to allow the series to end, seems unchanged by college; she would have done the same things without it. Helen Grant's purpose in going to college was purely vocational, and when she leaves, she gets a teaching job, continues her adventures, and finally marries.

It is the series books focusing on four years of college that have a problem indicative of the outside world and its realities. Given the practical motive that writer and publisher want to continue a successful series, what does one do with a popular hero after she graduates? The answer was consistent: bring her back to the green world and give her something to do there until her marriage, the acceptable closure for female adventure.

When Betty Wales graduates, she goes home to become the daughter of the house with no plans for anything else—a logical step for the character as she has been created. In four more volumes she joins two friends on a European tour, where she meets and solves problems for an irascible billionaire, whose son will marry Babe, one of her college friends. Returning from her travels, she and Madeline Ayres open a tea shop (or shoppe) in their college town, which Betty manages. The irascible Mr. Morton, however, who has been much impressed by Betty, decides to give Harding College the dormitory for students with financial needs which Betty has wanted, providing that she will come back to the campus to manage it.[16] Her return to the college functions in several ways: it allows the reader to find out more about her and the other chief characters, and, since she has friends who are still undergraduates, the author can continue to display college life. Since the story line remains with Betty and her friends, the campus events are episodic and tend to fall into the "larks and pranks" category.

Betty does not enter an established career, but becomes a businesswoman almost by accident. She had taken no courses in business administration—there were none to take—but clearly her creator and her friends have no doubt that her education has prepared her to take advantage of opportunity; she is ready for whatever happens. Managing the tea shop develops her business skills; managing the dormitory includes managing lives, and again she relies on the philosophy of her own undergraduate years: find one's talent and use it.

This ability to make the most of what life offers is apparent in the post-college life of Betty's friends as well. Those who had prepared for teaching find jobs, often jobs better than the average. (L. M. Montgomery's Anne Shirley, for example, becomes a high school principal, not just a teacher, because of her bachelor's degree.) Some wealthy young women discuss taking jobs so as not to waste their education, but most of them go home to "come out" in society. In the first of the Bryn Mawr stories, an alumna is getting material for an invited paper on college life, and she visits friends who graduated with her.[17] She finds them involved in what seems like a diversity of occupations and therefore options: active clubwomen, women doing in charitable work, women occupied with the arts. But all of them are wealthy; college enriched their lives, but none needs to earn her own living or depend on what she can earn. Too, they have returned to a city where presumably cultural opportunities exist, unlike the young women who must return to their country towns and villages.

Betty Wales goes back home to wait for whatever will happen next, and generally, her friends make lives centered at home or at the campus, with the assumption that marriage is somewhere in the future. Only Madeline is different; like other writers, especially in the collections, she is the one for whom a career is primary. Although she moves back and forth between New York and the campus, her writing comes first—and as the series ends, she is the only one left alone.

When billionaire Morton builds the dormitory, he hires a young architect, Jim Watson, brother of Betty's friend Eleanor. It is clear almost at once which way the series is going; Betty and Jim frequently ride together and he gradually replaces her close women friends, becoming her trusted confidant when problems are troublesome and assuming an increasingly important role in her life. The courtship is downplayed; however important to the people involved, it is a minor theme until the end, and Betty hesitates a long time about giving up her work. But the series ends with their wedding, having either married off, or indicated that marriage lies ahead for the other characters, except gifted Madeline, who feels her separateness: "I have an idea I'm going to miss you fearfully, Betty Wales. A career is an awfully lonely thing, the week your very best little pal is getting married." [18]

So although romance and marriage certainly become more important after graduation, there is no sense of waiting "gracefully passive" for the right man. All the young women are busy and happy, and they show a reluctance for the commitment of marriage. These women must be won, perhaps because they have learned to value themselves, perhaps because they are intelligent in their understanding of what marriage will mean. Characteristically, however, the series continuations are punctuated by weddings as the hero's friends marry, usually leaving her for the last. All make "good" marriages.

Molly Brown, too, returns to the campus, in four more volumes, first as a postgraduate student to prepare herself further for the teaching career she no longer wants; she and Nance share their former dormitory suite. Then she travels abroad and spends time at home before she marries Professor Green and returns as a young matron and faculty wife; she even has children. [19] As in Betty's tale, the author has two main purposes: to continue to talk about college life (Molly heads a student literary group which meets to read and criticize what they have written) and to conclude the adventures of Judy and Nance by getting them married. The outside world, specifically World War I, intrudes when Judy, studying art in Paris, is trapped there by the outbreak of the war with a letter of credit that cannot be honored, and when Molly's brother Kent, engaged to Judy, tries to rescue her, his ship is torpedoed and he is temporarily missing. In the last volume Molly's efforts are divided between patching up the rift between Nance and her longtime sweetheart, Andy, and, something totally new and rather out of character for this series, catching German spies on the campus. At the end she and her two children say good-bye to Professor Green, who has enlisted and is about to go off to the war. There was never a doubt in this series that the author was pointing her characters toward marriage, but even with the heavy romantic emphasis and the availability of men throughout the books, it remains a given that marriage must wait until college is over. No one leaves to marry. [20] Even here the four college years have been established as a woman's time and space, if a somewhat modified version.

For modern readers the negative side of all these good marriages is that young women with talents (other than writing) will not be encouraged or allowed to use them. Molly Brown's friend Margaret, an enormously capable politician and daughter of a senator, is the subject of discussion between her college president and a faculty member: "It will be interesting to watch her career if she only doesn't spoil everything by marrying" (S 34). But the author cannot or will not envision a career for her; in the continuations, Margaret announces her engagement to a young congressman whose star is rising; her political expertise will be used to advance his career, not hers.

Both Marjorie Dean and Grace Harlowe have continuations to their stories, and though their adventures verge on the absurd, the books are interesting for what they, too, say less directly about women's lives. Marjorie and her friends return to Hamilton College as "p.g.'s," postgraduates, though clearly they are in no legitimate degree program and nothing in their lives so far has suggested any dedication to learning. They live in a way unrecognizable to modern graduate students, since they keep their old dormitory rooms and remain active in undergraduate affairs. Whatever course work and studying they do goes unnoticed; they are still cleaning up the campus.

Marjorie in fact needs six more volumes before the campus is organized to her liking. Through her friendship with the elderly Miss Hamilton, she is invited to write the biography of Brooke Hamilton, the founder of the college. Though the reader has never been given a sign that Marjorie is capable of the task, no one doubts that she can do it. At the same time she is actively working to establish the dormitory for needy students, reforming a few who stray from college standards, combating and finally converting Leslie Cairns, and holding off her persistent suitor. Hal, who has loved her since their high school days, is sympathetically portrayed as he watches their friends pair off and marry while Marjorie remains adamant that she does not love him and is devoted to her work. When she has a change of heart and they do marry, Hal moves to the background; though Marjorie's friends comment on how sweetly she and her husband greet each other after a day's separation, her character remains so unaffected by marriage that it is difficult to contemplate any sexual activity between husband and wife. The couple live in Miss Hamilton's mansion at Harding and Marjorie continues her work for and devotion to the college; she will be Miss Hamilton's heir and will in time assume control. Hal, originally a strong character, joins Marjorie's other appendages.

Grace Harlowe and her friends also return to the campus as "p.g.'s" and keep their influence and connections with undergraduate life. Grace herself, like Betty, becomes manager of the dormitory a benefactor built for needy students. She too solves other people's problems and upholds the college standards while holding off her longtime suitor, Tom Gray, and has her moment of discovery, so the last of the college continuations ends with her wedding.

All the returns to the green world reinforce the idea that these women cannot cut the ties with their college life and reenter a world that has no place for them and offers them only empty lives as daughters at home. One of Marjorie Dean's friends, Lucy, who is very bright and goes through college on scholarships, does find a "career" job: she becomes secretary to the (male) president of the college. Molly Brown Green's return is perfectly logical, since she comes back as a faculty wife to the place of her husband's work; Betty Wales and Madeline Ayres try to establish their tea shop in New York, but cannot afford the real estate costs, so locating their tea shop at Harding, where they have a built-in clientele, is also logical. Grace's and Marjorie's reasons for returning are less convincing. It is a telling point that their authors, and indeed all the authors, in order to continue their series, must bring their characters back to the college world as if only there can they remain interesting and have a place. And both Grace and Marjorie, unlike Betty Wales and her friends, marry young men from home; their authors have never given them a chance to meet any others.

One characteristic of the young women in the pre-1930s books is that they are without any sense of a career. They are not preparing themselves to *be* anything specific. Grace Harlowe does wonder what her work will be: "She had no idea as to what life would mean to her when her college days were over. She had not yet found her work." She knows that her father and mother would like her at home, but feels she "ought to be 'up and doing with a heart for any fate' instead of being just a home girl" (J 217). She does not do anything to develop an expertise, but rather seems to expect that her work will descend upon her, as indeed it does. At another time Grace tells a friend, "To choose a profession is easier for boys than for girls. . . . Most boys enter college with their minds made up as to what their future work is going to be, but very few girls decide until the last minute." Her friend reminds her, "Girls whose parents can afford to send them to college don't have to decide, as a rule" (S 178).

Friends with special talents will use them; Anne, already an experienced actress, will join a Shakespearean company (a highly respected one, run by a gentleman-actor whose sister chaperones the cast) for a few years, but she is engaged to her high school sweetheart; Miriam, a gifted pianist, plans to study music in Germany. In the end, all will marry, as their high school friends have already done.

Grace's work, when it does come, is a reflection of society's view of women's role: altruistic and nurturing. Presumably Grace and Betty are paid salaries as house managers, although money is never mentioned, but what they are doing is an extension of volunteer work. In a sense they preside over another version of women's sphere, as do Molly and Marjorie who, though they do not have jobs, still watch over and control the lives of others.

After the high school and college volumes, there are three additional Grace Harlowe books that bring her back to the campus and lead up to her marriage. Then in six more, Grace goes to the battlefields of World War I, ostensibly to drive an ambulance for the Red Cross, but she immediately straightens out bad attitudes, catches spies, defeats regiments, and is generally a major factor in the final victory. Quite a few books for girls bring in World War I in varying degrees of importance; the times encouraged fiction about women "doing their bit" overseas. Many of the stories are silly, but none of the adventures can possibly be as magnificently illogical as are Grace's.[21] The war books are followed by Grace Harlowe's Overland Riders Series: eight books in which Grace and some of her friends, bored when the war ends, tour various parts of the country, chiefly the West, on horseback, solving problems and righting wrongs. Curiously, Grace's husband, a forester and a man of action, almost disappears into the trees; he is present, but the leadership is in Grace's hands (as is frequently her gun). She is supported by "Hippy," the former comic fat boy of the high school series.

These books are so bad that they are funny, but at the same time they are fascinating as they reveal how little there is to do for their strong, educated main character, who moves further and further away from plausibility. In high school and college Grace was an outstanding girl and young woman; in the war she was a superwoman, a Boadicea, but by the Overland Riders series, she has become a man. She outrides, outshoots, and outthinks everyone, and has all the masculine virtues. Tom is simply an adjunct, a wife. Though the author's name is the same and none of the earlier Grace Harlowe books are noted for good writing, the lack of logic and literary skill in the final volumes suggests that the name may have been picked up by a syndicate and the series given to hack writers to continue. Yet publishers do not act from eleemosynary motives, so someone must have bought the books to read of the adventures of mighty Grace and her friends.

It is refreshing, finally, to turn to Beverly Gray and her crowd, who retain their love for and loyalty to their college but who by graduation are quite ready to move on to the next stage; these competent young women go from college into the jobs for which their education has prepared them with no need to explain or apologize. By the 1930s career aimlessness was far less frequent, as indicated by the quantities of "career" books published then, books that take the hero through the steps needed to enter and succeed in her chosen field.

Soon after graduation and a short stay at home, Beverly and three of her friends, unlike their predecessors, head for New York City where they share an apartment and try to find jobs; the volume is even entitled *Beverly Gray's Career*.[22] Beverly's goals are clear: she wants to write, and more immediately she wants a job as a reporter. Her friends have similar ambitions. Shirley wants to act; Lois, a painter, wants a job as an illustrator; and the madcap Lenora becomes part owner of a fashionable gown shop. All four seek jobs and face failure, discouragement, and possible return home in defeat before the needed job materializes. Each acquires a young man (known collectively as "the boys"), and there is a mystery to solve as well. It is minor, however, and the emphasis remains on their establishing themselves in the city. It is paradoxical that at the end of Edna Howe's and Beverly Gray's college years, so distant in time, the characters depart to use their educations in making themselves a place in the world.

Beverly's career as a writer, too, is closer to reality, since hard work precedes success. Unlike Marjorie Dean, who can sit down and write a biography without any apparent preparation for the task, Beverly works seriously at her writing and despairs over the number of rejection slips she gets. She worries about doing well in her job, which in spite of the adventure plots is given the same importance it would have in real life; in fact her adventures, exaggerated as they may be, have a kind of realism in that they grow out of her reporting assignments in most of the remaining thirty volumes in the series.

In the postcollege volumes the emphasis, of course, is on adventure and mystery-solving; Beverly continues to resemble Nancy Drew or Judy Bolton more than Marjorie and Grace. Unlike the latter pair (and even Betty and Molly), who have one man whom they eventually marry, Beverly is popular and has dates, although only two men affect her seriously. Jim, her hometown boyfriend, is faithful and admirable, but she will eventually reject him, again unlike the earlier heroes, in favor of the dashing Larry, the aviator-Secret Serviceman she met in college. They share a love of adventure, and even while they become engaged and plan a home, they are busy tracking down smugglers, chasing robbers, finding spies, solving lost identities, and dealing with any other excitements that come along. In all these activities they are presented and their marriage is projected as an equal partnership.

The two books by Millay and Lapsley, with their intent to expose the evils of the women's colleges, are curiously muddled in their suggestion of a future. While the young women who suffer are chiefly those who truly want an education, there is not much indication of what they plan to do with it. Millay's Rebecca finally rejects the college entirely, leaving before she graduates, and though her gesture is impressive and clearly satisfying to her, the novel leaves her in the midst of the gesture with no hint of what happens next. In Lapsley's story the various main characters remain trapped in a situation that, the author suggests, is destroying them.

For the heroes of the coeducational stories, life after college is simple: they get married. Even Betty White's Dorinda, who leaves college in disgust, marries the brilliant, eccentric James whose qualities and attitudes made him unacceptable to the sorority-fraternity world that she is reject- ing. Her departure, like Rebecca's, is a gesture that satisfies her, but the marriage can be read as her only means of escape. Olive Hormel's Lucia, starting off with a healthy attitude and maturing through her four years, examines career choices and finally decides that she wants to bring what she has learned back to her hometown; her decision is confirmed after she returns and finds that she still loves the boy back home.

The Graper Girls also marry. Marian, for whom the prospect of a ca- reer or even a job never exists, marries almost at once; she is working out the first year of marriage and coming to terms with a very changed life while her younger sisters finish their last year in college. The bright, ac- tive Ernestine tries career and job in New York but gives them up when she realizes that she loves her childhood friend Bob, now finished medi- cal school and ready to begin his practice in their hometown. And Beth, the tennis star, defeated in her match at Forest Hills, marries a million- aire who suddenly appears in the story, presented in so detached and disconnected a manner that the reader can only assume the author must have been in a hurry to finish the last book and get those sisters married off.

Although this study ends with the 1930s, the books about the Graper girls lead logically to a brief look at later fictional accounts of college life for women.[23] Many such stories appear after World War II, and all are set in coeducational colleges. There is no doubt in anyone's mind why women go to college now: like those who enjoyed sorority life at Colossus U., they go to find husbands. They face such problems as deciding whether the high school boyfriend is indeed "Mr. Right," whether he still cares, or whether they should look around for something better. Jeal- ousy is a major motivation and misunderstandings predominate. Though these 1950s heroes are considerably more welcome at their coeduca- tional institutions, and though there is less emphasis on sororities, it is established overtly and without embarrassment that the great adventure of college provides women with wider fields from which to choose or be chosen. The books clearly reflect their era and the various post–World War II pressures to get women out of the work force and back into the home; this is the time of the "togetherness" campaign, the move to sub- urbia, and the creation of the station-wagon wife. After the 1960s, books for young people took on serious issues, often focusing on girls growing up in dysfunctional families or in a society filled with dangers for the young; going to college became simply one option.

To look at the fiction overall is to find some interesting conclusions. The small number of works set in the coeducational schools do not offer space that encourages women to discover their own strengths. Will and her friends are aliens, trying to claim a place as well as establish themselves; later, there is a women's place, but it is artificial and shaped by masculine perceptions of women's role. Education is there if a woman insists on having it, but it is not important enough to be talked about.

The series books set in the women's colleges, filling a gap between two similar efforts to present truth, essentially exploit the college backgrounds and the earlier fiction in order to entertain. As well, and probably unconsciously, stories like those of Marjorie and Grace uphold the noble-woman-as-nurturer image and carry over other earlier expectations about women. The Marjorie Dean books in particular mirror the clash between nineteenth- and twentieth-century values as they oppose good Marjorie to wicked Leslie, who is always defeated.

One must be careful about judging from fiction; nevertheless, it is suggestive that by the 1920s and 1930s much had changed. The college battlefields of Grace and Marjorie indicate that the magic, especially the magic of the women's colleges, was no longer available in the same way. The newness, challenge, adventure, and sense of a private woman's space had become, not commonplace since still only a small percentage of women attended college, but no longer a magical experience. Probably the determined trivializing by magazines like the *Ladies' Home Journal*, the new "fashionable" status of women's colleges and therefore the new kind of student who attended, and the failure or inability of society to provide places for educated women, all contributed to the differences; so did the changed reality of the outside world.

Historically these years were full of movement in women's lives and roles, and it is logical that the fiction reflects a loosening of restrictions. Women entered the work force, they became clubwomen, and, at the extreme, they agitated for women's rights. Activity in sports led to looser clothing; it was impossible to play tennis or ride the popular bicycle in corsets and miles of skirt.[24] The Gibson girl, in her shirtwaist and plain flared skirt, was at least one visual model of womanhood. Lois Banner calls the 1890s "years of transition, during which the advances women had made in the preceding decades began to add up to significant progress, and women's organizations entered a period of rapid growth"; this too is reflected in the fiction. Banner goes on to add, however, that "discrimination still existed in every area of women's experience." [25] Perhaps the awareness of that discrimination or simply the ambivalence of attitudes about women made the authors of the college fiction careful to avoid controversial issues.

The serious fiction about the women's colleges has nonetheless interesting messages for and about women as it explores their particular women's space and community. The early books celebrate an experience and opportunity for women that simply had not existed before; the "warmth and light and color" of what has been called here the green world, a space for women that, judging from the fiction, was at its most challenging in the earliest years and its most satisfying in the twenty years centering on 1900.

The writers of the fiction designated here as early, the pioneers like Helen Dawes Brown and the celebrators like Josephine Daskam Bacon or Margaret Warde, were making serious attempts to show the macrocosm what their college microcosm was really like. So, however, were Lapsley and Millay thirty years later, and the contrasts between the two presentations of women's space are significant. As women gained more freedom in their everyday lives, symbolized by bobbed hair, by changes in dress, by the vote, and certainly by the awareness of sex and the end of the nineteenth-century attitude that saw women as nonsexual beings, the colleges, with their rules and traditions, their preoccupation with image, and their determination to control what women might be permitted to know, seemed more and more restricting, so that the green world became, instead of a place of opportunity and growth, a place of confinement. The physical barriers—walls, gates, fortresslike buildings—were replaced by the restrictive "image" of the college product.

If what the early fictions presented was another version of women's sphere, it was one that encouraged women to develop self within a productive, ethical and stimulating universe. To compare these characters with some of the heroes of nineteenth-century women's fiction is perhaps farfetched, but it is an illuminating comparison. The nineteenth-century novel that deals with young girls growing toward maturity stresses constraint, the suppression or refinement of natural instincts, and the rejection of self in order to reach an ideal of womanly behavior. At the extreme, of course, is Ellen Montgomery of the enormously popular novel *The Wide, Wide World,* who must undergo one painful ordeal after another, each working to strip her of her will, her natural desires, and her self esteem.[26] The same kind of experience, though less painful, comes to Gerty in *The Lamplighter,* another longtime best seller, and to the heroes of Louisa May Alcott's juvenile novels.[27] Subordination of self to concern for others is a goal for these young women, and the corollary is that women will be happy if they are good and if they stop thinking about their own needs and desires. Mary Anne Ferguson describes the fictional world of women in the nineteenth-century novel: "The pattern for the female novel of development has been largely circular . . . women in fiction remain at home. Instead of testing their self-image through adventures in the outside world, they are initiated at home through learning the rituals of human relationships, so that they may replicate the lives of their mothers. . . . Women who rebel against the female role are perceived as unnatural and must pay the price of unhappiness."[28]

But this is just what the early serious portrayals of women in college do not do. Instead they break the pattern of nineteenth-century women's fiction, for this new world takes women away from their homes and weakens the function of mothers as role models. Social relationships and interaction occur and community develops from a different, wider, base. A new goal, learning, replaces older, more conventional ones. Most important, the women's college fiction, while it conforms to certain behavioral standards, emphasizes discovery and expansion of self, talent, and desire and glorifies the resulting happiness that comes from stretching the self and enjoyment of the process. Above all, interests need not conform; there is respect for individual talents and differences. Physical space may be confined and restricted; mental space is not.

Far from a sphere or space where women are encouraged to find their abilities and develop them, Lapsley and Millay create spaces that oppress because the aim is to mold the young women into conformity—to clone them into an image established as desirable by those who are more concerned with the outside world's judgments than with the needs of the students, who can leave the place, as Rebecca does, or can hang on with a kind of pitiful grimness to get the education—or the degree—that they want. Physical freedom is a given; the restrictions are on the use of the mind. While after *Two College Girls* the intellectual experience is not stressed, it is available; the caveat is that those who only study are missing a large part of the valuable experience and are not making their contribution to the college. But the exposés by Lapsley and Millay offer a world in which young women who want to feed their intellects must fight to do so. Critical thinking does not fit the image the college wants.

The early fiction as part of its thesis insists that higher education does not make women unfit for marriage, but it puts marriage after graduation and refuses to allow it, in the form of men and romance, to dominate or encroach on the unique experience. In contrast, the later fiction asserts an institutional and societal insistence that women must marry; Millay, especially, condemns Matthew College for its credo that any kind of marriage to any kind of man is better than no marriage at all. She implies, too, that the chief reason for this policy is to make the college look good in the statistics.

One would expect, in a study covering these years, to find a progression, and indeed the progression is there. Unfortunately it is not a record of steady gains and movement from restriction to freedom, but rather a mixture of views reflecting ambivalence about women—and, indeed, women's ambivalence about themselves. As just one example, in the same period that Betty Wales and her friends are exploring college life, learning to respect themselves and others, and enjoying every minute, Helen Grant is treating college as a vocational opportunity whose only real virtue is to train her to teach, and she and her friends are more concerned lest it affect their fitness for marriage than anything else.

But complex and inconsistent as it is, the progression marks the distance women traveled in those years—from the guarded green world with all its spacial restrictions which offered women more freedom and room to stretch themselves than anything else available to them and so much fulfillment that the college years were somehow unmatchable, to the place where, even though physical restrictions had all but vanished, the space was a prison compared to the outside world.

The pioneers, like Edna Howe, came to college able to learn facts and were taught to think with those facts in a green world that offered them far more opportunity than did the conventional one. The young women who people the turn-of-the-century collections, if less academic, came to stretch themselves, to develop their abilities and widen their understanding of a world full of difference. But Rebecca and her contemporaries, in search of knowledge, came to an image-bound institution that had crystallized in its attempt to produce an acceptable compromise between traditional and modern women.

The women's colleges as presented by the fiction display two parallel movements. One, a progression reflecting the outside world, is a steady loosening of the restrictions on women's behavior, a move toward more and more freedom and self-determination. The second is less attractive and even regressive. The early college experience pushed women to self-discovery and encouraged the expansion of their world. As part of the process, women made friends with and learned to appreciate other women, so that the sharing of experience and difference built a rich, rewarding community. But, as Nina Auerbach suggests, communities of women, so outside and independent of the patriarchal norm, are threatening:

> As a recurrent literary image, a community of women is a rebuke to the conventional ideal of a solitary woman living for and through men, attaining citizenship in the community of adulthood through masculine approval alone. The communities of women which have haunted our literary imagination from the beginning are emblems of female self-sufficiency which create their own corporate reality, evoking both wishes and fears.[29]

Auerbach's words apply to this fiction and to the world it reflects. The serious achievements of the pioneers and the joyous, self-contained worlds that followed were women's spaces that threatened the established order and therefore, one way or another, had to be controlled. Eventually the attempts at control could not succeed, but it is the stages along the way that fiction about women in college presented to its readers. It is fiction, not factual or historical accounts, that we have examined here, and while these tales should not be read as exact truth, they do reflect the conflicts, opportunities, pains, and joys of the as yet uncompleted movement toward women's equality and self-determination.

# *Notes*

The following abbreviations have been used in the annotation.

*Bryn Mawr*      *A Book of Bryn Mawr Stories*, ed. Margaretta Morris and Louise Buffum Congdon (Philadelphia: George W. Jacobs, 1901)

*LHJ*      *Ladies' Home Journal*

*Smith*      Josephine Daskam Bacon, *Smith College Stories* (New York: Charles Scribner's, 1900)

*Vassar*      Grace M. Gallaher, *Vassar Stories* (Boston: Richard G. Badger, 1899)

*Wellesley*      Grace L. Cook, *Wellesley Stories* (Boston: Richard G. Badger, 1904)

In the series books about the four college years of Betty Wales, Molly Brown, Grace Harlowe, Marjorie Dean, Beverly Gray, the different volumes will be identified by the following abbreviations, even when the titles do not always correspond.

F      Freshman
S      Sophomore
J      Junior
Sr      Senior

## Introduction

1. Sophia Kirk, "The College Girl and the Outside World," *Lippincott's Magazine* 65 (1900), 596–602.

2. I am particularly grateful to the work of such writers and critics as Nina Baym, Cathy Davidson, Judith Fetterly, Elaine Showalter, and others, who in different ways have taught us to widen our vision and read more wisely.

3. Alfred Habeggar, *Gender, Fantasy, and Realism in American Literature* (New York: Columbia University Press, 1982), viii–ix.

4. John O. Lyons, *The College Novel in America* (Carbondale: University of Southern Illinois Press, 1962), xvii. He discusses women's novels in chapter 3, "The Young Ladies and the Double Standard," 47–67.

5. Lyons's choices include many that are not college novels in my sense of the term. For example, he spends much time on Honoré Morrow's *Lydia of the Pines* (New York: Frederick A. Stokes, 1917). Though Lydia's education in the largest sense is the major theme of the novel, the experience of college is not. She is a country girl who lives at home and attends a nearby college, which seldom intrudes on her real life, since her developing maturity depends on her relationships with family and community. She is thrilled when she is elected to the Scholar's Club, of which the college president and "the best of the professors and only a few of the post-graduate pupils" are members—she calls them "highbrows"— (353–355) but the honor comes at her graduation and will not affect her college life; nor does it predict the future, since she has decided to marry a local farmer. Another choice Lyons makes is *Grey Towers: A Campus Novel* by Zoe Flannagan (Chicago: Covici-Magee, 1923), whose protagonist is a college instructor. Caroline Zilboorg in "Women before World War I: An Exploration of Their Awakening in the College Novel" (*Great Lakes Review* 7 [Summer 1981]: 29–38) explores much of the same material that Lyons examines. Such books as Mary Medeary's *College in Crinoline* (New York: Longmans Green, 1950), a well-researched historical novel of life at what was primarily a training college for teachers, also do not fit my definition.

6. Richard Tebbel, *A History of Book Publishing in the United States* (New York: R. R. Bowker, 1975), 2:647.

7. See Barbara Miller Solomon, *In the Company of Educated Women* (New Haven: Yale University Press, 1985); Helen Lefkowitz Horowitz, *Alma Mater: Design and Experience in the Women's Colleges from Their Nineteenth-Century Beginnings to the 1930s* (New York: Alfred A. Knopf, 1984); Lynn D. Gordon, *Gender and Higher Education in the Progressive Era* (New Haven: Yale University Press, 1990); Mabel Newcomer, *A Century of Higher Education for Women* (Boston: Houghton Mifflin, 1959). In several instances these authors use some of the same material that I use here; this is particularly true of Gordon but her reading and interpretation of the fiction differ from mine.

8. A useful source of information is Karen Nelson Hoyle, ed., *Girls Series Books: A Checklist of Hardback Books Published 1900–1975.* (Minneapolis: Children's Literature Research Collection, University of Minnesota Library, 1978).

9. Henry Noble MacCracken, *The Hickory Limb* (New York: Charles Scribner's, 1950), 45–46.

10. "New President Is Appointed at Barnard," *New York Times*, Mar. 22, 1994, B1, B8.

11. American Association of University Women, "How Schools Short-Change Girls," and "Hostile Hallways, the AAUW Study on Sexual Harassment in America's Schools" (Washington, D.C.: AAUW Educational Foundation, 1993).

12. "Women's Colleges Find a New Popularity," *New York Times*, Jan. 15, 1994, B1, B8.

## ONE  *Beginnings*

1. Olive San Louie Anderson, *An American Girl and Her Four Years in a Boy's College* (New York: D. Appleton, 1878), signed in the original "by SOLA"; Helen Dawes Brown, *Two College Girls* (Boston: Ticknor, 1886); Abbe Carter Goodloe, *College Girls* (New York: Charles Scribner's, 1895).

2. Elizabeth Stuart Phelps, "A Brave Girl," *Wide-Awake* 18, 19 (1884), published in book form by D. Lothrop, 1884; Elizabeth Champney, *Three Vassar Girls*

*in the Tyrol* (Boston: Estes and Lauriat, 1891). Since Champney graduated from Vassar in 1869, a member of the first class, it is unfortunate that she did not write more directly about the experience.

I thank Carol Farley Kessler for calling the Phelps story to my attention. I have not found a copy of the book, so all citations are from the magazine version.

3. Dorothy Guies McGuigan, *A Dangerous Experiment: 100 Years of Women at the University of Michigan* (Ann Arbor: University of Michigan Press, 1970).

4. The work, reprinted in Julia Ward Howe, ed., *Sex and Education: A Reply to Dr. E. H. Clarke's "Sex in Education"* (Boston: Roberts Brothers, 1874; repr. New York: Arno, 1972), will be discussed in Chapter 2.

5. At least the only one that I have found. There are certainly novels in which young women attend coeducational colleges, but the experience is one part of a whole life. Louisa May Alcott's Plumfield "college" in *Jo's Boys* is really an extended family that she constructed for her own literary purposes.

6. Review, *Atlantic Monthly* 57 (May 1886): 718.

7. Chapter 5, 56–71. This is the best scene in the novel, but it is too long to quote in full and excerpts alone do not convey the movement, coherence, and quality of the original.

8. They are reading Henry James, *The Portrait of a Lady*, chap. 7.

9. Nina Baym, *Women's Fiction* (Ithaca: Cornell University Press, 1979); for an excellent account of primitive initiation structures, though certainly not applied to women, see Mircia Eliade, *Rites and Symbols of Initiation* (New York: Harper and Row, 1958).

10. Edward Everett Hale's short story was printed in *Harper's Monthly* 80 (May 1870): 908–918. Frustrated at restrictions, college graduate Susan constructs a dummy escort, which eventually takes on a life of its own.

11. I have not found the date of her graduation, but she was born in 1867, so my 1888 date is a guess based on the assumption that she would graduate at 21.

12. Review of *College Girls, Critic* 28 (Apr. 18, 1896): 271.

13. Abbe Carter Goodloe, "Undergraduate Life at Wellesley," *Scribner's* 23 (May 1898): 520. This and its companion articles are discussed more fully in Chapter 2.

14. Alfred, Lord Tennyson, "The Princess" (1847) gently mocks the efforts of the Princess to found an intellectual enclave for women and assumes inevitable failure. See also William S. Gilbert and Arthur S. Sullivan, *Princess Ida.*

15. Nina Auerbach, *Communities of Women: An Idea in Fiction* (Cambridge: Harvard University Press, 1978), 11.

16. The review is of Josephine Daskam Bacon's *Smith College Stories, Book Buyer* 20 (May 1900): 326; this work will be discussed in Chapter 3 and following.

17. Lyons, *College Novel*, chap. 1, "The Doctrine of the Vernal Wood," 3–23.

18. Northrop Frye, "The Argument of Comedy," 79–89, in *Shakespeare: Modern Essays in Criticism*, ed. Leonard Dean (New York: Oxford University Press, 1957, 1967). See also Harry Berger Jr., *Second World and Green World: Studies in Renaissance Fiction-Making* (Berkeley: University of California Press, 1988). The green world is a concept so vital to the understanding of Shakespeare that it has become standard; sometimes it is hard to remember that the idea had a source.

19. Lida McCabe, *The American Girl at College* (New York: Dodd, Mead, 1893). No source is given for the lines, which serve as an epigraph for the volume.

20. Annis Pratt, *Archetypal Patterns in Women's Fiction* (Bloomington: Indiana University Press, 1981), 16–24.

21. Horowitz, *Alma Mater*, xv.

22. *Wellesley*, 234.

23. MacCracken, *Hickory Limb*, 194–205. Although I have not found the passage, MacCracken is quoting Ruskin, who in turn is modifying the words of John Donne's description of a university.

24. These college collections will be discussed more fully later. For full references see Chap. 3, n. 5.

25. *Vassar*, 10.

## TWO  *The World Outside*

1. Though the attitude seems strange today, it was prevalent. Penn State, founded in 1855, admitted women in the 1870s. They could major in the sciences, engineering, and home economics but were not allowed into liberal arts until 1912.

2. Susan Phinney Conrad, *Perish the Thought: Intellectual Women in Romantic America, 1830–1860* (New York: Oxford University Press, 1976), 5.

3. Clarke, *Sex in Education* in Howe, ed. *Sex and Education.* This collection presents the major writings for and against higher education for women.

4. Catharine Beecher in her *Treatise on Domestic Economy, for the Use of Young Ladies at Home or at School* (New York: Harper's, 1841, 1851) held another, less controversial position: women should be educated because they created homes and reared the citizens of the future, but that education should be geared to their special needs as homemakers. That philosophy led to the creation of such "women's courses" as home economics; it also justified many of the coeducational colleges' attempts to segregate women.

5. See especially Dio Lewis, *Our Girls* (New York: Harper's, 1871).

6. One juvenile series by Gertrude W. Morrison, *The Girls of Central High* (New York: Grosset and Dunlap, 1914), chronicles in its first volume the attempts to start athletic programs for high school girls in a small town where boys already have the opportunities for sports. The girls have to battle the opposition of both parents and townspeople, and the most controversial activity is basketball.

7. Frances Hodgson Burnett, *The Secret Garden* (New York: Grosset and Dunlap, 1910). Although certainly not a camping book and not intended as a juvenile, in a sense it is a prototype for the presentation of the healing powers of nature. Many girls' books were based on that same philosophy; a series that begins with *The Outdoor Girls of Deepdale* by Laura Lee Hope (New York: Grosset and Dunlap, 1913), a Stratemeyer book, for example, has its girls engaged in outdoor activites that are usually restricted to boys as well as involved in solving the occasional mystery; in the first volume they go on a walking trip, covering twenty miles a day. For what is possibly the best of this type, see Hildegard G. Frey's Campfire Girls series (New York: A. L. Burt, 1916).

8. Anne Maynard Kidder, "In Maytime," *Bryn Mawr*, 77.

9. Harriet Jean Crawford, "Catherine's Career," *Bryn Mawr*, 209–211.

10. "On Baccalaureate Sunday," *Vassar*, 254–256.

11. Marian T. Mackintosh, *Bryn Mawr*, 13–72.

12. Edith Campbell Crane, *Bryn Mawr*, 265.

13. Amelia Barr, *Girls of a Feather* (New York: R. Bonner, 1893), 15, 92.

14. Alumna, A. B., "Does the Girls' College Destroy the Wife?" *LHJ* 33 (June 1916): 27; William S. Sadler, M.D., "College Women and Race Suicide," *LHJ* 39 (Apr. 1922): 29, 58ff.

The first article, subtitled "A Frank Confession of Why One College Graduate Has Not Married," argues that not education but circumstances are at fault; young men have to establish themselves before they can marry, and by the time they are ready for marriage, like-aged women are considered too old. Sadler's piece, subtitled "Does Higher Education Unfit Them for Marriage and Mother-hood?" argues that educated women marry later and produce fewer children; therefore "race suicide confronts us if every childbearing mother does not . . . produce these four offspring." Fewer, even three, "would not enable the race to quite hold its own." Race here is used to mean nationality; Sadler is concerned with preserving what he calls "American stock" (in one place, "native-American stock") which he sees as superior to all others. His article, though more open than most, is fairly typical of this attitude.

15. Jean Webster, *Daddy Long-Legs* (New York: Century, 1912), 268.

16. C. S. Parrish, "The Womanly Woman," *Independent* Apr. 4, 1901, 776, 778. This is an excellent article, but discouraging, since many of its arguments are still being made today.

17. William DeWitt Hyde, *The College Man and the College Woman* (Boston: Houghton Mifflin, 1906), vii, 197, 201.

18. See Barbara Welter, "The Cult of True Womanhood, 1820–1860," *American Quarterly* 48 (1966): 151–174; Ronald W. Hogeland, "'The Female Append-age': Feminine Life-Styles in America, 1820–1860," *Civil War History* 17 (1971): 101–114.

19. Frances B. Cogan, *All-American Girl: The Ideal of Real Womanhood in Mid-Nineteenth Century America* (Athens: University of Georgia Press, 1989), 4.

20. Elizabeth K. Helsinger, Robin Lauterbach Sheets, and William Veeder, *The Woman Question: Society and Literature in Britain and America, 1837–1883* (New York: Garland, 1983), introduction, xi.

21. Gordon, *Gender and Higher Education*, 11.

22. "On Baccalaureate Sunday," *Vassar*, 245.

23. Amanda O. Douglas, *Helen Grant in College* (Boston: Lothrop, Lee and Shepard, 1906), 322.

24. MacCracken, *Hickory Limb*, 24.

25. Mabel Newcomer in *A Century of Higher Education for Women* (Boston: Houghton Mifflin, 1959) carefully examines histories of women college gradu-ates and finds no evidence to back up the claim that college destroys health.

26. Martha Pike Conant, *A Girl of the Eighties at College and at Home: The Family Letters of Charlotte Howard Conant* (Boston: Houghton Mifflin, 1931), 128.

27. S. Weir Mitchell, "When the College is Harmful to a Girl," *LHJ* 17 (June 1900): 4. The article prints an address he made to Radcliffe students; not surpris-ingly, he feels that harm comes when education interferes with women's ability to "be good wives and mothers." He adds, "I never saw a professional woman who had not lost some charm."

28. Bok was a major figure in the development of popular magazines; see Salme Harju Steinberg, *Reformer in the Marketplace: Edward W. Bok and the Ladies' Home Journal* (Baton Rouge: Louisiana State University Press, 1979). I chose this magazine because of Bok's importance, its wide circulation, and because it seems representative of the magazines of its type.

29. Adele-Marie Shaw, "Kate Douglas Wiggin As She Really Is As a Woman," *LHJ* 18 (May 1905): 5 ff.

30. Winfield Scott Moody, "Daisy Miller and the Gibson Girl," *LHJ* 21 (Sept. 1904): 17; Caroline Ticknor, "The Steel-Engraving Lady and the Gibson Girl," *Atlantic Monthly* 88 (1899): 105–108.

31. Bok, "Problems of Young Men," *LHJ* 12 (Jan. 1895): 12.

32. Bok, "My Quarrel with Women's Clubs," *LHJ* 27 (Jan. 1910): 5–6.

33. T. DeWitt Talmadge, "Male and Female Created He Them," *LHJ* 10 (Sept. 1893): 14.

34. An American Mother, "Is College the Best Thing for Our Girls?" *LHJ* 17 (July 1900): 15.

35. "Fetes of College Girls," *LHJ* 16 (June 1899): 3 ff.; "Inside the Rooms of College Girls" 15 (Mar. 1898): 7; Carolyn Halsted, "What a Girl Does in College" 18 (Dec. 1901): 26–27; 19 (Jan. 1902): 24–25, (Feb. 1902), 24–25, (Mar.), 26–27, (Apr.), 26–27, (May), 26–27, (Sept.), 26–27.

36. "College Scrapes We Got Into," *LHJ* 18 (Sept. 1901): 13–14 ff.; "College Girls' Larks and Pranks" 17 (Mar. 1900): 7–8, (Apr.), 16, (Aug.), 1–2; "When College Girls Have their Fun," 20 (Mar. 1903): 4; "Christmas Pranks of College Girls" 23 (Dec. 1906): 7; "The Dainties at College Girls' Spreads" 24 (Sept. 1907): 31; "Madcap Frolics of College Girls" 22 (Oct. 1905): 17 ff.; Mrs. S. T. Rorer, "What College Girls Eat" 22 (Nov. 1905): 13–14.

Margaret M. Caffrey in her biography, *Ruth Benedict: Stranger in This Land* (Austin: University of Texas Press, 1989), uses some of these same titles to create the atmosphere of her subject's years at Vassar.

37. Bok did, however, print serious articles about ways that young women could work their way through college and gave a certain amount of recognition to those who did; the assumptions were that these students would have to support themselves or others, or would never find a husband, and were just learning job skills.

38. Nell Speed, *Molly Brown's Senior Days* (New York: Hurst, 1913), 83–84.

39. See for example Emma E. Walker, "'Crushes' among Girls," *LHJ* 21 (Jan. 1904): 41. Walker's piece is part of a column entitled "Pretty Girl Papers." Crushes are discussed in Chapter 7.

40. Thomas Wentworth Higginson, "Ought Women to Learn the Alphabet?" *Atlantic Monthly* 3 (1859): 137–150. In his reminiscences called *Cheerful Yesterdays* (Boston: Houghton Mifflin, 1898) Higginson mentions editor James Russell Lowell's hesitation over printing so "radical" an essay, says that it turned out to be his most frequently reprinted article, and claims that it influenced the founders of the early women's colleges. See also his *Women and the Alphabet* (Boston: Houghton Mifflin, 1880; repr. New York: Arno Press, 1972) for this and his other writings on the subject of women and their rights.

41. Kirk, "College Girl," 596.

42. Margaret Sherwood, "Undergraduate Life at Vassar," *Scribner's* 23 (June 1898): 643–660. Included in the series are Goodloe, "Undergraduate Life at Wellesley," *Scribner's* 23 (May 1898): 515–538; Alice K. Fallows, "Undergraduate Life at Smith," *Scribner's* 24 (July 1898): 37–58.

43. Helen Gray Cone, "Women in American Literature," *Century* 40 (Oct. 1890): 921–930. Five years later Frances Doughty in the *Critic* (27 [Oct. 5, 1895], 209–210), brought up the subject again; college women, she wrote, have their "critical faculty" so highly trained that they either ignore fiction or are hesitant about their ability to do the best work. Or they use their productive years in employment, motherhood, or reform. Or, perhaps, the number of women college graduates who produce "creative literature" matches proportionately the number of men college graduates who do.

44. Arthur Bartlett Maurice, "The Undergraduate in Fiction," *Bookman* 11 (1900): 424–426. Maurice's review covered Bacon's *Smith College Stories* and *Stanford Stories* by Charles K. Field and Will H. Irwin (New York: Doubleday Page, 1901).

45. Dorothy Burgess for example in *Dream and Deed: The Story of Katharine Lee Bates* (Norman: University of Oklahoma Press, 1952) treats her subject's undergraduate years at Wellesley very seriously; she gives only a few indications that Bates and her friends had relaxed good times. Bates, who later taught at Wellesley, was a well-known poet as well as scholar.

46. "The Moulders of Public Opinion," *Vassar*, 60–61.

47. Josephine Daskam Bacon, "Point of View," *Her Fiancé, and Other Stories* (New York: Scribner's 1904).

48. Margaret Warde [Edith Kellog Duncan], *Betty Wales, Freshman* (Philadelphia: Penn Publishing, 1904), 90.

49. Edith Bancroft, *Jane Allen of the Sub-Team* (New York: Saalfield, 1917), 32–33. I assume that *Beatrice Horton's First Year at Exeley* is a made-up title.

## THREE   *Living Together: The Celebration of Community*

1. Margaret Warde [Edith Kellog Dunton], *Betty Wales, Freshman* (Philadelphia: Penn Publishing, 1904), *Betty Wales, Sophomore* (1905), *Betty Wales, Junior* (1906), *Betty Wales, Senior* (1907). The series was reprinted at least five times, the last time in 1932.

According to Annie Russell Marble (*Pen Names and Personalities* [New York: D. Appleton, 1930], 180), Warde used a pseudonym because she did not want her younger sister at Smith to "be annoyed by a connection with anyone writing stories about college life" and she did not want "Smith to be embarrassed by a graduate's impressions, wholly fictional but never so regarded by one's friends."

2. Jean Webster, *When Patty Went to College* (New York: Century, 1903). The Patty stories appeared in *Scribner's Magazine* and were collected in the college volume and later as *Just Patty* (1911); *Daddy Long-Legs* (New York: Century, 1912) had innumerable reprints: Nell Speed [Emma Speed Sampson], *Molly Brown's Freshman Days, Molly Brown's Sophomore Days, Molly Brown's Junior Days, Molly Brown's Senior Days* (New York: Hurst, 1912–1913).

3. In addition to writing stories, critical essays, and novels, Bacon became the first editor of the Girl Scout magazine, *The American Girl*, in 1917.

4. Waldron K. Post, *Harvard Stories* (New York: Putnam's, 1893; Freeport, New York: Books for Libraries Press, 1969); J. L. Williams, *Princeton Stories* (New York: Charles Scribner's, 1895); Charles K. Field and Will H. Irwin, *Stanford Stories: Tales of a Young University* (New York: Doubleday, Page, 1901); John Clair Minot and Donald Francis Snow, *Tales of Bowdoin* (Augusta, Me.: Press of the Kennebec Journal, 1901); John S. Wood, *Yale Yarns* (New York: Putnam, 1895, 1902); James Gardner Sanderson, *Cornell Stories* (New York: Scribner's, 1898). There may be others I have not seen.

5. As far as I can tell, this is the first series; advertising in the Helen Grant books however lists *Jean Cabot at Ashton* by Gertrude Fisher Scott, with three other titles, as a college series, and it would be contemporary with the Betty Wales books. I have been unable to locate any of the Jean Cabot series.

6. Marjorie Pryse, Afterword, *Selected Stories of Mary E. Wilkins Freeman* (New York: W. W. Norton, 1983), 322.

7. See, for example, the high school books in the Grace Harlowe and Marjorie Dean series (discussed in Chapter 5); both heroes "adopt" a poor girl into their crowd.

8. Goodloe, "Undergraduate Life at Wellesley," 522–523.

9. Fallows, "Undergraduate Life at Smith College," 41, 44.

10. Webster, *When Patty Went to College*, 62.

11. The play starred Ruth Chatterton as Judy and ran for 264 performances, beginning September 28, 1914; it later had a revival. As for the film, which I accidentally saw on television, it bears little relation to the original.

12. Inscriptions in secondhand copies show that they were given as Christmas or birthday presents or Sunday School prizes; many are carefully identified, and

some have penciled lists of the other books in the series, checked off as the owner acquired each new volume.

13. Margaret Emerson Bailey, *Good-Bye Proud World!* (New York: Century, 1945). Although the book does not meet my standard of immediacy, it is worth reading for itself and in connection with the fiction examined here, for both its similarities and differences. The hero of the novel comes to Bryn Mawr, where the green world exists but has to be discovered. Meg is a scholar, and she does not arrive full of anticipation. Used to the indigenous architecture of Harvard and Brown, where her father taught, she finds the brand-new Gothic style of Bryn Mawr artificial. Her professor's refusal to credit the existence of an American literature frustrates her, and she is dismayed when her well-written themes with familiar characters and settings are returned marked "provincial." It takes a while before the college becomes a real presence in her life.

Another book that is close to this category is a juvenile, *Babs at College*, by Alice Ross Colver (Philadelphia: Penn Publishing, 1920). Written twenty years later than the short story collections and set just before World War I, it shares the joyousness of the collections, but not their serious attempts to show more than one facet of college life; it is a celebration of Wellesley traditions into which the hero and her friends happily fit themselves. As in the pages of *Ladies' Home Journal*, going to college is one special event after another.

14. See Josephine Daskam Bacon, *Kathy* (New York: Longmans Green, 1934), 1–7.

## FOUR  *Living Together: Rewards and Limits*

1. "The Winning of the Cane" in Williams, *Princeton Stories* 1–35. There are similar "rushes" in other masculine collections and in *Stanford Sketches*, where the women students are spectators.

2. Burt L. Standish [William Gilbert Patten], *Frank Merriwell at Yale* (New York: Street and Smith, 1894), and innumerable other titles.

3. Owen Johnson, *Stover at Yale* (New York: Frederick A. Stokes, 1912); the story was serialized in *McClure's Magazine*, 1911–1912.

4. The histories confirm that student government came to different schools at different times; as a part of college life, it is most obvious in the Smith and Wellesley collections. It seems to have come to Vassar last; Bryn Mawr opened in 1883 with student government in place.

5. Hannah Lyman is mentioned in all the histories and in *Letters from Old-Time Vassar: Written by a Student in 1869–70* (Poughkeepsie: Vassar College, 1915). See particularly pages 103–105 and 146–147 of this charming collection of letters.

6. Women faculty are consistently called teachers everywhere but in the Wellesley stories; there they are professors. That collection also suggests an emphasis on friendships between faculty and students and generally presents faculty as happy and admired women. Wellesley was the first college to have a woman president, Alice Freeman (Palmer). Only the Molly Brown series has a woman head, but the significance of that fact is sadly undercut by the statement that she "succeeded her father" as president (S 74).

7. Frances L. Warner (*On A New England Campus* [Boston: Houghton Mifflin, 1937], 114–115) writing about Mount Holyoke, tells of "Miss Lyon's young ladies stepping out their 'mile a day no matter what weather,' " using the half-mile posts on the surrounding roads as their measure (115).

8. "Her Position," *Vassar*, 86–87.

9. Gordon, *Gender and Higher Education*, 4.

10. See 186–188. Several other books portray or suggest the acting out of the election process. Since women could not yet vote, perhaps this was a forward-looking sign.

11. Cora Armistead Hardy, *Bryn Mawr*, 169–193.

12. Harriot Stanton Blatch, *Challenging Years* (New York: Putnam's, 1940), 35–36.

13. "The Clan, *Vassar*, 215, and "A Family Affair," *Smith*, 184.

14. Liva Baker, *I'm Radcliffe! Fly Me: The Seven Sisters and the Failure of Women's Education* (New York: Macmillan, 1976), 11–12.

15. Dorothy W. Cantor and Toni Bernay, with Jean Stoess, *Women in Power: The Secrets of Leadership* (Boston: Houghton Mifflin, 1992). This recent study of women in politics points out that a large percentage of women elected to office went to single-sex schools: "Women's colleges have been found to be twice as likely as comparable coed schools to produce achievers" (204–208).

16. Annabel Sharp, *Peggy Parsons, A Hampton Freshman* (New York: M. A. Donahue, 1916). There was a previous volume to this well-written story, but I have not been able to find it; this is the only author not even listed in the Library of Congress holdings.

17. This is perhaps another version of the fear of success noted by Matina Horner, "Fail: Bright Women," *Psychology Today*, Nov. 1969, 36 ff. There is the same reluctance to compete or to be perceived as stepping out of place. See also Valerie Miner and Helen E. Longino, eds., *Competition: A Feminist Taboo* (New York: Feminist Press, 1987).

18. "On Baccalaureate Sunday," *Vassar*, 239–269.

19. "A Lyrical Interlude," *Wellesley*, 189–239.

20. Elva Lee, *Bryn Mawr*, 124.

21. Georgiana Goddard King, "Free among the Dead," *Bryn Mawr*, 159.

22. Cornelia Otis Skinner, *Family Circle* (Boston: Houghton Mifflin, 1948), 274. Skinner finishes: "She [the Bryn Mawr ideal] was typified by the girl who, selected as the best all-round, jolly-good person of the year was awarded a prize known, I regret to say, as the 'Sunny Jim,' a distinction rating as much local publicity as the European Fellowship given for academic distinction."

23. Margaret F. Thorp, *Neilson of Smith* (New York: Oxford University Press, 1956), 253.

24. Ada M. Comstock, *The American College Girl* (Boston: L. C. Page, 1930), 295.

25. Even the movement toward and the establishment of settlement houses and work, a serious involvement for many students and graduates by this time, is never mentioned.

## FIVE   *Living Together: The Disintegration of Community*

1. Dates given range from the 1890s to the 1920s. *College Girls* assumes social differences that will affect choice of friends without making a point of snobbery.

2. Thorp, *Neilson*, 253–254

3. The situation echoes one briefly suggested in *Smith*, 306–310, indicating that the two authors might have encountered similar circumstances as students.

4. Margaret Warde, "The Freshman Freak," *St. Nicholas Magazine* 40 (1912–1913): 1013–1018.

5. Carol Billman, *The Secret of the Stratemeyer Syndicate* (New York: Ungar, 1986)

is an interesting study of this publishing phenomenon. See also Dierdre Johnson, ed., *Stratemeyer Pseudonyms and Series Books* (Westport, Conn.: Greenwood Press, 1982).

6. Amanda O. Douglas, *Helen Grant in College* (1906) and *Helen Grant, Senior* (1907). Douglas was a prolific and popular writer of fiction for a wide audience; most of her fiction, whether for adult or juvenile readers, concerns girls growing into womanhood.

7. Jeanette Marks, *A Girl's Student Days and After* (New York: Fleming H. Revell, 1911), 29.

8. Jessie Graham Flower, A.M. [sic], *Grace Harlowe's Plebe Year at Overton College* (Philadelphia: Henry Altemus, 1914), *Grace Harlowe's Second Year at Overton College* (1914), *Grace Harlowe's Third Year at Overton College* (1914), *Grace Harlowe's Fourth Year at Overton College* (1914); and Pauline Lester, *Marjorie Dean, College Freshman* (New York: A. L. Burt, 1922), *Marjorie Dean, College Sophomore* (1922); *Marjorie Dean, College Junior* (1922); *Marjorie Dean, College Senior* (1922).

9. Daisy Newman, *A Golden String* (New York: Harper and Row, 1986), says that in planning a children's story she usually followed editorial advice: "The child had to be a boy—girls, it was generally assumed, would like reading about him but boys wouldn't want to read about a girl" (45). Newman was a novelist who also wrote juveniles.

10. Neither series is listed as part of Stratemeyer's productions; probably Lester read Flower and both had read the earlier works. Although the writing is poor in both series, they have a greater sense of authenticity and much more liveliness than the Helen Grant books.

11. Treatment and life of first-year students are detailed in Alice K. Fallows, "The Girl Freshman," *Munsey's Magazine* 25 (Sept. 1901): 818–828. Meeting new students had by this time grown into an important and pleasant ritual, and one expected by the newcomers.

12. In both cases the high school books are somewhat more interesting because they put more emphasis on character development.

13. Carroll Smith-Rosenberg, *Disorderly Conduct* (New York: Alfred A. Knopf, 1985). Other works that examine the changes in women's lives during these years are Barbara Kuhn Campbell, *The "Liberated" Woman of 1914* (UMI Research Press, 1979); George H. Douglas, *Women of the Twenties* (Dallas, Tex.: Saybrook Press, 1986); Paula S. Fass, *The Damned and the Beautiful* (New York: Oxford, 1977); Susan Ware, *Holding Their Own: American Women in the 1930s* (Boston: Twayne, 1982).

14. Thorp, *Neilson*, 247–248.

15. Katherine Stokes, *The Motor Maids' School Days* (New York: Hurst and Co., 1911); Margaret Penrose, *The Motor Girls* (New York: Cupples and Leon, 1917); Laura Dent Crane, *The Automobile Girls* (Philadelphia: Henry Altemus, 1912). These titles are the first volumes of their respective series.

16. Dana Gaitlin, *Harper's Bazar* 47 (1913): 69.

17. Edith Bancroft, *Jane Allen of the Sub-Team* (New York: Saalfield, 1917); *Jane Allen, Right Guard* (1918); *Jane Allen, Center* (1920); *Jane Allen, Junior* (1921); *Jane Allen, Senior* (1922). I have not been able to find a copy of the last volume.

18. Gertrude W. Morrison, *The Girls of Central High* (New York: Grosset and Dunlap, 1914), 197.

19. Alice B. Emerson, *Ruth Fielding at College* (New York: Cupples and Leon, 1917).

20. See Margaret Deland, *Small Things* (New York: D. Appleton, 1919), which talks about the college women who went overseas.

21. Clair Blank, *Beverly Gray, Freshman* (New York: Grosset and Dunlap, 1934), 8; the remaining books in the series are *Beverly Gray, Sophomore* (1934), *Beverly Gray, Junior* (1934), *Beverly Gray, Senior* (1934). There are about thirty postcollege volumes, including several based on a cruise around the world.

22. Billman, *Secret of the Stratemeyer Syndicate,* 108.

23. Helen Doré Boylston, *Sue Barton, Student Nurse* (Boston: Little, Brown, 1936) and *Sue Barton, Senior Nurse* (1937). Other volumes continue her career in nursing before and after her marriage; later ones have some interesting discussions of the use of talents after marriage and children.

Even in the career books, with their focus on jobs, however, there is always a man in the background and the promise of marriage in the future.

24. Bacon, *The Luck of Lowry* (New York: Junior Literary Guild, 1931).

## SIX  *Worlds Not So Green*

1. For a discussion of the developmental novel, see Elizabeth Abel, Marianne Hirsch, and Elizabeth Langford, eds., *The Voyage In: Fictions of Female Development,* (Hanover, N.H.: University Press of New England, 1983).

2. McGuigan, *Dangerous Experiment,* and Charlotte Conable, *Women at Cornell: The Myth of Equal Education* (Ithaca: Cornell University Press, 1977), are my sources of information for these paragraphs. There is some overlap, and I have summarized from both texts.

3. Olive Hyde Foster, "With the 'Co-eds' at Cornell," *Harper's Bazar* 45 (July 1911): 315–316, describes Sage College as lavish and comfortable and beloved by the girls who live in it.

4. Conable, *Women at Cornell,* 117.

5. Helen Wright, *Sweeper in the Sky: The Life of Maria Mitchell* (New York: Macmillan, 1949), discusses Mitchell's years at Vassar.

6. See Marjorie H. Dobkin, ed., *The Making of a Feminist: Early Journals and Letters of M. Carey Thomas* (Kent, Ohio: Kent State University Press, 1979); George H. Palmer, *The Life of Alice Freeman Palmer* (Boston: Houghton Mifflin, 1908), by her husband, and a new and better biography, Ruth Bordin, *Alice Freeman Palmer: The Evolution of a New Woman* (Ann Arbor: University of Michigan Press, 1993); Louise Fargo Brown, *Apostle of Democracy. The Life of Lucy Maynard Salmon* (New York: Harper and Brothers, 1943). Thomas is badly in need of a new biography.

7. Field and Irwin, *Stanford Stories.*

8. Sanderson, *Cornell Stories.*

9. Dorothy Canfield Fisher, *The Bent Twig* (New York: Grosset and Dunlap, 1915), 151.

10. Margaret T. Van Epps, *Nancy Pembroke, Sophomore at Roxford* (New York: A. L. Burt, 1930). The character is viewed as absurd because he is so extreme, but even these poorly written books suggest that women students remained somewhat segregated.

11. See, for example, Edwin E. Slosson, "Traitors to Cornell," *Independent* 104 (Dec. 18, 1920): 396–397; Olivia Howard Dunbar, "Women at Man-Made Colleges" *Forum* 70 (Nov. 1923): 2049–2058; "Confessions of a Coed," *Independent* 65 (Oct. 10, 1907): 871–874.

12. Edith Rickert, "The Fraternity Idea among College Women," *Century* 85 (1912): 100, 106. Rickert taught at Vassar and was a well-known Renaissance scholar. For the opposite view and an example of gushy prose, see "'Court' Circles at Wisconsin," *Collier's* 45 (July 23, 1910): 14–16.

13. Olive Deane Hormel, *Co-ed* (New York: Charles Scribner, 1926); Betty White, *I Lived This Story* (Garden City, N.Y.: Doubleday, Doran, 1930); and Elizabeth Corbett, *The Graper Girls* (New York: Century, 1932), *The Graper Girls Go to College* (1933), *Growing Up with the Grapers* (1934), *Beth and Ernestine Graper* (1936).

14. Margaret Mead, *Blackberry Winter* (New York: William Morrow, 1972), 90–95.

15. Lyons, *College Novel*, 53.

16. Anzia Yezierska, *Bread Givers* (New York: Grosset and Dunlap, 1925), 211, 213. One chapter of this developmental novel describes Sara's years at a nameless coeducational college where she has gone to become a teacher.

17. Corbett, *Growing Up*, 144.

18. Corbett, *Growing Up*, 134.

19. Bess Streeter Aldrich, *A White Bird Flying* (New York: D. Appleton, 1931), 107–108.

20. Lela Horn Richards, *Caroline at College* (Boston: Little, Brown, 1922). Richards also wrote a preceding book called *Then Came Caroline* and a third, *Caroline's Career*, but I have not been able to find them. The narrative is different and interesting because of the city setting, which creates an entirely different atmosphere.

21. Edna Yost, "The Case for the Co-Educated Woman," *Harper's Magazine*, July 1927, 195, 199. This article will be discussed more fully in Chapter 7.

22. Gladys Hasty Carroll, *To Remember Forever* (Boston: Little Brown, 1963).

23. There is reinforcement and a parallel in Mary Ellen Chase's account of her years at the University of Maine, *A Goodly Heritage* (New York: Henry Holt, 1932), 272–285. She says, "Of the four hundred students who constituted the University of Maine during my four years there, ninety per cent were from the state and of that ninety per cent, the vast majority came from country places" similar to her own background (274).

24. L. M. Montgomery, *Anne of the Island* (Boston: L. C. Page, 1915). The CBC television version of Anne's story, which violently distorts the text, places no emphasis on her college education, even though the books note that she is the first young woman from Prince Edward Island to go to college.

25. Helen Hull, *Quest* (New York: Macmillan, 1922), 221.

26. Mary Lapsley, *The Parable of the Virgins* (New York: Richard Smith, 1931), 197–198.

27. Martha Gellhorn, *What Mad Pursuit?* (New York: Frederick A. Stokes, 1934), 7, 11, 21–22. Gellhorn, a well-respected journalist and author, has been best known, sadly, as one of Ernest Hemingway's wives.

28. Kathleen Millay, *Against the Wall* (New York: Macauley, 1929).
Biographical information on Millay and Lapsley is sparse. Kathleen Millay (1897–1943) was the younger sister of Edna St. Vincent Millay. She published several volumes of poetry and another novel, *The Wayfarer* (New York: William Morrow, 1926); Mary Lapsley (Caughey) Guest has no other publication listed. Given their dates of birth and assuming that they graduated at 21, they would have been in college from 1914 to 1918 and 1917 to 1921 respectively.

29. Helen M. Bennett, "Seven Colleges—Seven Types," *Women's Home Companion*, Nov. 1920, 13; quoted in Baker, *I'm Radcliffe*, 3. See also MacCracken, *Hickory Limb*, 56–57.

30. See Brown, *Apostle of Democracy*, 213, 223. Though her biographer is tactful, it is clear that Salmon and President Taylor did not like each other, while Taylor's successor, MacCracken, though he sometimes found Salmon difficult, admired and respected her; see his references to her in *The Hickory Limb* (24–25, 45–46, 65–66).

Reading Lapsley's weak, public-relations-driven president as Taylor may not be correct, however; he was president from 1886 to 1914 (Salmon came to Vassar in 1886), but Lapsley was born in 1900, which would have brought her to college after Taylor retired. From all accounts, MacCracken, president while she was there, bears little resemblance to the president she depicts. Still, Lapsley was writing fiction, not history.

31. Lee, "Within Four Years," *Bryn Mawr,* 113.

32. *New York Times,* July 18, 1926, Books, 11; *Boston Transcript,* June 16, 1926, 4.

33. *New York Times,* Aug. 3, 1930, 7. The review also noted that the book had won "the prize offered jointly by Doubleday, Doran and College Humor for a story of American college life written by an undergraduate or a graduate of not more than a year."

34. *New York Times,* Aug. 25, 1929, 14; *Outlook* 152 (Aug. 28, 1929): 710; *New Republic* 60 (Nov. 6, 1929): 331.

35. *New York Times,* Apr. 19, 1931, 6.

36. Fallows, "Undergraduate Life," 41, 53.

37. "A Sense of Obligation," *Vassar,* 107.

## SEVEN   *Men and Other Loves*

1. Goodloe, *College Girls,* 210. The Eva Hungerford stories are "Her Decision" (145–161), "A Telephoned Telegram" (205–211) and "A Short Study in Evolution" (227–242).

2. Katharine R. Ellis, *The Wide-Awake Girls in Winstead* (Boston: Little, Brown, 1909), presents just that situation: Catherine's parents are both practicing physicians, and the text notes that her "physician parents were everybody's friends" (10). This short series has young women who are connected through *Wide-Awake* Pen Pals feature going to college together, but there is little emphasis on the college itself.

3. At Ruth Fielding's college "a girl could have a young man call on her Sunday evening, provided he took her to service at chapel" (Emerson, 152).

4. Harriet Jean Crawford, *Bryn Mawr,* 216–218.

5. Bacon, *Her Fiancé,* 17. Although not a sequel to *Smith College Stories,* this collection offers four tales about the same characters.

6. Warde, *Betty Wales Decides,* 230–232.

7. Warner, *On a New England Campus,* 141.

8. Alice Ross Colver, *Babs at College* (Philadelphia: Penn Publishing, 1920), 274–290. The chapter is entitled "The First Man-Dance."

9. Douglas, *Helen Grant in College,* 7.

10. Carol leaves college owing money to everyone, including Helen, in a situation that is clearly lifted from "Clorinda" in the Wellesley collection.

11. Though Bacon celebrates the freedom of the college years and the postponing of marriage until later, here and there she offers a thread of pity for unmarried women faculty. In "The Education of Elizabeth" (*Smith,* 123–147) a faculty woman's boredom with her isolation among women is clear, and in a short story, "A Reversion to Type" (*Scribner's* 31 [Apr. 1902]: 453–460), the hero, having taught for nine years and now approaching thirty, regrets a refusal to marry made years ago. The story ends in marriage, since the man is still waiting. Bacon makes an interesting distinction:

> The youngest among the assistants [faculty], themselves fresh from college, mingled naturally enough with the students; they danced and skated and enjoyed their girlish authority. The older women, seasoned to the life, set-

tled there indefinitely, identified themselves more or less with the town, amused themselves with their little aristocracy of precedence, and wove and interwove the complicated, slender strands of college gossip. But a woman of barely thirty, too old for friendships with young girls, too young to find her placid recreation in the stereotyped round of social functions, that seemed so perfectly imitative of the normal and yet so curiously unsuccessful at bottom—what was there for her? (456)

12. Christina Catrevas, *That Freshman* (New York: D. Appleton, 1910), 89.

13. *Wellesley*, 3–52, and *Smith*, 247–275.

14. See William S. Alger, *The Friendships of Women* (Boston: Roberts, 1868), and Carroll Smith-Rosenberg, "The Female World of Love and Ritual: Relations between Women in Nineteenth-Century America," in *Disorderly Conduct*, 53–76.

15. Nancy Sahli, "Smashing: Women's Relationships before the Fall," *Chrysalis* 8 (1979): 25.

16. See for example two *LHJ* articles: Ruth Ashmore, "The Intense Friendships of Girls," 15 July 1898: 20; and Emma E. Walker, "Crushes among Girls," 21 ( Jan. 1904): 21. Ashmore objects to the "so-called ecstatic friendships that are just now fashionable," condemning the "ecstatic girl lover" as one who not only regards man as her "natural enemy," but is incapable of real friendship with women. Walker talks of "mushroom affection," saying that these "morbid emotions" are "sham" friendships. Both women wrote regular columns in the magazine.

17. Lillian Faderman, *Surpassing the Love of Men: Romantic Friendship and Love between Women from the Renaissance to the Present* (New York: William Morrow, 1981).

18. H. B. Adams, "Letters of a Wellesley Girl," *New England Magazine* 37 (1907): 161–163. Other letters appear throughout this volume and volume 38. In general the events described are in the "larks and pranks" category.

19. Edna Yost, "The Case for the Co-Educated Woman," *Harper's*, July 1927, 194–202.

20. Faderman, *Surpassing the Love*, 227. She cites Elaine Kendall, *Peculiar Institutions: An Informal History of the Seven Sisters Colleges* (New York: G. P. Putnam's, 1976), 127–128.

21. Faderman, *Surpassing the Love*, 252. According to her notes the quoted passages are from *Whose Fault Is It?*, a Danish novel by Meienreis, excerpted in *Jahrbuch für sexuelle Zwischenstufen* 5 (Leipzig, 1903); and *The Disinherited of Love's Happiness*, discussed in 'Wie ich es sehe,' *Jahrbuch* 3 (Leipzig, 1901).

## EIGHT  *Afterward*

1. For an excellent account of the struggle of Englishwomen for education and then for degrees, see Vera Brittain, *The Women at Oxford: A Fragment of History* (London: G. G. Harrap, 1960).

2. Mary Panton Roberts, "When the College Girl Comes Home to Stay," *New York Times Magazine*, Jan. 26, 1913, 8 ff.

3. Marion Harland, "The Passing of the Home Daughter," *Independent* 71 July, 13, 1911, 88–91.

4. Anne O'Hagen, "The Over-Educated Heart," *Harper's Bazar* 47 (May 1913): 238.

5. Alice Bartlett Stimson, "When the College Girl Comes Home," *Harper's Bazar* 42 (Aug. 1908): 799.

6. Jane M. Bancroft, "Occupations and Professions for College-Bred Women," *Education* 5 (1885): 485–495.

7. Charles F. Thwing, "What Becomes of College Women?" *North American Review* 161 (1895): 546–553. Thwing concludes his article with a list of "eminent" graduates.

8. Frances M. Abbott, "A Generation of College Women," *Forum* 20 (1895): 377–384.

9. Marian Kent Hurd and Jean Bingham Wilson, "When She Came Home from College," *LHJ* 26 (May 1909): 11 ff., (June 1909), 13 ff.; (July 1909), 16 ff. Quoted passages come from May, 11; June, 13, 14; July, 42.

10. Elaine Ginsberg, "The Female Initiation Theme in American Fiction," *Studies in American Fiction* 3 (Spring 1975): 27–38.

11. Abbe Carter Goodloe, "Was It Her Duty?" *LHJ* 16 (Aug. 1898): 9 ff; (Sept. 1898), 10 ff.

12. George Hodges, "The College Girl in the Country Town," *LHJ* 23 (June 1906): 18. The comments did not go unanswered: Kate M. Cone's "The College Woman in the Country Town" (Nov. 1906), presents the same situation more positively and intellectually: "To the college-trained feminine mind the country town may present itself as a social unit of great interest" (44). Laura E. Richards, "The After-College Girl" (Oct. 1906) agrees that the well-educated young woman will find a way to use her education (12).

13. Harriet Hanson Robinson, *Loom and Spindle* (New York: T. Crowell, 1896; repr. Kailua, Hawaii: Press Pacifica, 1976); see also Benita Eisler, *The Lowell Offering* (New York: Harper's, 1977). There is a parallel between the adventurous behavior of the mill girls and the later college students; both were involved in what seemed at first to be "dangerous experiments" for women. For example, one shocking aspect of the mill girls' behavior was that many of them had their own bank accounts.

In Ellis's *Wide-Awake Girls* the hero, home from college for the summer, leads her friends in founding a town library.

14. Mateel Howe Farnham, *Rebellion* (New York: Dodd Mead, 1927).

15. "On Baccalaureate Sunday," *Vassar*, 245

16. Margaret Warde, *Betty Wales, B.A.* (Philadelphia: Penn Publishing, 1908), *Betty Wales & Co.* (1909), *Betty Wales on Campus* (1910), *Betty Wales Decides* (1911).

17. Marian T. Macintosh, "Her Masterpiece," *Bryn Mawr*, 13–72.

18. Warde, *Betty Wales Decides*, 349.

19. Nell Speed, *Molly Brown's Post-Graduate Days* (New York: A. L. Burt, 1914), *Molly Brown's Orchard Home* (1915), *Molly Brown of Kentucky* (1917), *Molly Brown's College Friends* (1921).

20. The only exception I found comes in *The Four Corners at College* by Amy E. Blanchard (Philadelphia: Penn Publishing, 1926), an undistinguished series about sisters whose last name is Corner. They attend a college that sounds like Wellesley, and one of their friends, a very bright student who has put herself through college on scholarships, is suddenly noticed by the man with whom she has been secretly in love for years; he wants to marry at once, and she drops everything in the middle of her senior year and leaves. Minor characters may leave to marry in other college tales, but this is the only case I have seen of such action by a major character.

While this manuscript was in production, I discovered a small book entitled *Three Freshmen, Ruth, Fran, and Nathalie*, by Jessie Anderson Chase (Chicago: A. C. McClurg, 1898). This is a gentle account of three girls who go to Smith; their first year is a pleasant matter of becoming familiar with college customs. Written in a

curiously lifeless style, the narrative offers no conflict, little character development, and not much sense that college is a different experience. The only departure from the norm is that one of the girls, Nathalie, leaves at the end of her first
year to marry.

21. The Grace Harlowe war books have titles such as *Grace Harlowe with the
Marines at Chateau Thierry*. Many women did go overseas, of course, to drive ambulances and work with with the Red Cross; often there were units of women
from the same college.

22. Claire Blank, *Beverly Gray's Career* (New York: Grosset and Dunlap, 1935).
There are about thirty more titles in Beverly's adventurous life and series.

23. Although I did not read many of these books, those I did look at were
much the same. See, for example, a writer named Rosamond DuJardin, author
of many books about characters with names like Marcie and Tobey. Through high
school their problems are learning to date, finding the right man, and then deciding whether or not to go steady. In college, dating and men dominate, and
graduation is followed immediately by a wedding. College in these stories presents everything from sororities to studies as taken-for-granted parts of the background while the hero focuses on the important business of finding the right
man. See also fiction by Betty Cavanna and a seductively good writer named Janet
Lambert; their heroines never even consider college and all marry young.

24. For an excellent look at the kinds of changes occurring during these years,
see Patricia Marks, *Bicycles, Bangs, and Bloomers* (Lexington: University Press of
Kentucky, 1990).

25. Lois Banner, *Women in Modern America: A Brief History* (New York: Harcourt
Brace Jovanovich, 1984), 1. See also Marks, *Bicycles*, and Gordon, *Gender and
Higher Education*, for different facets of women's experiences at this particularly
interesting time.

26. Susan Warner, *The Wide, Wide World* (New York: G. P. Putnam, 1850). For
the best analysis of this novel, which I am following here, see Jane Tompkins,
*Sensational Designs* (New York: Oxford University Press, 1985), chap. 6.

27. Maria S. Cummins, *The Lamplighter* (Boston: J. R. Jewett, 1852); and Louisa
May Alcott, *Little Women* (Boston: Roberts, 1868), *Jack and Jill* (Boston: Roberts,
1880), *Eight Cousins* (Boston: Roberts, 1875). The progress of these heroes is less
painful than is Ellen Montgomery's, but the goals are similar.

28. Mary Anne Ferguson, "The Female Novel of Development and the Myth
of Psyche," in *The Voyage In:* eds. Elizabeth Abel, Marianne Hirsch, and Elizabeth
Langland, 228.

29. Auerbach, *Communities of Women*, 5.

# Bibliography

## College Fiction

*Note: For series books, titles are given only for those discussed in the text; publishers will be named in the first entry but not again unless they change.*

ADAMS, H. B. "Letters of a Wellesley Girl." *New England Magazine* 37 (1907): 32–36, 161–166, 360–365, 433–436; 38 (1908): 82–87.

ALDRICH, BESS STREETER. *A White Bird Flying.* New York: D. Appleton, 1931.

ANDERSON, OLIVE SAN LOUIE. *An American Girl and Her Four years at a Boys College.* New York: D. Appleton, 1878.

BACON, JOSEPHINE DASKAM. *Smith College Stories.* New York: Scribner's, 1900; Freeport, N.Y.: Books for Libraries Press, 1969.

———. *Her Fiancé, and Other Stories.* New York: Scribner's, 1904; Freeport, N.Y.: Books for Libraries Press, 1970.

———. *Kathy.* New York: Longmans Green, 1934.

———. "A Reversion to Type." *Scribner's* 31 (Apr. 1902): 453–460.

BAILEY, MARGARET EMERSON. *Good-Bye Proud World!* New York: Century, 1945.

BANCROFT, EDITH. *Jane Allen of the Sub-Team.* New York: Saalfield, 1917. *Jane Allen, Right Guard,* 1918; *Jane Allen, Center,* 1920.

BLANCHARD, AMY E. *The Four Corners at College.* Philadelphia: Penn Publishing, 1926.

BLANK, CLAIR. *Beverly Gray, Freshman.* New York: Grosset and Dunlap, 1934. *Beverly Gray, Sophomore,* 1934. *Beverly Gray, Junior,* 1934. *Beverly Gray, Senior,* 1934. *Beverly Gray's Career,* 1935.

*Book of Bryn Mawr Stories, A.* Edited by Margaretta Morris and Louise Buffum Congdon. Philadelphia: George W. Jacobs, 1901.

BOYLESTON, HELEN DORÉ. *Sue Barton, Student Nurse.* Boston: Little, Brown, 1936. *Sue Barton, Senior Nurse,* 1937.

BROWN, HELEN DAWES. *Two College Girls.* Boston: Ticknor, 1886.

CATREVAS, CHRISTINA. *That Freshman.* New York: D. Appleton, 1910.

CHAMPNEY, ELIZABETH. *Three Vassar Girls in the Tyrol.* Boston: Estes and Lauriat, 1891.

COLVER, ALICE ROSS. *Babs at College.* Philadelphia: Penn Publishing, 1920.

COOK, GRACE L. *Wellesley Stories.* Boston: Richard G. Badger, 1901.

CORBETT, ELIZABETH. *The Graper Girls.* New York: Century, 1932. *The Graper Girls Go to College,* 1933. *Growing Up with the Grapers,* 1934. *Beth and Ernestine Graper,* 1936.

DOUGLAS, AMANDA. *Helen Grant in College*. Boston: Lothrop, Lee and Shepard, 1906. *Helen Grant, Senior*, 1907.

ELLIS, KATHARINE R. *The Wide-Awake Girls at Winstead*. Boston: Little, Brown, 1909.

EMERSON, ALICE B. *Ruth Fielding at College*. New York: Cupples and Leon, 1917.

FARNHAM, MATEEL HOWE. *Rebellion*. New York: Dodd, Mead, 1927.

FIELD, CHARLES K. and WILL H. IRWIN. *Stanford Stories: Tales of a Young University*. New York: Doubleday, Page, 1901.

FISHER, DOROTHY CANFIELD. *The Bent Twig*. New York: Grosset and Dunlap, 1915.

FLOWER, JESSIE GRAHAM. *Grace Harlowe's First Year at Overton College*. Philadelphia: Henry Altemus, 1914. *Grace Harlowe's Second Year at Overton College*, 1914. *Grace Harlowe's Third Year at Overton College*, 1914. *Grace Harlowe's Fourth Year at Overton College*, 1914.

GALLAHER, GRACE M. *Vassar Stories*. Boston: Richard G. Badger, 1899; Freeport, N.Y.: Books for Libraries Press, 1970.

GELLHORN, MARTHA. *What Mad Pursuit?* New York: Frederick A. Stokes, 1934.

GOODLOE, ABBE CARTER. *College Girls*. New York: Charles Scribners, 1895.

———. "Was It Her Duty?" *Ladies' Home Journal* 16 (Aug. 1898): 9 ff.; (Sept. 1898): 10 ff.

HOPE, LAURA LEE. *The Outdoor Girls of Deepdale*. New York: Grosset and Dunlap, 1913.

HORMEL, OLIVE DEAN. *Co-ed*. New York: Charles Scribner, 1926.

HULL, HELEN. *Quest*. New York: Macmillan, 1922.

HURD, MARIAN KENT AND JEAN BINGHAM WILSON. "When She Came Home from College," *Ladies' Home Journal* 26 (May 1909): 11 ff.; (June 1909), 13 ff.; (July 1909), 16 ff.

JOHNSON, OWEN. *Stover at Yale*. New York: Frederick A. Stokes, 1912.

LAPSLEY, MARY. *The Parable of the Virgins*. New York: Richard Smith, 1931.

LESTER, PAULINE. *Marjorie Dean, College Freshman*. New York: A. L. Burt, 1922. *Marjorie Dean, College Sophomore*, 1922. *Marjorie Dean, College Junior*, 1922. *Marjorie Dean, College Senior*, 1922.

MILLAY, KATHLEEN. *Against the Wall*. New York: Macauley, 1929.

MINOT, JOHN CLAIR and DONALD FRANCIS SNOW. *Tales of Bowdoin*. Augusta, Me.: Press of the Kennebec Journal, 1901.

MONTGOMERY, L. M. [LUCY MAUD]. *Anne of the Island*. Boston: L. C. Page, 1915.

MORRISON, GERTRUDE W. *The Girls of Central High*. New York: Grosset and Dunlap, 1914.

PHELPS, ELIZABETH STUART. "A Brave Girl." *Wide-Awake* 18 (1884): 27 ff.; 19 (1884): 27 ff.

POST, WALDRON K. *Harvard Stories*. New York: Putnam's, 1893; Freeport, N.Y.: Books for Libraries Press, 1969.

RICHARDS, LELA HORN. *Caroline at College*. Boston: Little, Brown, 1922.

SANDERSON, JAMES GARDNER. *Cornell Stories*. New York: Charles Scribner's, 1898.

SHARP, ANNABEL. *Peggy Parsons, A Hampton Freshman*. New York: M. A. Donahue, 1916.

SPEED, NELL [EMMA SPEED SAMPSON]. *Molly Brown's Freshman Days*. New York: Hurst, 1912. *Molly Brown's Sophomore Days*, 1912. *Molly Brown's Junior Days*, 1912. *Molly Brown's Senior Days*, 1913.

STANDISH, BURT L. [WILLIAM GILBERT PATTEN]. *Frank Merriwell at Yale*. New York: Street and Smith, 1894.

VAN EPPS, MARGARET. *Nancy Pembroke, Sophomore at Roxford*. New York: A. L. Burt, 1930.

WARDE, MARGARET [EDITH KELLOG DUNTON]. *Betty Wales, Freshman*. Philadelphia:

Penn Publishing, 1904. *Betty Wales, Sophomore,* 1905. *Betty Wales, Junior,* 1906. *Betty Wales, Senior,* 1907. *Betty Wales Decides,* 1911.

———. "The Freshman Freak." *St. Nicholas Magazine* 40 (1912–1913): 1013–1018.

WEBSTER, JEAN. *Daddy Long-Legs.* New York: Century, 1912.

———. *When Patty Went to College.* New York: Century, 1903.

WHITE, BETTY. *I Lived This Story.* New York: Doubleday, Doran, 1930.

WILLIAMS, J. L. *Princeton Stories.* New York: Charles Scribner's, 1895.

WOOD, JOHN SEYMOUR. *Yale Yarns.* New York: Putnam, 1895, 1902.

## Works Consulted

ABBOTT, FRANCES M. "A Generation of College Women." *Forum* 20 (1895): 377–384.

ABEL, ELIZABETH, MARIANNE HIRSCH, and ELIZABETH LANGLAND, eds. *The Voyage In: Fictions of Female Development.* Hanover, N.H.: The University Press of New England, 1983.

ALUMNA, A. B. "Does the Girls' College Destroy the Wife?" *Ladies' Home Journal* 33 (June 1916): 27.

AMERICAN MOTHER, AN. "Is College the Right Thing for Our Girls?" *Ladies' Home Journal* 17 (July 1900): 15.

ASHMORE, RUTH. "The Intense Friendships of Girls." *Ladies' Home Journal* 15 (July 1898): 20.

AUERBACH, NINA. *Communities of Women: An Idea in Fiction.* Cambridge, Mass.: Harvard University Press, 1978.

BAKER, LIVA. *I'm Radcliffe! Fly Me: The Seven Sisters and the Failure of Women's Education.* New York: Macmillan, 1976.

BANCROFT, JANE M. "Occupations and Professions for College-bred Women." *Education* 5 (1885): 486–495.

BANNER, LOIS. *Women in Modern America: A Brief History.* New York: Harcourt Brace Jovanovich, 1984.

BARR, AMELIA. *Girls of a Feather.* New York: R. Bonner, 1893.

BAYM, NINA. *Women's Fiction.* Ithaca: Cornell University Press, 1979.

BEECHER, CATHARINE. *Treatise on Domestic Economy, for the Use of Young Ladies at Home or at School.* New York: Harper & Brothers, 1850.

BERGER, HARRY, JR. *Second World and Green World: Studies in Renaissance Fiction-Making.* Berkeley: University of California Press, 1988.

BILLMAN, CAROL. *The Secret of the Stratemeyer Syndicate.* New York: Ungar, 1986.

BLATCH, HARRIOT STANTON. *Challenging Years.* New York: Putnam's, 1940.

BOAS, LOUISE S. *Women's Education Begins: The Rise of the Women's Colleges.* Norton, Mass.: Wheaton College Press, 1935.

BOK, EDWARD. "My Quarrel with Women's Clubs." *Ladies' Home Journal* 27 (Jan. 1910): 5–6.

———. "Problems of Young Men," *Ladies' Home Journal* 12 (Jan. 1895): 12.

BRIGGS, LEBARON. *Girls and Education.* Boston: Houghton Mifflin, 1911.

BROWN, LOUISE FARGO. *Apostle of Democracy. The Life of Lucy Maynard Salmon.* New York: Harper and Brothers, 1943.

BURGESS, DOROTHY. *Dream and Deed: The Story of Katharine Lee Bates.* Norman: University of Oklahoma Press, 1952.

CALL, ANNIE PAYSON. "The Greatest Need of College Girls," *Atlantic Monthly,* Jan. 1892, 102–109.

CAMPBELL, BARBARA KUHN. *The "Liberated" Woman of 1914*. Ann Arbor: UMI Research Press, 1979.

CANTOR, DOROTHY W. and TONI BERNAY, with JEAN STOESS. *Women in Power: The Secrets of Leadership*. Boston: Houghton Mifflin, 1992.

CARROLL, GLADYS HASTY. *To Remember Forever*. Boston: Little, Brown, 1963.

CHASE, MARY ELLEN. *A Goodly Heritage*. New York: Holt, 1932.

"Christmas Pranks of College Girls." *Ladies' Home Journal* 23 (Dec. 1906): 7.

CLARKE, EDWARD H. *Sex in Education*. Reprinted in Julia Ward Howe, ed., *Sex and Education: A Reply to Dr. E. H. Clarke's "Sex in Education."* Boston: Roberts, 1874; New York: Arno Press, 1972.

COGAN, FRANCES B. *All-American Girl: The Ideal of Real Womanhood in Mid-Nineteenth Century America*. Athens: University of Georgia Press, 1989.

"College Girls' Larks and Pranks," *Ladies' Home Journal* 17 (Mar. 1900): 7–8; (Apr. 1900): 7–8; (Aug. 1900): 1–2.

"College Scrapes We Got Into," *Ladies' Home Journal* 18 (Sept. 1901): 13 ff.

COMSTOCK, ADA M. *The American College Girl*. Boston, L. C. Page, 1930.

CONABLE, CHARLOTTE. *Women at Cornell: The Myth of Equal Education*. Ithaca: Cornell University Press, 1977.

CONANT, MARTHA PIKE. *A Girl of the Eighties at College and at Home: The Family Letters of Charlotte Howard Conant*. Boston: Houghton Mifflin, 1931.

CONE, HELEN GRAY. "Women in American Literature." *Century* 40 (Oct. 1890): 921–930.

"Confessions of a Coed." *Independent* 63 (Oct. 10, 1907): 871–874.

CONRAD, SUSAN PHINNEY. *Perish the Thought: Intellectual Women in Romantic America, 1830–1860*. New York: Oxford University Press, 1976.

"Dainties at College Girls' Spreads." *Ladies' Home Journal* 24 (Sept. 1907): 31.

DAVIS, CHARLES. " 'Court' Circles at Wisconsin," *Collier's Magazine* 45 (July 23, 1910): 14–16.

DELAND, MARGARET. *Small Things*. New York: D. Appleton, 1919.

DOTY, MADELINE Z. "What a Woman's College Means to a Girl." *Delineator* 75 (1910): 209, 265–266.

DOUGHTY, FRANCES A. "The College Woman in Literature." *Critic* 27 (Oct. 5, 1895): 209–210.

DOUGLAS, GEORGE H. *Women of the Twenties*. Dallas: Saybrook Press, 1986.

DUNBAR, OLIVIA H. "Women at Man-Made Colleges." *Forum* 70 (Nov. 1923): 2049–2058.

FADERMAN, LILLIAN. *Surpassing the Love of Men: Romantic Fiction and Love between Women from the Renaissance to the Present*. New York: William Morrow, 1981.

FALLOWS, ALICE K. "The Girl Freshman," *Munsey's Magazine* 25 (Sept. 1901): 818–828.

———. "Undergraduate Life at Smith College." *Scribner's* 24 (July 1898): 37–58.

FASS, PAULA S. *The Damned and the Beautiful*. New York: Oxford University Press, 1977.

FERGUSON, MARY ANNE. "The Female Novel of Development and the Myth of Psyche." In *The Voyage In: Fictions of Female Development*, eds. Elizabeth Abel, Marianne Hirsch, and Elizabeth Langland. Hanover, N.H.: University Press of New England, 1983.

"Fetes of College Girls." *Ladies' Home Journal* 16 (Jan. 1899): 3 ff.

FOSTER, OLIVE HYDE. "With the 'Co-eds' at Cornell." *Harper's Bazar* 45 (July 1911): 315.

FRYE, NORTHROP. "The Argument of Comedy." In *Shakespeare: Modern Essays in Criticism*, ed. Leonard Dean. New York: Oxford University Press, 1957; 1967.

GAITLIN, DANA. "Women Who Achieve." *Harper's Bazar* 47 (1913): 69.

GINSBERG, ELAINE. "The Female Initiation Theme in American Fiction." *Studies in American Fiction* 3 (Spring 1975): 27–38.

GOODLOE, ABBE CARTER. "Undergraduate Life at Wellesley." *Scribner's* 23 (May 1898): 515–538.

GORDON, LYNN D. *Gender and Higher Education in the Progressive Era.* New Haven: Yale University Press, 1990.

HABEGGAR, ALFRED. *Gender, Fantasy and Realism in American Literature.* New York: Columbia University Press, 1982.

HALE, EDWARD EVERETT. "Susan's Escort." *Harper's Monthly* 80 (May 1870): 908–918.

HALSTEAD, CAROLYN. "What a Girl Does in College." *Ladies' Home Journal* 18 (Dec. 1901): 26–27; 19 (Jan. 1902): 24–25; (Feb. 1902): 24–25; (Mar. 1902): 26–27; (Apr. 1902): 26–27; (May 1902): 26–27; (Sept. 1902): 26–27.

HARLAND, MARIAN. "The Passing of the Home Daughter." *Independent* 71 (July 13, 1911): 88–91.

HELSINGER, ELIZABETH K., ROBIN LAUTERBACH SHEETS, and WILLIAM VEEDER. *The Woman Question: Society and Literature in Britain and America, 1837–1883.* New York: Garland Press, 1983.

HIGGINSON, THOMAS WENTWORTH. "Ought Women to Learn the Alphabet?" *Atlantic Monthly* 3 (1859): 137–150.

———. *Women and the Alphabet.* Boston: Houghton Mifflin, 1880; New York: Arno Press, 1972.

HODGES, GEORGE. "The College Girl in the Country Town." *Ladies' Home Journal* 23 (June 1906): 18.

HOGELAND, RONALD W. "'The Female Appendage': Feminine Life-Styles in America, 1820–1860." *Civil War History* 17 (1971): 101–114.

HORNER, MATINA. "Fail: Bright Women." *Psychology Today* (Nov. 1969): 36 ff.

HOROWITZ, HELEN LEFKOWITZ. *Alma Mater: Design and Experience in the Women's Colleges from Their Nineteenth-Century Beginnings to the 1930s.* New York: Alfred A. Knopf, 1984.

HOWE, JULIA WARD, ed. *Sex and Education: A Reply to Dr. E. H. Clarke's "Sex in Education."* Boston: Roberts, 1874.

HOYLE, KAREN NELSON, ed. *Girls Series Books: A Checklist of Hardback Books Published 1900–1975.* Minneapolis: Children's Literature Research Collection, University of Minnesota Library, 1978.

HYDE, WILLIAM DEWITT. *The College Man and the College Woman.* Boston: Houghton Mifflin, 1906.

"Inside the Rooms of College Girls," *Ladies' Home Journal* 15 (Mar. 1898): 7.

JOHNSON, DIERDRE, ED. *Stratemeyer Pseudonyms and Series Books: An Annotated Checklist of Stratemeyer and Stratemeyer Syndicate Publications.* Westport, Conn.: Greenwood Press, 1982.

KIRK, SOPHIA. "The College Girl and the Outside World." *Lippincott's Magazine* 65 (1900): 596–602.

*Letters from Old-Time Vassar: Written by a Student in 1869–1870.* Poughkeepsie: Vassar College, 1915.

LEWIS, DIO. *Our Girls.* New York: Harper's, 1871.

LYONS, JOHN O. *The College Novel in America.* Carbondale: Southern Illinois Press, 1962.

MACCRACKEN, HENRY NOBLE. *The Hickory Limb.* New York: Scribner's, 1950.

"Madcap Frolics of College Girls." *Ladies' Home Journal* 22 (Oct. 1905): 17 ff.

MAGALIFF, CECILE. *The Junior Novel: Its Relationship to Adolescent Reading.* Port Washington, N.Y.: Kennikat Press, 1964.

MARBLE, ANNIE RUSSELL. *Pen-Names and Personalities.* New York: D. Appleton, 1930.

MARKS, JEANETTE. *A Girl's Student Days and After.* New York: Fleming H. Revell, 1911.

MARKS, PATRICIA. *Bicycles, Bangs, and Bloomers.* Lexington: University Press of Kentucky, 1990.

MASON, BOBBIE ANN. *The Girl Sleuth: A Feminist Guide.* Old Westbury, N.Y.: Feminist Press, 1975.

MAURICE, ARTHUR BARTLETT. "The Undergraduate in Fiction." *Bookman* 11 (1900): 424–426.

McCABE, LIDA. *The American Girl at College.* New York: Dodd, Mead, 1893.

McGUIGAN, DOROTHY G. *A Dangerous Experiment: 100 Years of Women at the University of Michigan.* Ann Arbor: University of Michigan Press, 1970.

MEAD, MARGARET. *Blackberry Winter.* New York: William Morrow, 1972.

MEDEARY, MARY. *College in Crinoline.* New York: Longmans Green, 1950.

MINER, VALERIE, and HELEN E. LONGINO, eds. *Competition: A Feminist Taboo.* New York: Feminist Press, 1987.

MITCHELL, S. WEIR. "When the College is Harmful to a Girl." *Ladies' Home Journal,* June 1900, 14.

MOODY, WINFIELD SCOTT. "Daisy Miller and the Gibson Girl." *Ladies' Home Journal* 17 (Sept. 1904): 17.

NEWCOMER, MABEL. *A Century of Higher Education for Women.* Boston: Houghton Mifflin, 1959.

NEWMAN, DAISY. *A Golden String.* New York: Harper and Row, 1986.

O'HAGAN, ANNE. "The Over-Educated Heart." *Harper's Bazar* 47 (May 1913): 238.

ORTON, JAMES. *The Liberal Education of Women.* New York: A. S. Barnes, 1873.

PARRISH, C. S. "The Womanly Woman." *Independent* (Apr. 4, 1901): 775–778.

PRATT, ANNIS. *Archetypal Patterns in Women's Fiction.* Bloomington: Indiana University Press, 1981.

PRYSE, MARJORIE. Afterword. *Selected Stories of Mary E. Wilkins Freeman.* New York: W. W. Norton, 1983.

Review of *College Girls. Critic* 28 (Apr. 18, 1896): 271.

Review of *Smith College Stories. Book Buyer* 20 (May 1900): 326.

Review of *Two College Girls. Atlantic Monthly* 57 (May 1886): 718.

RICKERT, EDITH. "The Fraternity Idea among College Women." *Century* 85 (1912): 97–106.

ROBERTS, MARY PANTON. "When the College Girl Comes Home to Stay." *New York Times Magazine,* Jan. 26, 1913, 8.

ROBINSON, HARRIET HANSON. *Loom and Spindle.* New York: T. Crowell, 1896; Kailua, Hawaii: Press Pacifica, 1976.

RORER, MRS. S. T. "What College Girls Eat." *Ladies' Home Journal* 22 (Nov. 1905): 13–14.

SADLER, W. S. "College Women and Race Suicide," *Ladies' Home Journal* 39 (Apr. 1922): 29.

SAHLI, NANCY. "Smashing: Women's Relationships before the Fall." *Chrysalis* 8 (1979): 17–27.

SHAW, ADELE-MARIE. "Kate Douglas Wiggin As She Really Is As a Woman. *Ladies' Home Journal* 22 (May 1905): 5 ff.

SHERWOOD, MARGARET. "Undergraduate Life at Vassar." *Scribner's,* June 1898, 643–660

SKINNER, CORNELIA OTIS. *Family Circle.* Boston: Houghton Mifflin, 1948.

SLOSSON, EDWIN E. "Traitors to Cornell." *Independent* 104 (Dec. 18, 1920): 396–397.

SMITH-ROSENBERG, CARROLL. *Disorderly Conduct.* New York: Alfred A. Knopf, 1985.

SOLOMON, BARBARA MILLER. *In the Company of Educated Women.* New Haven: Yale University Press, 1985.

STARRETT, HELEN E. *After College, What? for Girls.* New York: Crowell, 1896.

————. *The Future of Educated Women.* Chicago: Johnson, McClurg, 1885.

STEINBERG, SALME HARJU. *Reformer in the Marketplace: Edward W. Bok and the Ladies' Home Journal.* Baton Rouge: Louisiana State University Press, 1979.

STIMSON, ALICE BARTLETT. "When the College Girl Comes Home." *Harper's Bazar* 42 (Aug. 1908): 797–799.

TALMADGE, T. DeWITT. "Male and Female Created He Them." *Ladies' Home Journal* 10 (Sept. 1893): 14.

TEBBEL, JOHN WILLIAM. *The American Magazine.* New York: Hawthorn Press, 1969.

THORP, MARGARET F. *Nielson of Smith.* New York: Oxford University Press, 1956.

THWING, CHARLES. *The College Woman.* New York: Baker and Taylor, 1894.

————. "What Becomes of College Women?" *North American Review* 161 (1895): 546–553.

TICKNOR, CAROLINE. "The Steel-Engraving Lady and the Gibson Girl," *Atlantic Monthly* 88 (1901): 105–108.

TOMPKINS, JANE. *Sensational Designs.* New York: Oxford University Press, 1985.

VERBRUGGE, MARTHA H. *Able-Bodied Womanhood.* New York: Oxford University Press, 1988.

WALKER, EMMA E. "Crushes among Girls." *Ladies' Home Journal* 21 (Jan. 1904): 21.

WARE, SUSAN. *Holding Their Own: American Women in the 1930s.* Boston: Twayne, 1982.

WARNER, FRANCES L. *On a New England Campus.* Boston: Houghton Mifflin, 1937.

WEIN, ROBERT. "Women's Colleges and Domesticity, 1875–1918." *History of Education Quarterly* 14 (Spring 1974): 31–47.

WELTER, BARBARA. "The Cult of True Womanhood, 1820–1860." *American Quarterly* 48 (1966): 151–174.

"When College Girls Have Their Fun." *Ladies' Home Journal* 20 (Mar. 1903): 4.

WHITE, BARBARA A. *Growing Up Female: Adolescent Girlhood in American Fiction.* Westport, Conn.: Greenwood Press, 1985.

WHITE, LYNN T. "Do Women's Colleges Turn Out Spinsters?" *Harper's Bazar*, Oct. 1952, 44–48.

WRIGHT, HELEN. *Sweeper in the Sky: The Life of Maria Mitchell.* New York: Macmillan, 1949.

YEZIERSKA, ANZIA. *Bread Givers.* New York: Grosset and Dunlap, 1925.

YOST, EDNA. "The Case for the Co-Educated Woman," *Harper's Bazar*, July 1927, 194–202.

ZILBOORG, CAROLINE. "Women before World War I: An Exploration of their Awakening in the College Novel." *Great Lakes Review* 7 (Summer 1981): 29–38.

# Index

# About the Author

**Shirley Marchalonis** is a professor of English and Women's Studies at Penn State, where she teaches at the Berks Campus. She is the author of a biography, *The Worlds of Lucy Larcom, 1824–1893*, and editor of *Patrons and Protégées: Gender, Friendship, and Writing in Nineteenth-Century America* and *Critical Essays on Mary Wilkins Freeman.* She is interested in women writers and women's lives in the latter half of the nineteenth and the early years of the twentieth centuries.